P9-DFN-546

Natural rights theories

Natural rights theories
Their origin and development

RICHARD TUCK

University Lecturer in History and
Fellow of Jesus College, Cambridge

CAMBRIDGE UNIVERSITY PRESS

CAMBRIDGE

LONDON   NEW YORK   NEW ROCHELLE

MELBOURNE   SYDNEY

Published by the Press Syndicate of the University of Cambridge
The Pitt Building, Trumpington Street, Cambridge CB2 IRP
32 East 57th Street, New York, NY 10022, USA
296 Beaconsfield Parade, Middle Park, Melbourne 3206, Australia

© Cambridge University Press 1979

First published 1979
First paperback edition 1981

Printed in Great Britain at the
University Press, Cambridge

British Library Cataloguing in Publication Data

Tuck, Richard
Natural rights theories.
1. Natural law – History
I. Title
323.4'01   KA415   78-73819

ISBN 0 521 22512 4 hard covers
ISBN 0 521 28509 7 paperback

Contents

For Levis

Preface

To provide full acknowledgements for the help I have received on this book would ideally require the public recognition of assistance given to me by innumerable people at home, school and university – all the people who would have to figure in any complete explanation of why *I* have written *this* book. Short of providing that complete explanation, the acknowledgements must necessarily be inadequate. But it is right to single out the following people as having had a special role in its genesis. Quentin Skinner must of course have pride of place: it was he who originally sharpened my interest both in this kind of history and in political philosophy, and who since then has been a constant critic and friend – the perfect audience for whom to write. His own book, *The Foundations of Modern Political Thought* (Cambridge, 1978) appeared too late to be more than briefly acknowledged, but much of what I say takes on a new significance in the light of his survey. What I know about political philosophy in general and rights theories in particular I owe to many conversations over the years with him and with other friends – especially John Barber, John Skorupski, John Urry, Ron Smith, Jane Heal, Albert Weale, Philip Pettit, Jeremy Butterfield, Jonathan Lear and Stefan Collini. As for the more strictly historical material in the work, I owe a great debt to J. H. Plumb, who was the original supervisor of the Cambridge Ph.D. thesis on which the book is ultimately based, to the other members of his last seminar – notably John Brewer, Derek Hirst, Simon Schama and Roy Porter – and to John Walter, Nicholas Jolley and Mark Goldie. Moses Finley has provided constant support and encouragement, and insights into many things in addition to ancient history, while Peter Garnsey helped me greatly over the knotty problems of classical Roman law. In writing the sections on medieval theory, I benefited very much from conversations with Timothy Reuter and my brother Anthony Tuck. The examiners of the original thesis, Wolfgang von Leyden and Peter Stein, encouraged me to think that the ideas in it were worth developing, and in the process of doing so I received an enormous amount of help and inspiration from Jim Tully, whose conviction as to the importance of this kind of enterprise repeatedly lifted my flagging spirits and left me with a debt I will find hard to repay. Alan Ryan read the manuscript in its final form and provided me with many of his characteristically cogent and useful insights. All my dealings with Cambridge University Press have been smoothed by Patricia Williams, whose help (for me as for so many others) has been invaluable. My thanks go to them all, and to many others inevitably missing from the list. Institutions which have helped me as much, though necessarily in a more impersonal way, include first Jesus College, Cambridge, which not only financed some of the research by electing me to a research fellowship, but also possesses in its Old Library an invaluable and constantly accessible collection of relevant books; the Cambridge University Library, the best library in the United Kingdom in which to work; the British Library and the Bodleian. No one could wish for more help and kindness than has been shown me by the members or staff of all of them.

Jesus College, Cambridge
July 1978

Introduction

This book began as an attempt to solve some of the problems which twentieth-century philosophers have found in writing about rights. The thirty years since the war have witnessed a curious phenomenon: the language of human rights plays an increasingly important part in normal political debate, while academic political philosophers find it on the whole an elusive and unnecessary mode of discourse. With the exception of Robert Nozick,[1] no major theorist in the Anglo-Saxon world for almost a century has based his work on the concept of a right, and when most philosophers have looked closely at the concept it has seemed to collapse quickly into other, less intractable notions. One argument in particular has meant that the language of rights is difficult to use straightforwardly: it is the famous argument stemming ultimately (as we shall see) from Samuel Pufendorf, though generally associated with Bentham, that to have a right is merely to be the beneficiary of someone else's duty, and that all propositions involving rights are straightforwardly translatable into propositions solely involving duties. If this is true, then the language of rights is irrelevant, and to talk of 'human rights' is simply to raise the question of what kinds of duty we are under to other human beings, rather than to provide us with any independent moral insights.[2] The residual Utilitarianism of many Anglo-American political theorists has made this argument particularly attractive, but its force has always largely been that it appears to embody a logical truth. And yet to dismiss such a key area of political thought in this way seems a foolhardy enterprise – there must be *something* to the language of rights.

The conviction that these problems, like much in the area of moral and political philosophy, could be solved *historically*, by an investigation of how the relevant language had developed, led to a consideration of what such an investigation might look like. One thing it seemed that it should not be is simply an exercise in historical lexicography. We cannot satisfactorily talk about the meaning of a particular word in the past merely by giving examples of its use, and constructing the dictionary with which

---

[1] R. Nozick, *Anarchy, State, and Utopia* (Oxford, 1974).
[2] For a fuller discussion of this, see below, pp. 4–7.

contemporaries never provided us.[3] Because the meaning of a term such as
a right is theory-dependent, and we have to be sure about what role the
term played in the various theories about politics which engage our
attention, we will in practice be writing something much more like the
traditional history of ideas. This is true even to the extent that much of our
material will be provided by the literature traditionally studied as part of
that history. The elucidation of a complex notion such as a right requires a
fairly full account of the possible theories about politics which involve the
concept, and in general those theories (given the obvious facts about our
culture) are embodied in particular texts. The pursuit of a set of common
assumptions possessed by people independently of or outside the historical
literature and informing that literature is likely to be fruitless: in a culture
such as ours has been since the Roman period, understanding a political
language involves understanding the literature of political theory, and that
applies to the speakers of the language as much as to its historians.

Given this, there seemed to me to be two important periods which have
to be studied if we are to make sense of the language of rights. The first is
clearly the period in which the language first appeared and developed into
something close to what we see today, and as I show in the first chapter,
that was essentially the early and high middle ages. The second is the
period of what can be termed the classic texts of rights theory, stretching
from Grotius through to Locke. In order to link these two periods
together, I provide in Chapter Two a discussion of why the rights theories
which were developed in the later middle ages failed at the Renaissance,
and what the circumstances were which led to their revival at the very end
of the century in both Catholic and Protestant Europe.

For obvious reasons, my enterprise has certain parallels with that of
Professor C. B. Macpherson in *The Political Theory of Possessive
Individualism*. He too turned to the seventeenth-century rights theorists in
an attempt to understand the confusions of contemporary political theory,
in his case liberal democratic theory as a whole. A continual assumption of
Macpherson is that the great nineteenth-century democratic thinkers such
as Bentham and even Mill built on the seventeenth-century rights theorists' foundations, and that the seventeenth-century theory is therefore
basic to all current liberal and democratic political thinking. The oddity of
this claim (for, as we have seen, one of the things which characterises a
Utilitarian view of politics is a deep scepticism over the validity of a
language of rights – a scepticism which we can see emerging as part of an
explicit repudiation of the classic seventeenth-century theories) does not
however vitiate his enquiry: it remains true that at least one powerful way
of talking about politics is correctly rooted in those writings, even if there
is an important kind of democratic theory which is not.

[3] To some extent, this is the failing of a work such as Raymond Williams's *Keywords*
(London, 1977).

Moreover it is also true that Macpherson correctly divined the 'posses-sive' character of the classic works; a concept of man as the *owner* of his liberty and other moral attributes is undoubtedly central to them. But this is a much more complex matter than might appear from Macpherson's book. He was content to explain it in terms of the social realities of the day – 'the relation of ownership, having become for more and more men the critically important relation determining their actual freedom and actual prospect of realising their full potentialities, was read back into the nature of the individual'.[4] But as we can see from my first chapter, from its inception the language of rights had an ambiguous character, and already by the fourteenth century it was possible to argue that to have a right was to be the lord or *dominus* of one's relevant moral world, to possess *dominium*, that is to say, *property*. To have a strongly individualistic theory of rights was inevitably, given this political language, to have a *possessive* theory. If it is true that the difficulties of modern liberal–democratic theory are attributable to the possessive quality of the individualism at its heart (a belief which I do not share), then those difficulties cannot be solved by seeing how we stand in relationship to the classic seventeenth-century texts; they are far more fundamental and long-standing.

Furthermore, it is very far from clear that any sort of *liberal* political theory can easily be traced back to these works. An important conclusion to which one is forcibly led is that most strong rights theories have in fact been explicitly authoritarian rather than liberal. Hobbes is representative, not exceptional. The medieval rights theorists, Molina, Grotius, Selden (one of the most important and yet neglected of the seventeenth-century figures), Selden's followers and Hobbes all openly endorsed such institu-tions as slavery and the absolutist state. It is true that more liberal rights theories developed out of this conservative and authoritarian tradition, and that Grotius was the vital figure here; in his early works and to some extent in *De Iure Belli ac Pacis* itself he provided a theory which could be read in a liberal way, as it was in their different manners by the English radicals of the 1640s and by John Locke. But the Grotian origins of these liberal theories cannot be ignored, for they were always uneasily close to their authoritarian counterparts. When Rousseau repudiated the entire tradition as conservative, and chose Grotius as his main target, his instincts were absolutely right, however unfair he may have been to the more liberal thinkers such as Locke.[5]

A change in the conventional view of how far someone like Hobbes was

[4] C. B. Macpherson, *The Political Theory of Possessive Individualism* (Oxford, 1962), p. 3. There is, of course, a vast literature on Macpherson's thesis; for one of the most comprehensive lists of the contributions to it, see J. Dunn, *The Political Thought of John Locke* (Cambridge, 1969), pp. 271–84. Macpherson's *Democratic Theory: Essays in Retrieval* (Oxford, 1973) should be added to the list.

[5] The best study of Rousseau's relationship with this tradition is still R. Derathé, *Rousseau et la science politique de son temps* (Paris, 1950).

a deviant and unorthodox thinker should indeed be one important result of
this enquiry. As I show in the central chapters of the book, in both his
political theory and his ideas on the English constitution, Hobbes should
be seen against a background of fundamentally like-minded theorists. But
unlike the context in which Quentin Skinner has located Hobbes,[6] the
milieu I propose – Selden and Selden's friends and followers – was both an
influential and important element in the English political scene from 1640
to 1680, and one in which we know that Hobbes himself moved at a
formative period of his intellectual life. It thus has some explanatory
power over Hobbes's theories, which the Engagement writers (as Skinner
has always been careful to stress) do not possess. Moving a 'Hobbesian'
ideology (broadly defined, in the way explained in those chapters) into the
centre of the intellectual and political stage in this way might in turn affect
our ideas about the character of the English Revolution: but to draw that
conclusion is outside the scope of the present study.

[6] That is to say the writings of English pamphleteers in defence of the Engagement in 1650.
See for the best statement of Skinner's thesis 'Conquest and Consent: Thomas Hobbes and
the Engagement Controversy' in *The Interregnum*, ed. G. E. Aylmer (London, 1972). His
argument was first put forward in the classic article, 'The Ideological Context of Hobbes's
Political Thought', *Historical Journal*, IX (1966).

I

The First Rights Theory

I

In 1515 a Dominican theologian, Silvestro Mazzolini da Prierio, summarised a debate which had been conducted over the previous two hundred years about the relationship between the concepts of *dominium* and *ius*, two words usually translated as 'property' and 'right', though to do so may sometimes obscure the history we need to clarify.

Dominium, according to some people, is the same thing as *ius*. So that anyone who has a *ius* in something, has *dominium* over it; and anyone who has a *ius* to the use of something, has *dominium* in it, and vice versa... According to other people, it is not identical, for an inferior does not have *dominium* over a superior, but he may have a *ius* against him. Thus for example a son has a *ius* to be fed by his father, and the member of a congregation has a *ius* to receive the sacrament from a prelate, etc. So they say, to have *dominium* implies that one has a *ius*, but not vice versa; for in addition to a *ius* one must have superiority.[1]

Important issues were at stake in this argument. The first and more innovatory group (to which Mazzolini himself belonged) thought that any *ius* has to be something the operation of which its possessor could control himself – it had to be *dominium* with its implications of control and mastery. It was not simply a claim on other people, the justice of which ought to be recognised by them. The second group, on the other hand, thought that it was possible for men to have *iura* which they could not themselves control, and which relied exclusively for their operation on their recognition by other people. Already, at the beginning of the sixteenth century, we seem to have an argument which has recurred repeatedly in the history of rights theories: the question of the relationship between (in David Lyons's terminology) 'active' and 'passive' rights.[2]

---

[1] 'Dominium secundum aliquos, est idem quod ius. Unde qui ius habet in re, habet in re dominium: & qui habet ius in usu rei, in eo habet dominium, & econverso ... Secundum alios vero non est idem quod ius, quia inferior in superiorem non habet dominium, & tamen habet ius, puta, filius in patrem ius alimentorum, & subditus in prelatum ius sacramentorum, & huiusmodi: ideo, secundum eos, dominium omne est ius, non econtra: sed super ius addit superioritatem.' S. Mazzolini da Prierio, *Summa Summarum quae Silvestrina nuncupatur*, 1 (Lyons, 1539), p. 159v. (1st edn, Bologna, 1515.)

[2] D. Lyons, 'The Correlativity of Rights and Duties', *Nous*, 4 (1970), p. 48. See also D. D. Raphael's distinction between rights of action and rights of recipience, 'Human Rights', *Aristotelian Society* Supplementary Vol. XXXIX (1965), p. 207.

To have a passive right is to have a right to be given or allowed something by someone else, while to have an active right is to have the right to do something oneself. The distinction between the two is not always as clear as it might be, as there is at least one common theory about rights the implication of which is that all rights have at any rate a 'passive' component. This theory is that all rights entail and are entailed by duties on other people to secure the possessor of the right that which he has a right to.

Thus my (in formal characteristics, active) right to walk about the street correlates necessarily with a duty imposed on other people to allow me to do so, and thus to have a right to walk about the street is simply to have a right to be allowed to walk about when I want to do so. Any active right can thus be re-phrased as a passive right of this kind.

The notorious problem with this theory (leaving aside such potentially soluble difficulties as the case of the third-party beneficiary)[3] is that it appears, as I suggested in the Introduction, to render the language of rights nugatory. If any right can be completely expressed as a more or less complex set of duties on other people towards the possessor of the right, and those duties can in turn be explained in terms of some higher-order moral principle, then the point of a separate language of rights seems to have been lost, and with it the explanatory or justificatory force possessed by references to rights. This result has been acceptable to many political philosophers, but others have been worried by it, feeling (along with Hart) that the point of attributing rights to people is to attribute to them some kind of 'sovereignty' over their moral world.[4] According to this view, to have a right to something is more than to be in a position where one's expressed or understood want is the occasion for the operation of a duty imposed upon someone else: it is actually in some way to impose that duty upon them, and to determine how they ought to act towards the possessor of the right.

Precisely because the notion of a passive right appears to deny this, in that it leaves no scope for the exercise of any kind of 'sovereignty' by the possessor of the right, any theory about rights which lays stress on such a notion tends to develop into some form of the theory that rights and duties are mutually entailed. While conversely, any theory which stresses the idea of an active right will tend to have at its heart the idea of the individual's sovereignty within the relevant section of his moral world. It will also tend as a consequence to stress the importance of the individual's own capacity

[3] See J. Feinberg, 'Duties, Rights, and Claims', *American Philosophical Quarterly*, 3 (1966), pp. 137–44 and D. Lyons, 'Rights, Claimants and Beneficiaries', *American Philosophical Quarterly*, 6 (1969), pp. 173–85.
[4] H. L. A. Hart, 'Are There Any Natural Rights?' *Philosophical Review*, 64 (1955), pp. 175–91. His use of the term 'sovereignty', interestingly close to *dominium*, is on p. 184. For his later views, see 'Bentham on Legal Rights', in A. W. B. Simpson ed., *Oxford Essays in Jurisprudence. Second Series* (Oxford, 1973), pp. 171–201.

to make moral choices, that is to say his *liberty*. If passive rights are taken as paradigmatic, then liberty is a relatively unimportant concept; other people may have a duty to secure my free choice in certain matters, but that is a duty which is parallel (and not fundamental) to their duty to secure me other goods, where my free choice is only important in so far as it may be a condition of their being confident that I really want the good. And not even that, much of the time – do we have to be sure that every child would freely choose to be educated, to be sure that they all have a right to education? But if active rights are paradigmatic, then to attribute rights to someone *is* to attribute some kind of liberty to them. Moreover it is this sort of rights theory which is the most important and interesting, for it is the only sort in which the concept of a right has a truly independent role to play.

The issues at stake in the debate which Mazzolini summarised were thus the crucial ones for any understanding of the concept of a right, and the great seventeenth-century rights theories depended on its outcome. But it is on the face of it curious that such a debate had to be conducted: why was there a problem about rights at all? Why has the language of rights developed in such a way that these kinds of puzzle about fundamental features of a right have been generated, and have remained unsolved? We can only answer these questions by looking more fully at the background to this late medieval controversy.

II

The first point to make is an obvious one, but one nevertheless of great significance: it is, that the language of reflective political discussion in the middle ages was Latin. Thus we are considering developments in a language which already by 1500 had a literary history of some nineteen hundred years (taking the Twelve Tables of 450–400 B.C. to be the first relevant record of Roman legal terminology, or even of the Latin language as such). So it already had a longer history as a written language than English has yet had as a spoken language. It is not to be expected that in the course of such a long history the meanings of even central terms should be at all stable, and this applies very much to the term which is bound to be central to our discussion, the word *ius*.

Over the past thirty years, Michel Villey has published a series of works which have as their common argument the claim that the Romans and the early glossators on the Roman law did not possess any subjective concept of right (to use the useful Continental distinction between 'subjective' and 'objective' *ius*, *recht* or *droit*, a distinction necessitated precisely by the post-Roman changes in the meaning of *ius* and its cognates).[5] He has

---

[5] See 'L'idée du droit subjectif et les systèmes juridiques romains', *Revue historique de droit* Series 4v 24–5, (1946), pp. 201–28; 'Du sens de l'expression jus in re en droit romain

argued that they always meant by *ius* something *objective*, 'that which is right' in a particular situation, and he has adduced as evidence for this not only the fact that a translation of *ius* by (subjective) 'right' often fails to make sense, but above all that the Romans did not regard *dominium*, property, as a *ius*. If property was not a *ius*, Villey claims, then *ius* simply cannot have meant 'right'. It is certainly true that the word *ius* did not mean for the Romans what it meant for the men of the middle ages; whether this implies that the Romans did not possess the concept of a subjective right (which ought have been expressed through another term, or through no term at all) is a more difficult question, to which (as Villey's early critic Giovanni Pugliese pointed out)[6] Villey has not given a clear answer.

The term *ius* was used by the early Romans in the context of a primitive method of divine judgement. Disputants took oaths as to the righteousness of their claims, one of which was upheld in a subsequent ordeal or other supernatural judgement. The favourable verdict was a *ius*.[7] This is a significant origin in two ways. First, it shows that a *ius* was taken to be something objectively right and discoverable, and in this sense it remained as a kind of synonym for 'law' throughout the history of Latin as an effective language. Thus Paulus, the early third-century A.D. jurist, said that *ius* means either 'what is always fair or good (*ius naturale*) . . . or what is best for all or most in a particular society (*ius civile*)';[8] while at a lower level particular rules of law could be described as *iura* – thus a single woman with more than three children was exempt *iure liberorum* from the requirement that she should have a male *tutor*, that is to say by the *ius* in question.[9] But the early use of the term *ius* also shows that it was generally taken to be the right way in which two disputants should behave towards each other, and did not (for example) cover criminal matters. This connexion with private, bilateral relationships seems to have remained an important feature of the classical Roman use of the term, particularly in the central cases involving land.

A good illustration of this is provided by the *iura praediorum*. These were

[6] G. Pugliese, '"Res corporales", "res incorporales" e il problema del diritto soggettivo', *Studi in Onore di Vincenzo Arangio-Ruiz,* III (Naples, 1954), pp. 223–60.
[7] See P. Stein, *Regulae Iuris* (Edinburgh, 1966), p. 4.
[8] 'Id quod semper aequum ac bonum est ius dicitur, ut est ius naturale. Altero modo, quod omnibus aut pluribus in quaque civitate utile est, ut est ius civile.' *Digest* I.1.11.
[9] See W. W. Buckland, *A Text-Book of Roman Law,* 3rd edn revised by P. Stein (Cambridge, 1963), p. 167.

classique' in *Mélanges Fernand de Visscher,* II, *Revue internationale des droits de l'antiquité,* 2 (1949), pp. 417–36; 'Le "jus in re" du droit romain classique au droit moderne', *Publications de l'Institut de droit romain de l'université de Paris,* 6 (1950), pp. 187–225; 'Suum jus cuique tribuens' in *Studi in onere di Pietro de Francisci,* II (Milan, 1956), pp. 361–71; 'Les origines de la notion du droit subjectif' in M. Villey, *Leçons d'histoire de la philosophie du droit* (Paris, 1962), pp. 221–50 (1st edn, 1957); 'La genèse du droit subjectif chez Guillaume d'Occam', *Archives de philosophie du droit* 9 (1964), pp. 97–127; *La Formation de la Pensée Juridique Moderne* (Paris, 1968).

the products of arrangements made between the inhabitants of the tightly packed cities, or between villagers in the country, about the shared services and access which they needed across each other's property. Gaius, writing one of the best-preserved Roman legal treatises under the Emperor Hadrian, listed the *iura* connected with urban property as follows:

the *ius* of building houses higher and obstructing the light of neighbouring houses, or not doing so, because it obstructs their light; the *ius* of streams and gutters, that is, of a neighbour taking a stream or gutter overflow through his yard or house; and the *ius* of admitting into one's property someone else's drains and not depriving them of light.[10]

These *iura* are plainly not rights in the modern sense: a householder did not have the right to put up with the overflowing gutter of his neighbour, he had the duty. Gaius in fact remarked later that the *iura praediorum* 'are also called *servitutes*',[11] which would most reasonably be translated as liabilities rather than rights, were it not that the *ius altius tollendi* and of blocking a neighbour's light was scarcely a liability incident on a property.

All these *iura praediorum* were the product of agreement between neighbours, and without such an agreement they would not come into being. This seems in fact to be the key to the puzzling character of the list: for the unit with which the Roman lawyer dealt was the agreement *as such*, and he was often indifferent as to which of a number of competing descriptions he would employ. This can be seen in a variety of instances of particular *iura*. For example, the term *obligatio* did not generally mean obligation in our sense. Rather, to have an *obligatio* normally meant to be in the position where one benefited from an agreement which laid an obligation (in our sense) on the other party. The *obligatio* was the *vinculum*, the chain which bound the two parties together, rather than the duty laid on only one of them.[12] In general, any such agreement was describable mainly from the point of view of the man who benefited by it: to have an *obligatio* was to benefit by one, and to have a *ius* was to do the same. In certain cases this could alter, as Gaius's list shows, mainly because the *iura* on his list were attached to the property of one of the parties, and could therefore be seen as 'his' even though he might not benefit by them.

Gaius gave another and more comprehensive list of *iura* elsewhere, in the course of a discussion about corporeal and incorporeal *res*. Straightforward physical objects were corporeal:

incorporeal things cannot be touched, and comprise those things which subsist *in iure*, such as an inheritance, a usufruct, or obligations contracted in some way. It is

[10] 'Praediorum urbanorum iura sunt velut ius altius tollendi aedes et officiendi luminibus vicini aedium aut non extellendi, ne luminibus vicini officiatur; item fluminum et stilicidiorum ius, id est ut vicinus flumen vel stilicidium in aream vel in aedes suas recipiat; item cloacae immittendae et luminum immittendorum.' F. de Zulueta ed., *The Institutes of Gaius*, 1 (Oxford, 1946), p. 68.

[11] 'Haec iura ... servitutes vocantur.' *ibid*.

[12] See Buckland, *Roman Law*, pp. 405-6.

irrelevant that corporeal things are inheritable, or that the produce extracted from an estate is corporeal, or that what we owe as the result of an obligation may be, such as an estate, a man, or money. The *ius* of succession and the *ius* of usufruct and the *ius* of obligation are incorporeal. So are the *iura praediorum* and *rusticorum*.[13]

All the *iura* on this list were generally the product of agreements or promises made between specific and independent parties (this is true even of the *ius* of inheritance, which in Roman law was not of course automatically from parent to child). This fact about the way in which *iura* were actually generated or incurred within the legal system was to be of great importance in the area of property rights.

Classical lawyers made a clear and to later eyes puzzling distinction between having *dominium* in something and having a *ius* in it. Gaius (again) remarked that

in the *stipulatio damni infecti*, the claim of those who are absent in good faith is not to be ignored, if the power of notification is given to them on their return, as equity demands. This is the case whether they are *domini*, or whether they have a *ius* in the matter – such as a creditor, a usufructuary or a superficiary.[14]

Ulpian, of the generation after Gaius, made the point explicitly in the case of usufruct: 'the *ius* of using and taking the crop can only be attributed to the man who has the usufruct; the *dominus* of an estate does not have it, since anyone who enjoys the ownership of something does not have a separate *ius* to use it and take its produce'.[15] This caused great confusion later, as surely a proprietor had the right to take his own crop! But the explanation of the distinction was that *dominium* was not constituted by an agreement or other transaction between independent and private parties. It did not come into being because one person promised something to someone else (though it could be transferred in such a way, like most *res* in Roman law, including some *iura*), but was simply given by the fact, as it seemed to the Romans, of a man's total control over his physical world – his land, his slaves or his money.

In the later Empire, such an independent and total control began to seem increasingly implausible. The Emperor was now someone with whom all citizens had bilateral relationships, and who claimed to be able to intervene in their social and economic life in a wide variety of ways. The conse-

---

[13] 'Incorporales sunt quae tangi non possunt, qualia sunt ea quae iure consistunt, sicut hereditas, ususfructus, obligationes quoquo modo contractae. nec ad rem pertinet quod in hereditate res corporales continentur, et fructus qui ex fundo percipiuntur corporales sunt, et quod ex aliqua obligatione nobis debetur, id plerumque corporale est, veluti fundus, homo, pecunia: nam ipsum ius successionis et ipsum ius utendi fruendi et ipsum ius obligationis incorporale est. eodem numero sunt iura praediorum urbanorum et rusticorum.' *Institutes*, p. 68.

[14] 'Eorum quo bona fide absunt in stipulatione damni infecti ius non corrumpitur, sed reversis cavendi ex bono et aequo potestas datur, sive domini sint, sive aliquid in ea re ius habeant, qualis est creditor et fructuarius et superficiarius.' *Digest*, XXXIX.2.19.

[15] 'Uti frui ius sibi esse solus potest intendere, qui habet usum fructum, dominus autem fundi non potest, quia qui habet proprietatem, utendi fruendi ius separatum non habet.' *Digest* VII.6.5.

quence is easy enough to understand: *dominium* came to be seen as another kind of *ius*, not as something outside the area of *iura*. The first signs of this are there even in the time of Gaius himself, though not in the heartland of the Empire: the Emperor Hadrian gave squatters on virgin land in his imperial domain of North Africa the '*ius* to possess it, take its crop and transmit it to heirs'.[16] Such a *ius* came very close in scope to classical *dominium*, and is indeed the nearest any sources of the period come to describing *dominium* as a *ius*. But it was a *ius* because it was constituted by a gift from the Emperor to his tenants. He was not transferring to them some of his own *dominium*, otherwise the virgin lands would have been removed from his imperial control. Instead, he was creating a *ius* related to his *dominium*, but one which in practice had all the salient features of *dominium* as understood in the city of Rome. Such settlers are indeed referred to as *domini* in other documents.

The expansion of imperial institutions into every detail of the law, and the assimilation of Roman and non-Roman citizens, led inevitably to this process being repeated throughout the Empire. The lawyers were now able to describe anything which we would call a property right as a *ius*, because all property could be interpreted as subsisting in bilateral relationships between citizen and Emperor. Levy has traced this process in impressive detail,[17] and it is clear that by the time the Western provinces were lopped off by the Germanic kings, the classical theory of the Digest writers had completely disintegrated.

Not only was *dominium* now a *ius*, but classical *dominium* appeared as only the extreme end of a continuum which included a wide variety of possible property rights – absolute rights for a limited term, rights to transmit only within a circumscribed set of possible legatees, absolute rights tied to a particular trade, etc. There was no obvious barrier between *dominium* and these kinds of property, and so the extension of the term tended to expand (though always with some sense of strain – classical *dominium* remained *dominium perfectum*, and the other uses were seen to be in some way parasitic upon the classical case).[18]

At the same time as *dominium* became a kind of public *ius*, so the old private *iura* came to be interpreted as quasi-public. A good illustration of this is the late imperial lawyers' treatment of praedial servitudes: increasingly, they were understood as *public* rights like modern rights of way, and the idea of their private and bilateral character was lost.[19] A *ius* was now something which one possessed as a result of one's relationship with the state, the public or the Emperor, and as a consequence had become much more like a modern right *in rem*, that is to say an indeterminate right

[16] 'isque qui occupaverint possidendi ac fruendi heredique suo relinquendi id jus datur.' T. Frank ed., *An Economic Survey of Ancient Rome*, IV (Peterson, N. J., 1959), p. 94.

[17] E. Levy, *West Roman Vulgar Law. The Law of Property* (Philadelphia, 1951).

[18] Levy, *Law of Property*, pp. 40–3.

[19] Levy, *Law of Property*, pp. 55–9.

against all the world, as distinct from a right *in personam*, available against determinate individuals.[20] Continuity with the classical concept was given by the fact of the Emperor, a Roman citizen with whom all other Roman citizens had the most extensive relationships; the disappearance of such an institution in the West left this vocabulary suddenly cut off from its roots.

If this is the history of the development of the ideas of *ius* and *dominium* in the ancient world, how far is it true to say, as Villey wants to, that the Romans did not possess any concept of a subjective right, active or passive? There are a number of methodological problems here: first, are we committed to saying that the word *ius* changed its meaning over this period? It is clear that what were classed as *iura* altered, but *prima facie* it looks as if that was because a wider theory about the political world altered, and as if it was precisely because the meaning of *ius* within a narrower section of the theory remained relatively stable that its extension could change. For its extension not to have changed, *would* have implied a change of meaning. But by the end of the period, we have *ius* being used in a way that might lead Villey reasonably to regard it as meaning a right, while in Gaius's work we certainly do not. This reveals graphically the impossibility of talking about the meaning of a word, or about a concept, detached from the theories which are actually putting the word or concept to use.

This in turn raises the problem of whether, despite the fact that the classical Romans did not have a theory about legal relationships in which the modern notion of a subjective right played any part, they can nevertheless be said to have had the concept. In general, the mere absence of a word or phrase translatable into modern terms proves nothing – all human beings (presumably) possess the concept of three-dimensionality, but there is no reason to suppose that all languages contain something which can be translated as such. But we are dealing here with a particular kind of concept, one whose essence is that it plays some justificatory or explanatory role in the social life of the people who possess it. And it is difficult to see how such a concept can operate if there is no way of signalling its use verbally. So it would seem that we have to produce some linguistic evidence if we are to be able to say that the Romans did have the concept of a right.

Pugliese has made the point that it is to *dominium* rather than to *ius* that we should look to find the idea of a subjective right among the Romans.[21] This is a powerful argument, as it is at the heart of Villey's case (as it has been at the heart of my rather different position) that *dominium* was not an example of a *ius*, and if this fact does any work for our cases it must be because *dominium* has many of the features one would expect to see in a

---

[20] For a discussion of this distinction in the modern law, see P. J. Fitzgerald ed., *Salmond on Jurisprudence*, 12th edn (London, 1966), pp. 235–8.
[21] Pugliese, *Studi Arangio-Ruiz*, p. 254.

right. Against Pugliese, one could say that *dominium* could do only some of the work done by the concept of a right; it was never extended to cover any relationships other than those of *total* control. But I want to argue that it is misleading to look (as both Pugliese and Villey have tended to) at the meaning of words taken in a fairly high degree of isolation. The fact that a particular term is being used in a way which is comparable to the way in which we use a term of our own, tells us nothing unless we can understand *why* it is being used in such a way. *Dominium* and *ius* were both used under the later Empire, as we have seen, in ways very similar to the way in which we use the term 'right': but the explanation of this is to be found in a very different kind of theory from any that we use the term 'right' to expound. Consequently, although linguistic evidence is necessary, it is never going to be sufficient to establish that the classical Romans possessed the concept of a right; and the evidence of their theory suggests that they did not. But the traces of their alien and unfamiliar concepts remained embedded in such things as the Digest, and created a constant set of problems for the theoreticians of subsequent ages.

III

It is among the men who rediscovered the Digest and created the medieval science of Roman law in the twelfth century that we must look to find the first modern rights theory, one built round the notion of a passive right. Their problem was to balance the legal language of their own time, derived from the vulgar law of the late Empire and the Germanic kingdoms, with what they found in the Digest, and in a sense the history of Roman law studies in the middle ages is the history of how the lawyers moved between these two poles. There is one feature which remained constant throughout the period, however, and which to some extent serves to mark medieval law studies off from those of the Renaissance: the medieval lawyer always regarded *dominium* as a *ius*, and hence was prepared to talk about *property* rights. He was not prepared to read the Digest in the counter-intuitive way practised by the Renaissance lawyer, nor to let it lead him to a fundamental modification of his existing legal concepts. As Irnerius, the founder of the law school at Bologna at the turn of the eleventh and twelfth centuries, said, '*dominium* is a kind of *ius*',[22] and that remained a basic assumption until the Renaissance.

But in some ways, an understanding of *dominium* as a kind of *ius* led to great problems when these early lawyers tried to produce their systematic accounts of *iura*. The theory they employed to elucidate and extend the concept of a *ius* was embodied for them most neatly in the famous phrase of Ulpian and the *Institutes*, 'Justice is the continuous and lasting determi-

---

[22] 'Dominium tale ius est quo res ipsa corporalis mea fit.' E. Besta ed., *L'Opera d'Irnerio*, II (Turin, 1896), p. 85.

nation to assign to everyone their *ius*.'[23] Ulpian had presumably meant by
this simply that a judge should always seek the just outcome to a dispute,
and he enumerated later the criteria for a just outcome (including, but not
exclusively, giving everyone their *suum* – their *own*). The medieval commentators, however, took it to mean that people should recognise and
respect one another's *claims*. As Azo, the head of the Bolognese school a
hundred years after Irnerius, put it in his explanation of this passage, 'their
ius, that is, their claim *(meritum)*. For in law one is deprived of one's *ius* by a
crime or a breach of contract or such like.'[24]

Azo referred in elucidation of this to a rule embodied in the Digest that a
creditor who took unilateral and illegal action to seize the goods owing to
him lost his *ius* in them, and it was in fact as a gloss on this rule that the
twelfth-century lawyers had developed their theory of *iura*. To Azo's
teacher, Johannes Bassianus, was attributed in this context one of the most
potent observations in medieval jurisprudence: he it was who first (apparently) classified *iura* as either *in re* or *pro re* (later *ad rem*) when he said that
'the creditor loses all the *ius* he has either in the thing or to the thing which
he has recovered'.[25] The notion of a *ius ad rem* would have been utterly
incomprehensible to the Roman jurist, but it obviously followed from the
idea of a *ius* as a claim. Many people have claims on something which they
do not yet possess, and the medieval jurists quickly extended the notion to
cover such things as the claim by an elected ecclesiastic to the benefice into
which he had not yet been inducted, and the claim by the eldest son of a
king to his father's throne. Such claims were essentially claims against
specific people or institutions, who had it in their power to allocate the
benefit in question.

The *ius in re*, on the other hand, covered all the *iura* where someone was
actually in possession of something, and in particular the *iura* of *dominium*
and usufruct. In these cases, there was some kind of right which the
possessor could claim against everyone, even the person from whom he
held his tenancy: these rights were therefore the successors to the late
Roman *iura*. As a mid-twelfth-century commentary on the Codex put it,
in a phrase remarkable not only for illustrating the point neatly but also for
employing the vernacular synonym for *ius*, 'one has a *drictura* in something, if one can use it to claim *(petere)* the thing from all men'.[26] Not only

---

[23] 'Iustitia est constans et perpetua voluntas ius suum cuique tribuendi.' *Digest* I.I.10. See also
Institutes I.I.I.
[24] '*suum ius*, id est, hominis meritum. nam et de iure propter delictum vel pactum non
servatum vel similia quis privatur iure suo.' F. W. Maitland ed., *Select Passages from the
Works of Bracton and Azo*, Selden Society, 8 (London, 1895), p. 22.
[25] 'amittit creditor ius suum tantum quam habet in re illa vel pro re illa quam recuperavit.' E.
M. Meijers, 'Le Soi-Disant "Jus ad Rem"' in his *Etudes d'Histoire du Droit*, IV (Leiden, 1966),
p. 176.
[26] 'ipse habet dricturam in re illa, quare potest eam petere omnibus hominibus.' See E.
Meynial, 'Notes sur la Formation de la Théorie du Domaine Divisé', *Mélanges Fitting,* II
(Montpellier, 1908), p. 422.

were *iura in re* indeterminate in this way, they were also (and as a consequence) transferable by an act of their possessor, unlike *iura ad rem* which depended for their modification on an act of someone else. These twelfth- and early thirteenth-century lawyers, however, were very clear that not all *iura in re* were cases of *dominium*, let alone any *ius ad rem*. While a usufructuary had an indeterminate and transferable right to his estate, it was not a right of total control: the classical distinction between *dominium* and usufruct was entirely to their liking.

The theory of the early glossators was a formidable and plausible one. All rights were claim rights: they all required other men to act in some way towards the claimant, to grant him something. Distinctions between rights could be given by distinguishing either between the people they were claims on, or between what was being claimed; and true property, *dominium*, was defined as a claim to total control against all the world. In other words, they had evolved a consistent theory of passive rights. To a large extent, this must be bound up with the increasing sophistication and elaboration of *canon* law. It was the canon lawyers who developed and applied such important maxims as the principle that 'personal *iura* [i.e. *iura ad rem*] cannot be transferred to others nor be the subject of contracts'[27] which picked out the central difference between the two categories. Ecclesiastical law was of course greatly concerned with general questions of welfare: in the Church, Europe had an institution unprecedented in the Roman world in that it was actually designed (at least in part) for charitable purposes. It is not surprising that a theory about rights as claims should have evolved from within an institution which was so concerned with the claims made on other men by the needy or deserving.[28]

IV

But this theory lasted in its classical form with no competition for only a hundred years or so – Azo was in fact one of its last spokesmen. During the thirteenth century various writers made alterations to it, such that by the fourteenth century it was possible to have the kind of debate which Mazzolini summarised and from which this investigation started. The alterations did not go unchallenged, and the full story of the debate over them is still to be told. But we can at least see what its broad outlines were, and the circumstances in which doubts about the 'passive' theory emerged.

The twelfth-century lawyers, as I said earlier, were clear about the difference between *dominium* and usufruct. One was property in its true sense, the other was not, and they raised the question of whether a usufructuary had *dominium* in his estate only to dismiss it. But their

[27] Largely as a gloss on the *Decretum* I. 100 on the *pallium* and (later) on the *Decretales Gregorii* IX 1.7.8. This whole matter, like so much in the history of canon law, needs further investigation.
[28] See W. Ullmann, 'Public Welfare and Social Legislation in the Early Medieval Councils', *Studies in Church History*, 7 (Cambridge, 1971), pp. 1–39.

successors felt obliged to disagree. The first person to move clearly away
from this position, and to use the term *dominium utile* to describe what the
usufructuary possessed, as distinct from the *dominium directum* enjoyed by
the superior lord, seems to have been the great Bolognese glossator
Accursius, working in the second and third decades of the thirteenth
century.[29] Throughout his Great Gloss the terms occur, apparently without any sense on his part of conceptual strain. But there was clearly a lot of
opposition to his move, which seems to have been connected with a
personal feud in the Bolognese law school between Accursius and another
master, Jacobus Balduini.

We know about Balduini's opposition to Accursius's ideas only in-
directly: Balduini taught both Hostiensis the famous canonist, and Guido
de Ginis who became head of the law school at Orleans in the middle of the
century. Hostiensis records that Balduini described *dominium utile* as 'a
chimaera', while it was at Orleans that the theory that there is only one
kind of *dominium* was to be defended. There are a number of stories about
the personal hostilities between Balduini and Accursius, but we know very
little about the arguments Balduini employed.[30] In itself, this is an indication of the rapidity and completeness with which Accursius's ideas con-
quered the law schools.

But the recognition of the category of *dominium utile* was to transform
rights theories. For now *dominium* was taken to be any *ius in re*: any right
which could be defended against all other men, and which could be
transferred or alienated by its possessor, was a *property* right, and not only
rights of total control. The process had begun whereby all of a man's
rights, of whatever kind, were to come to be seen as his property. This
obscure thirteenth-century feud had these tremendous consequences:
there is a direct line linking Accursius with the late medieval rights
theorists, and through them with the great seventeenth-century figures. It
was not in fact Accursius himself who provided a full elaboration of the
idea of *dominium utile*; that work was done first by two late thirteenth-
century professors at (surprisingly) Orleans, Jacques de Révigny and
Pierre de Belleperche, and given its final summation by their successor as a
leader of the new kind of jurisprudence, Bartolus de Sassoferrato
(1314–57).[31] The idea was still under attack – Bartolus mentions an

[29] See Meynial, *Mélanges Fitting*, especially p. 419.
[30] See Meijers, 'L'Université d'Orleans au xiiie siècle' in his *Etudes d'Histoire du Droit*, iii
(Leiden, 1959), p. 33 for the feud between Balduini and Accursius; see Meynial, *Mélanges
Fitting*, pp. 427 and 443 for Hostiensis and the Orleans school. The remark 'dominus meus
dicit quod utile dominium est chimaera' is an addition by Hostiensis to the *Summa* of Pillius
which he was otherwise following word for word. See the edition by G. B. Palmieri,
Scripta Anecdota Glossatorum, ii (Bologna, 1892), p. 190.
[31] See F. Calasso, *Medio Evo del Diritto*, i (Milan, 1954), pp. 569–73 for a discussion of the
origin of Bartolism in the work of Révigny and Belleperche. See also G. Chevrier, 'Jacques
de Révigny et la Glose d'Accurse', *Atti del Convegno Internazionale di Studi Accursiani*, iii
(Milan, 1968), pp. 979–1004.

unidentified German lawyer as cohtinuing the old Orleanist line[32] – but it was the dominant theory.

Why had Accursius and his successors felt obliged to extend the concept of *dominium* in this way? The answer which Meynial gave in his study of this issue still seems to be the plausible one: the complexity of feudal relationships had reached such a point by the mid-thirteenth century that either all lords had *dominium* of some kind or the notion ceased to have much sense.[33] A great web of sub-infeudations, mutual infeudations and so on covered Europe: it was reasonably clear what kind of person had traditionally counted as a *dominus*, but according to the classical theory one such *dominus* might well not have *dominium* of any kind over his land, while his neighbour (indistinguishable in all other respects) would have. In such a society, *dominium* had to be taken in a looser or more extended sense.

As a natural adjunct to this process, the later heirs to Accursius began to look on all *iura* as much more active than earlier lawyers had done. Bartolus produced an entirely active definition of *dominium directum* as 'the unrestricted *ius* of disposing of a corporeal object unless prohibited by law',[34] while Jacques de Révigny went as far as interpreting *iura ad rem* not as passive claims on other people but as active rights to demand things from them: 'it is a *ius* to demand something, as when you promise me a horse I have the *ius* to demand it, but not a *ius* in it'.[35] So far it was not really possible to claim explicitly that all *iura* including *iura ad rem* were *dominia*, all rights were active; but the foundation for such a claim had been laid at the point at which *dominium* expanded to cover all *iura in re*, since it took with it precisely the idea of control over one's world which the notion of *dominium* had always implied. But we must look elsewhere for the explanation of why that move was made; it came about not because of the exigencies of fitting a legal terminology to the realities of a feudal society, but because political theorists arguing in particular about the naturalness or otherwise of *poverty* began to exploit the terminology for their own purposes.

V

We can see the beginnings of this exploitation in the work of thirteenth-century theologians, especially Thomas Aquinas. To understand their position, we must return to classical Roman theory, this time about the natural life of man. The ancient jurists had been unwilling to allow that men might naturally have *dominium* over other men (slaves) or goods.

---

[32] Meynial, *Mélanges Fitting*, p. 443.

[33] Meynial, *Mélanges Fitting*, p. 450.

[34] 'Ius de re corporali perfecte disponendi, nisi lex prohibeat.' Bartolus on *Digest* XLI.2.17, *Differentia. In Ius Universum Commentarii*, II (Basle, 1562), p. 214.

[35] 'est enim ius ad petendam rem ut si promisisti mihi equum habeo ius ad rem petendam sed non habeo ius in re.' See Meijers *Etudes*, IV, p. 177.

Ulpian had remarked in a famous phrase that 'everyone was born free under the law of nature' – slavery came in by the *ius gentium*, the agreement of men over what redounded to their mutual benefit. Similarly Hermogenianus had argued that the *ius gentium* lay behind 'wars, separate nations, the origin of kingdoms, private property (*dominia distincta*), the division of land, grouping of houses, commerce', etc. Under the *ius naturale* everything had been held and used in common.[36] These stray ideas received their most influential synthesis in the work of Isidore of Seville, whose formulation of the classical position was taken up by Gratian in the *Decretum* and became the basic text around which later argument centred.

The *ius naturale* is common to all nations; it is what is received everywhere by natural instinct, and not by any convention. It includes the union of men and women, the bringing up of children, common possession of everything (*communis omnium possessio*), and freedom for everyone.[37]

Isidore and Gratian's use of the term *possessio* is crucial: they understood by it something which was *not dominium*. Under classical law, of course, *possessio* and *dominium* were necessarily contrasted: to possess something was to occupy it and use it but not to have private property rights in it. This fact has led a number of historians (including A. J. Carlyle) into a misunderstanding of what the pre-Accursian theorists argued about the naturalness of property. They generally assumed that a usufructuary could be said to have *natural* possession of his estate, but not *civil* possession of it, and this meant precisely that he did not have *dominium* over it. He obviously had natural possession of it, since he was actually walking over it, growing things on it and harvesting them, but he did not have civil possession of it, that is, he lacked the right of property, claimable against other men in his society. This is perfectly compatible with a belief that *dominium* came in by agreement, or even by sin, under a different *ius* from the *ius naturale*, and so we find Irnerius (to Carlyle's astonishment) arguing both that *dominium* is the product of the *ius civile* and may well be inequitable, and also that there is natural as well as civil possession.[38] Under the *ius naturale*, such a theory implies, all men had at best usufructuary rights: they all had natural possession of the earth and its fruits, but they lacked *dominium* over it, that is, they could not have natural property rights.

After the development of the concept of *dominium utile*, such a straightforward presentation of this theory was no longer possible. If a usufructu-

[36] 'Iure naturali omnes liberi nascuntur.' *Digest* 1.1.14. 'Ex hoc iure gentium introducta bella, discretae gentes, regna condita, dominia distincta, agris termini positi, aedificia collocata, commercium ...' *Digest* 1.1.5.
[37] 'Jus naturale est commune omnium nationum. et quod ubique instinctu naturae, non constitutione aliqua habetur, ut: viri et feminae conjunctio, liberorum susceptio et educatio, communio omnium possessionum, et omnium una libertas.' Isidore of Seville, *Etymologiarum*, v.4, Migne Patrologia Series, II 82, col. 199. Gratian, *Decretum* 1.1.7, *ibid.*, 187, col. 31.
[38] A. J. & R. W. Carlyle, *A History of Medieval Political Theory in the West*, II (London, 1928), pp. 43–4. For the Roman notion of *possessio*, see Buckland, *Roman Law*, pp. 196–9.

ary has *dominium* of a kind, then natural *dominium* of a kind is also possible. And perhaps the best example of a theorist who drew precisely this conclusion is Aquinas in his *Secunda Secundae*. As he said,

We can consider a material object in two ways. One is with regard to its nature, and that does not lie within human power, but only the divine power, to which all things are obedient. The other is with regard to its use. And here man does have natural *dominium* over material things, for through his reason and will he can use material objects for his own benefit.[39]

Aquinas was born at about the time Accursius was working on his Gloss, and it is clear that he had assimilated the new way of talking about *dominium* by the time he came to write the *Secunda Secundae* in 1271–2.

There has been a certain amount of argument over whether Aquinas in fact possessed the concept of a subjective right at all,[40] and it is true that he does not often (if at all) talk about *iura* as other than objective moral rules. But in so far as he was able to understand what contemporary lawyers were doing, and was able to appropriate their idea of natural *dominium utile*, then he must be reckoned to have had at least the basic concept of a right. But despite his use of the idea of natural *dominium*, his general theory (and this is of course true of all thirteenth-century theories) was not a genuine natural rights theory. This can be seen if we look at a further claim of his about the natural life of man, which was to be of considerable influence later.

Something can be said to be according to the *ius naturale* in two ways. One, if nature inclines us to it: such as not to harm another human being. The other, if nature does not prescribe the opposite: so that we can say a man is naked under the *ius naturale*, since he received no clothes from nature but invented them himself. In this way 'the common possession of all things, and the equal liberty of all' is said to be according to the *ius naturale*: for distinctions between possessions and slavery were not the products of nature, but were made by human reason for the advantage of human life.[41]

---

[39] 'Res exterior potest dupliciter considerari. Uno modo quantum ad ejus naturam, quae non subjacet humanae potestati, sed solum divinae, cui omnia ad nutum obediunt. Alio modo quantum ad usum ipsius rei, et sic habet homo naturale dominium exteriorum rerum, quia per rationem et voluntatem potest uti rebus exterioribus ad suam utilitatem.' T. Aquinas, *Summa Theologia 2a 2ae*, 66.1, ed. M. Lefébure (London, 1975), p. 64.

[40] Arguing that he did not: P. Lachance, *Le Concept de Droit selon Aristote et St. Thomas d'Aquin* (Montreal, 1933); Villey, 'La genèse', p. 103; D. Composta, 'La "moralis facultas" nella filosofia giuridica di F. Suarez', Part II, *Salesianum*, XIX (1957), p. 9. Arguing that he did: H. M. Hering, 'De iure subjective sumpto apud Sanctum Thomam', *Angelicum*, XVI (1939), pp. 295–7.

[41] 'Aliquid dicitur esse de jure naturali dupliciter: uno modo, quia ad hoc natura inclinat, sicut non esse injuriam, alteri faciendam; alio modo, quia natura non inducit contrariam, sicut possemus dicere quod hominem esse nudum est de jure naturali, quia natura non dedit ei vestitutum, sed ars adinvenit. Et hoc modo communis omnium possessio et una libertas dicitur esse de jure naturali, quia scilicet distinctio possessionum et servitus non sunt inductae a natura, sed per hominum rationem ad utilitatem humanae vitae.' Aquinas, *Summa Theologiae la 2ae*, 94.5, ed. T. Gilby (London, 1966), p. 94. See also *2a 2ae*, 66.2, in Lefébure ed., p. 68.

The point about this argument, however, is that it is not designed to attribute rights to people in a state of nature. As Aquinas said, the *ius naturale* is neutral in the areas of personal servitude and private property, and that cuts both ways. There is no *prima facie* right to either servitude *or* liberty, either private property *or* common possession. It is the essence of a natural rights theory that it attributes *prima facie* rights to natural men; Aquinas explicitly avoided doing so, and refrained from following up the implications of a natural *dominium utile*. The most important area which his theory left out, and which was left unconnected with any rights theory for a hundred years or so, was the area of natural liberty. In Aquinas, men do not have a *prima facie* natural right to liberty any more than they have a *prima facie* natural right to dominate other men.

VI

It is clear that one of the objects of Aquinas's theory of natural *dominium* was to cast doubt on the life of apostolic poverty as practised particularly by the great rivals of his Dominican order, the Franciscans. There was a long controversy over precisely this point, which raged from the late thirteenth century through to the middle of the fourteenth century; its importance is that the late medieval natural rights theories undoubtedly grew out of it, and it went on being an obligatory issue for rights theorists to discuss even into the early seventeenth century.

The history of the argument has already been traced in detail by Leff, and there is no need to repeat what he has said on the matter.[42] Briefly, what happened was that the leaders of the Franciscan order in the second half of the thirteenth century tried to evolve a systematic doctrine of apostolic poverty, which would allow them to use all the commodities necessary for their daily lives without entailing that they had property rights, *dominium*, in them. Such a doctrine was obviously vital if the Franciscans were to be both highly organised and faithful to the ideals of their founder. Given its formulation in the works of Bonaventura, it received its classic statement in a bull of Pope Nicholas III, the former protector of the order, issued in 1279 and entitled *Exiit*.

The bull enumerated five kinds of relationship between a man and a material object: *proprietas, possessio, usufructus, ius utendi* and simple use, *simplex usus facti*. The first four could all count as cases of *dominium*, and were therefore unavailable to the Franciscans, but they could have the fifth. The difference was that in the first four cases, there was some commodity which could be disposed of *ad libitum* by an agent – either land and its products, or simply its products (as in the case of usufruct). But in the fifth case, the agent could only *consume* the commodity, he could not trade it or give it away. By asserting that such consumption did not count as the

[42] G. Leff, *Heresy in the Later Middle Ages*, 1 (Manchester, 1967), pp. 51–255.

exercise of a property right, the Franciscans implied that the possibility of alienation or exchange relationships was necessary to property. Because their order was able to step outside the network of exchange relationships, it was able to claim genuine apostolic poverty. To a great extent, although their terminology was different, the Franciscans were faithful to the pre-Accursian tradition: property was something which had to come in with social, civil man, and could not be possessed by a man in himself and his immediate world.

Although this has seldom been noted by the historians of this controversy, there is little doubt that the major theoretical explanation of the Franciscan doctrine was given not by any of the direct participants in the pamphlet war, but by another more famous member of the order, Duns Scotus. He argued in effect against Aquinas, and on lines that served as a justification of the Franciscan position (which at the time he was writing, the first decade of the fourteenth century, was still the papal orthodoxy), that

> by the law of nature or God, there are not distinct *dominia* over things in a state of innocence, indeed everything is in common... One reason for this is that, since the use of things following right reason is allowed to men in so far as it conduces to harmony, peaceful intercourse and necessary sustenance, in the state of innocence common use without distinct *dominium* is more valuable for everyone than distinct *dominium*, as no one will then take over what is necessary for another, nor will they have to defend it by violence, but he who first found it necessary to occupy it, will use it as far as he needs ...[43]

Scotus thus argued that the *ius naturale* was not simply neutral with regard to *dominium*: it positively ruled it out, since common use was the optimum strategy for men in a state of innocence. Common use, for Scotus, was not common *dominium*: it was not the case that the human race collectively had the kind of right over the world which (say) a Benedictine monastery had over its estates. Rather, each human being was simply able to take what he needed, and had no right to exclude another from what was necessary for him. But the crucial point is that such necessary use is not a case of *dominium utile*: Scotus took *dominium* to be necessarily private, something which not only could be exchanged, but which could also be defended against the claims of the needy, and quite possibly by violence. Such an account of man's natural life was absolutely in line with Franciscan

---

[43] 'Lege naturae vel divina, non sunt rerum distincta dominia pro statu innocentiae, imo tunc omnia sunt communia ... Ratio ad hoc duplex est: Prima, quia usus rerum secundum rectam rationem ita debet competere hominibus, sicut congruit ad congruam et pacificam conversationem, et necessariam sustentationem; in statu autem innocentiae communis usus sine distinctione dominiorum ad utrumque istorum plus valuit, quam distinctio dominiorum, quia nullus tunc occupasset quot fuisset alii necessarium, nec oportuisset illud ab ipso per violentiam extorqueri, sed quilibet hoc quod primo occurrisset necessarium, occupasset ad necessarium usum ...' J. Duns Scotus, *Quaestiones in librum Sententiarum*, 15.2, *Opera Omnia*, XVIII (Paris, 1894), pp. 256–7.

poverty: in the terms of *Exiit*, natural man had the *simplex usus facti*, but not *dominium*. As a corollary, the Franciscans in the early fourteenth century were supposed to be living a natural or innocent life (mirrored also, of course, in the poverty of the apostles).

To answer the Franciscan case presented in these terms, it was necessary to clarify the assumptions about *dominium* implicit in (for example) Aquinas, and to develop a rival account of the life of man under the laws of nature or God. The idea that a man could have property as an individual, and that it was not purely a feature of a *social* life, had to be put forward. And this is precisely what happened when the papacy began to move against the Franciscans in the 1320s, alarmed (apparently) by the radical conclusions which could now be drawn from the doctrine of poverty. After all, the Franciscan theory had a normative point: if it was possible for some men to live in an innocent way, then it should be possible for all men to do so. The papacy under John XXII retreated from this radicalism; but in the process it evolved what was to be in the long run the equally radical doctrine of full natural rights. The early fourteenth century saw in this respect a curious anticipation of what was to happen three hundred years later, when natural rights theories were developed by conservative thinkers as a defence of property, competition and other related values.

The apogee of John XXII's campaign was reached in 1329, with the promulgation of his bull *Quia vir reprobus*. In this he met the Franciscan argument at its roots, claiming that God's *dominium* over the earth was conceptually the same as man's *dominium* over his possessions, and that Adam 'in the state of innocence, before Eve was created, had by himself *dominium* over temporal things', even when he had no one to exchange commodities with.[44] A history could be told of the transition of such *dominium* after the fall down to the present day: property was thus natural to man, sustained by divine law, and could not be avoided. For John, all relationships between men and their material world were examples of *dominium*: for some lonely individual to consume the products of his countryside was for him to exercise property rights in them. Property had begun an expansion towards all the corners of man's moral world.

The response to this came in the most famous work produced during the whole controversy, William of Ockham's *Opus Nonaginta Dierum*, written as a blow-by-blow refutation of *Quia vir reprobus*. Villey has seen this work as of fundamental importance in the evolution of rights theories, in that it was the first work in which a systematic account of subjective rights is to be found.[45] However, as the context in which I have begun to locate the work suggests, Villey may have got this (in a sense) completely the wrong

[44] 'Adam in statu innocentiae, antequam Eva formaretur, solus habuerit dominium rerum temporalium.' Leff, *Heresy*, p. 247.
[45] See Villey, 'Les origines' and 'La genèse'. A. S. McGrade in *The Political Thought of William of Ockham* (Cambridge, 1974), p. 16, promises (but does not later deliver) a critique of Villey on this matter.

way round. He took the fact that Ockham consistently elucidates the notion of a *ius* in something by using the word *potestas* to be significant; but as we have seen, if we are to look anywhere for evidence that *ius* is being used in an active sense (which is the kind of subjective right which interests Villey), then we must look first for the assimilation of such a *ius* and *dominium* – and that had occurred already in the writings of the post-Accursians, and in *Quia vir reprobus* itself. By describing a *ius* as a *potestas*, Ockham was merely signalling that he too was using *ius* in an active sense. As Leff has said, 'Ockham was fighting on the pope's ground; and although he contested every position he was still accepting the pope's doctrine and the pope's arguments as the basis for his own replies.'[46]

In fact, if anything, Ockham was inclined to modify the active sense of *dominium*, though not that of *ius*. It was by doing so that he made his case against the *prima facie* plausible arguments of John: *dominium* for Ockham had to be human because

that *dominium* which in jurisprudence and in the writings of people who follow a jurisprudential way of talking is called 'property', is a feature of some person or group of people by virtue of which they can take some other person or group to court, prosecute them or defend themselves, if they have sold or occupied the thing in which they have *dominium*.[47]

Because *dominium* was thus logically tied to human judicial institutions, it followed that natural man could not have it. What he did have, Ockham conceded (thereby transforming the Franciscan case), was the *ius utendi* – *ius naturale* to use commodities as seemed necessary, which was not *dominium*. But there was no litigation possible about such a *ius*. Clearly, Ockham was walking a dialectical tightrope with this argument: it was highly implausible, in that there was no reason in the existing political language to restrict *dominium* solely to a capacity to operate a human judicial machinery. Any *ius in re* for almost a hundred years had been seen as a case of *dominium*, and Ockham's attempt to re-introduce a *ius* to use things, which was not *dominium*, was desperate and unconvincing. Moreover Ockham had made the major concession when he allowed that natural man had active *iura* over the material world, for in effect that was all that the opponents of the Franciscans had been trying to argue when they claimed that natural man had *dominium* over his world. Ockham rescued the form of the Franciscan case, that they need not have *dominium* in their possessions, only to lose the substance, that they need not have *iura* in them. It is not surprising that the *Opus Nonaginta*

[46] Leff, *Heresy*, p. 250.
[47] 'Illud autem dominium, quod in scientiis legalibus et in scripturis modum loquendi scientiarum legalium servantibus vocatur "proprietas", est proprium alicui personae singulari vel collegio speciali, virtute cuius contra aliam personam vel collegium, si rem, cuius habet tale dominium, vendicaverit vel detinuerit, potest in iudicio litigare, agendo vel defendo.' G. de Ockham, *Opera Politica*, II, ed. R. F. Bennett and H. S. Offler (Manchester, 1963), p. 484.

Dierum was to be virtually the last shot from the Franciscan side in the campaign.

The end result of this debate was that the conservative theorists had been led to say that men, considered purely as isolated individuals, had a control over their lives which could correctly be described as *dominium* or property. It was not a phenomenon of social intercourse, still less of civil law: it was a basic fact about human beings, on which their social and political relationships had to be posited. The application of post-Accursian legal concepts to the problems of the essential character of men had led pretty directly to a strongly individualistic political theory which had to undergo only a few modifications to emerge as something very close to the classic rights theories of the seventeenth century.

VII

It was men thinking about the role of God in the papalist theory who made those modifications. By resting his defence of universal and perpetual property on a claim about the nature of God's relationship with his creation, John had unwittingly introduced a theme which was to occupy writers during the remainder of the century (and which, ironically, was to be taken up as an argument for his new heresy by John Wycliffe). It was this theme which bulked large in the book which was to be the occasion for the development of a full natural rights theory, Richard Fitzralph of Armagh's *De Pauperie Salvatoris*, written in the 1350s as a summary of the anti-Franciscan case. In his analysis of terminology, Fitzralph tried to come to an agreement with Ockham; thus he did not argue that all *iura* were *dominia*, but accepted that a *ius utendi* could be excluded from the category. However, he insisted that such a *ius* was only possessed by the agents of the owner of something when they were acting on his behalf – thus an ostler had the right to use a horse in order to stable it, without having *dominium* in it. There had to be *some* owner of everything.[48]

A *ius utendi* was not what natural men possessed to the use of the world; to explain why this was so, Fitzralph brought in his theology. In the beginning, God had 'the full *ius* of possessing the world and using it fully and freely with all things therein contained, by means of possession solely; so that *ius* is the genus of *dominium*, and all else in it is as the specific difference whereby God's *dominium* is distinguished from all *dominium* of his creatures'.[49] This *dominium* of God was the same kind of thing as man's; God admitted man to *share* in his *dominium*, in the same way as commoners

---

[48] R. L. Poole ed., *Iohannis Wycliffe De Dominio Divino* (London, 1890), pp. 475–6.

[49] 'Divinum dominium est ius plenum possidendi mundum, et mediante possessione sola plene ac libere utendi, cum omnibus contentis in ipso; ita ut ius sit genus dominii, et totum residuum tanquam differencia specifica per quam divinum dominium ab omnibus creaturarum dominiis est distinctum.' Poole ed., *Wycliffe*, p. 290; translation p. xxxviii.

can admit a new member to share in their rights without losing them themselves. By thus putting man on a level with God in his rule over the world, Fitzralph might have seemed to be elevating man's own inherent qualities to a divine status: but he avoided doing so by stressing that God admitted men to share out of his *grace*, and that it was thus only men who enjoyed God's grace who could be said to have *dominium*. This was the source of his famous claim that *dominium* is founded on grace, the claim which Wycliffe was to seize on as a weapon with which to beat the clergy – an unregenerate church, having forfeited God's grace, had forfeited its earthly *dominium* likewise.

It was as a reaction to this last belief of Fitzralph's, though still within the general framework of the anti-Franciscan argument, that the transition was made to a fully fledged natural rights theory. Fitzralph's natural human *dominium* was too morally circumscribed: the category had to be widened if it was to be of any use. This was the work of the French nominalists and conciliarists Pierre d'Ailly and (above all) Jean Gerson, and their achievement was refined and developed by their followers during the fifteenth and early sixteenth centuries. D'Ailly adumbrated the basic theory in two tracts written about 1381; his argument was that sinners could have *dominium* because, although Fitzralph's basic theory of *dominium* derived from God through grace was true, the kind of grace involved was that which (for example) an ungodly priest still possessed when it came to administering the sacraments. It was not the grace needed for personal salvation; it was ministerial and not personal, *gratia gratis data* rather than *gratia gratum faciens*.[50]

But it was d'Ailly's successor as Chancellor of the University of Paris, Jean Gerson, who really created the theory. He did so in a work entitled *De Vita Spirituali Animae*, dedicated to d'Ailly and written partially with his help during the early months of 1402. It contains the following remarkable analysis of the concept of a *ius*.

Ius is a dispositional *facultas* or power, appropriate to someone and in accordance with the dictates of right reason ... This definition includes '*facultas* or power', since many things are in accordance with right reason which do not count as *iura* of those that have them, such as penalties for the damned or punishment for mortal men. Nor do we say that anyone has a *ius* to harm themselves, although that is not far removed from what sacred scripture records about the ordinances of divine providence, as in the passage of I Kings about the *ius regis*, etc. And we do say that demons have the *ius* to punish the damned. The definition includes 'dispositional', since many things allow someone to do something in accordance with right reason, ... as a mortal sinner has the *facultas* or power of meriting eternal life; but it is not a dispositional *facultas*, or as we normally say, it is not in accordance with present justice [i.e. the sinner has the capacity but not the actual dispositional ability to merit salvation] ... I want to say that an entity has *iura*, defined in

---

[50] See F. Oakley, *The Political Thought of Pierre d'Ailly. The Voluntarist Tradition* (New Haven, 1964), pp. 74–92.

this way, equivalent to those positive qualities which constitute its identity and therefore its goodness. In this way the sky has the *ius* to rain, the sun to shine, fire to burn, a swallow to build its nest, and every creature to do what is naturally good for it. The reason for this is obvious: all these things are appropriate to these beings following the dictate of the divine right reason, otherwise none of them would survive. So man, even though a sinner, has a *ius* to many things, like other creatures left to their own nature ... This analysis of *ius* is modified by political theorists, who use the term only of what suits rational creatures using their reason. [51]

This is an important passage in many ways. One is that it was the first time that an account of a *ius* as a *facultas* had been given. The idea of a *facultas*, an *ability*, had belonged hitherto mainly to non-moral discourse – Fitzralph indeed had insisted that *dominium* must be an *auctoritas* and not a *facultas* for that very reason, for non-moral and irrational creatures had faculties or abilities. And it clearly still had that sense, but Gerson was not worried about drawing the conclusion that all creatures have rights, of a kind. In the process, however, he was able to make a further move of great importance. I have already stressed that for neither the Romans nor the early medieval lawyers could liberty be a *ius*, a *right*. The Romans had in fact contrasted *libertas* with *ius*, and emphasised its natural, non-moral character. As Florentinus said in a famous remark, later incorporated in the *Institutes*, liberty is the '*facultas* to do what one wants, unless prevented by force or *ius*'. [52] But by claiming that *ius* was a *facultas*, Gerson was able to assimilate *ius* and *libertas*. As he said in another work, his *Definitiones Terminorum Theologiae Moralis* (written between 1400 and 1415), '*Ius* is a *facultas* or power appropriate to someone and in accordance with the dictates of right reason. *Libertas* is a *facultas* of the reason and will towards

[51] 'Ius est facultas seu potestas propinqua conveniens alicui secundum dictamen rectae rationis ... Ponitur "facultas seu potestas", quoniam multa conveniunt secundum dictamen rectae rationis aliquibus quae non dicuntur jura eorum, ut poena damnatorum, et punitiones viatorum; non enim dicimus aliquem jus habere ad ejus nocumentum. Tamen non est penitus alienum a Scriptura Sacra quod ea dicantur jura quae divina providentia sapienter ordinat, sicut 1 Reg. dicitur quod hoc erit jus regis, etc. Et daemones dicimus habere jus ad punitionem damnatorum. Ponitur "propinqua" quoniam multa possunt alicui competere secundum dictamen rectae rationis ... ut existens actualiter in peccato mortali habet potestatem seu facultatem merendi vitam aeternam, non tamen propinquam vel, ut dici solet, non secundum praesentem justitiam ... Dicamus ergo quod omne ens positivum quantum habet de entitate et ex consequenti de bonitate, tantumdem habet de jure sic generaliter definito. In hunc modum coelum jus habet ad influendum, sol ad illuminandum, ignis ad calefaciendum, hirundo ad nidificandum, immo et quaelibet creatura in omni eo quod bene agere naturali potest facultate. Cujus ratio perspicua est: quoniam omnia talia conveniunt eis secundum dictamen rectae rationis divinae, alioquin nunquam persisterent. Sic homo etiam peccator jus habet ad multa sicut et aliae creaturae naturis suis derelictae ... Contractior tamen est ejus acceptio apud polizantes, ut jus dicatur solum de illis quae competunt creaturis rationalibus ut utuntur ratione.' J. Gerson, *Oeuvres Complètes*, III, ed. P. Glorieux (Paris, 1962), pp. 141–2.

[52] 'Libertas est naturalis facultas eius quod cuique facere libet, nisi si quid vi aut iure prohibetur.' *Digest* 1.5.4; see *Institutes* 1.3.1. For Roman ideas on *libertas*, see C. Wirszubski, *Libertas as a Political Idea at Rome during the Late Republic and Early Principate* (Cambridge, 1950).

whatever possibility is selected ... *Lex* is a practical and right reason according to which the movements and workings of things are directed towards their ordained ends.'[53] He was thus even able to make that distinction between *ius* and *lex* which seventeenth-century natural rights theorists thought they had invented.

He was able to go further, and treat liberty as a kind of *dominium*, when he came to apply his analysis of *ius* to the problem of natural *dominium*. As he put it in his *De Vita Spirituali Animae*,

There is a natural *dominium* as a gift from God, by which every creature has a *ius* directly from God to take inferior things into its own use for its own preservation. Each has this *ius* as a result of a fair and irrevocable justice, maintained in its original purity, or a natural integrity. In this way Adam had *dominium* over the fowls of the air and the fish in the sea ... To this *dominium* the *dominium* of liberty can also be assimilated, which is an unrestrained *facultas* given by God ...[54]

The strongly naturalistic aspect of his account allowed him to refute Fitzralph very easily: when God withdrew grace from a sinner, he obviously did not withdraw the sinner's natural ability to do things, so why should he withdraw his *iura*? His substantive position was thus the same as d'Ailly's, but its theoretical foundations were far more fully developed.

Having suggested this theory, Gerson left it to his successors to develop it fully. It was at the universities of Tübingen and Paris, both famous in the fifteenth and early sixteenth centuries as centres of Gerson's kind of nominalism, that the work was done.[55] In some ways the most interesting contribution was made by Conrad Summenhart, a colleague of the famous nominalist theologian Gabriel Biel at Tübingen. Summenhart had been a student at Paris in the 1470s, and then became a master in the arts faculty at Tübingen in 1478, where he remained until his death in 1502. His main work in social theory was a massive *Septipertitum opus de contractibus*, an extensive discussion in Gersonian terms of all the problems associated with contracts and the transfer of *dominium*. In the preliminary material, he systematised Gerson's insights into the nature of *ius* and *dominium*, but he also tried to deal with a number of obvious objections. He took Gerson,

---

[53] 'Jus est facultas seu potestas competens alicui secundum dictamen rectae rationis. Libertas est facultas rationis, et voluntatis ad utrumlibet oppositorum ... Lex est recta ratio practica secundum quam motus et operationes rerum in suos fines ordinatae regulantur.' Gerson, *Oeuvres Complètes*, IX, ed. P. Glorieux (Paris, 1973), p. 134.

[54] 'Erit igitur naturale dominium donum Dei quo creatura jus habet immediate a Deo assumere res alias inferiores in sui usum et conservationem, pluribus competens ex aequo et inabdicabile servata originali justitia seu integritate naturali. Hoc modo habuit Adam dominium super volucres coeli et pisces maris ... Ad hoc dominium spectare potest dominium libertatis, quae est facultas quaedam libere resultans ex dono Dei ...' Gerson, *Oeuvres*, III, p. 145.

[55] See H. A. Oberman, *The Harvest of Medieval Theology; Gabriel Biel and Late Medieval Nominalism* (Cambridge Mass., 1963), and A. Renaudet, *Préréforme et humanisme à Paris pendant les premières guerres d'Italie (1494–1517)*, Bibl. de l'Inst. français de Florence, Series I, vol. 6 (Paris, 1916).

quite rightly, to have implied that all *iura* are *dominia*, that the categories of *ius* and *dominium* are identical. But if this were so, then what about *iura ad rem*, the claims which people make on other people, which had been rather lost sight of in the debates about apostolic poverty?

Summenhart admitted that

an inferior may have a *ius* against a superior, for a superior is obligated to an inferior in many ways. A son has a *ius* against his father ... and a wife has a *ius* against her husband. But we do not strictly say that an inferior has *dominium* in his superiors, nor a son in his parents, nor a wife in her husband. But I do not accept that one should have such a strict concept of *dominium*. It can be taken in a larger sense, and seen as equivalent to a *ius*, in the following way. Whoever has a *ius* in something, can be said to be the *dominium* of it, and therefore *ius* is the same as *dominium* ... For if something is stolen or abstracted from someone who has a *ius* in it, against their will, then a theft has been committed – and it is part of the definition of a theft that the object has been abstracted against the will of a *dominus* ...[56]

This is of course a pretty bad argument, but it shows the determination with which this group were prepared to push through their case. They had converted the claim-right theory of the twelfth century completely into an active right theory, in which to have any kind of right was to be a *dominus*, to have sovereignty over that bit of one's world – such that even a child had sovereignty over its parents when it came to questions of its welfare.

It was the Parisian nominalists who systematised and developed the other aspect of Gerson's idea, its consequences for the theory of natural *dominium*. Thus John Major remarked in his commentary on the Sentences of Peter Lombard (1509) that one of the results of the theory was that in a sense *private* property was natural. Given that *dominium* was simply the *ius* to use something, it might be that the most effective way of using something was to appropriate it privately: hence there was no categorical break in this respect between the state of innocence under the law of nature and the present day.[57] His pupil Jacques Almain said the same:

Dominium as such is nothing other than the *ius* of using something in accordance with right reason. And *ius* (as Gerson says) is nothing other than a dispositional power or *facultas* which everyone has as a result of the rule of right reason ... Natural *dominium* is thus the dispositional power or *facultas* of using things which people can employ in their use of external objects, following the precepts of the law

---

[56] 'Nam inferior habet ius in superiorem: quia superior tenetur inferiori in multis. Et filius habet ius in patrem ... Et uxor habet ius in virum. Et tamen proprie non concederemus inferiorem habere dominium in superiores, aut filium in parentes, aut uxorem in virum. Sed ista stricte hic non accipemus. Et autem possit ita large accipi ut convertitur cum iure; probo: quia quiscunque habet ius in aliqua re; potuit dici dominus illius rei; igitur illud ius poterit dici dominium ... Si ei surripietur vel subtraheretur res illa eo invitō surripiens diceretur furtum commisisse; & si sic; quomodo surripiens contrectavit rem alienam invito domino; tenet consequentia per diffinitionem furti ...' C. Summenhart, *Septipertitum Opus de Contractibus* (Hagenau, 1515), sig. E5. Summenhart died in 1502.

[57] See J. Major, *Quartus Sententiarum* (Paris, 1509), p. 86r.

of nature – by which everyone can look after their own bodies and preserve themselves.[58]

The difference between natural and non-natural *dominia* was simply that natural *dominia* were necessary (i.e. covered basic commodities) while non-natural *dominia* were the product of convention – a modification in Gersonian terms of Aquinas's position.

We can see from the history of this movement how the attack on apostolic poverty had led to a radical natural rights theory. If one had property in anything which one used, in any way, even if only for personal consumption and with no possibility of trade, then any intervention by an agent in the outside world was the exercise of a property right. Even one's own liberty, which was undoubtedly used to do things in the material world, counted as property – with the implication that it could, if the legal circumstances were right, be traded like any other property.[59] *Dominium* did not appear when the laws allowed appropriation and exchange; it had been present from the beginning of time, even when appropriation and exchange were unnecessary, and there was no conceptual break at the point at which men decided to trade their property rather than merely consume it. God's relationship with the world was paradigmatic for these writers: isolated, with no comparable being with which to exchange his possessions, God nevertheless had property in the world, and man could in this respect resemble his maker.

By the second decade of the sixteenth century, the Gersonian theory of rights seemed to reign supreme. When Mazzolini came to write his *Summa*, despite the fact that he was a Dominican and therefore inclined to a Thomist view of the world, he nevertheless accepted the Gersonian arguments as modified and presented by Summenhart. There is very little evidence of any serious opposition to them throughout the fifteenth century; it seemed that the debate whose progress we have been following had come to an end, and that what looks in many ways like a seventeenth-century theory of rights had been achieved. This was of course an illusion: as we shall see in the next chapter, the Renaissance pulled the foundations out from underneath the theory, and it had to be laboriously rebuilt at the end of the sixteenth century. But there can be no doubt of the theory's strength in the fifteenth century.

---

[58] 'Dominium in toto genere, nihil aliud est: quam ius utendi aliqua re secundum rectam rationem. & ius (ut dicit Gerson) nichil aliud est: quam potestas, vel facultas propinqua competens alicui secundum dictamen rectae rationis . . . Dominium naturale nihil aliud est: quam potestas seu facultas propinqua utendi rebus: alicui competens, circa usum aliquarum rerum, secundum regulas legis naturalis. His supponitur: quod de lege naturali, quilibet quantum sibi possibile est. tenetur corpus suum: & se conservare in esse.' J. Almain, *Aurea opuscula omnibus theologis perquam utilia* (Paris, c. 1525), p. 28v.

[59] Mazzolini, *Summa Summarum*, II, p. 256v.

VIII

This raises certain questions about the reasons for its success, and about its relationship to the wider issues involved in the nominalism and conciliarism which its exponents all espoused. The theory in fact seems to have played very little part in the communitarian, conciliarist case to arguing which d'Ailly, Gerson, Almain and Major all devoted so much of their time. Its implications were, after all, potentially individualistic, while it was a crucial feature of their kind of conciliarism that a community was the source of political authority. Moreover, it was presented not in any of the works which they wrote in defence of the conciliarist line, but rather in works of moral theology – like Gerson's *De Vita Spirituali Animae* – or in works of legal and not political theory like Summenhart's *De Contractibus*. This suggests that it is to their theology that we should look first to find the reasons for the theory's success.

The central area of convergence between the Gersonian rights theory and Gersonian theology comes in the belief that man's relationship to the world is conceptually the same as God's. Basic to Gerson's theology, as Ozment has shown, was a conviction that by using all his intellectual and spiritual resources, and with sacramental grace, man could come to be the same kind of being as God, and that the union of man with God (which Gerson presented in quasi-mystical terms) was an expression of this generic unity.[60] Gerson kept a distance between God and man, but it was not a categorical break between two different kinds of being, as it was to be in Luther's theology. Clearly, it was the similarity in the *dominium* which God and men possess over the world which led d'Ailly and Gerson to take up, though in a modified form, Fitzralph's theory in *De Pauperie Salvatoris*. This theology also led Gerson to see the relationship between God and man as a reciprocal one between equals. Thus he argued for a natural covenant between God and man, which – and this is the crucial point – generated rights on *both* sides. According to Gerson, men have rights against God as a result of God's promise to them: 'the humble have been given a right to all things which are to be possessed and held in *dominium*, not by civil law but by divine law'.[61] In this area too, men in some sense confronted God as an equal. Because of this, we can see how freedom became an important value for Gerson: like Ockham (though with a number of important differences) he elevated the free wills of both man and God together. The arbitrary freedom of God's will was necessarily matched by a similar freedom of man's will – there could be no opposition between them.

If this theological position, from which so much of Gerson's thought

---

[60] See S. E. Ozment, *Homo Spiritualis* (Leiden, 1969), p. 83.

[61] 'jus tradi humilibus ad omnia quae dominantur possidenda, non quidem civili lege sed divina.' Ozment, *Homo Spiritualis*, p. 58.

derived, was also the starting-point for his rights theory, then despite its success in the fifteenth century its foundations were indeed extremely fragile. When the Protestants turned against the whole project of assimilating God and man in this way, then much of the plausibility of this rights theory would disappear; while it was simultaneously weakened by the Renaissance and the revival of other forms of scholasticism, notably a purer Thomism. It is to this multiple assault that we must now turn.

2

The Renaissance

I

The same period which saw the culmination of the Gersonian rights theory at Paris saw also the beginning of the movements which were quickly to lead to its abandonment. At Wittenberg in 1515–16, Martin Luther was writing a critique of Gerson's theology into his marginal notes on Tauler's sermons and preparing his seminal lectures on Paul's Epistle to the Romans. At Paris itself Francisco de Vitoria, the creator of the new scholasticism which was to dominate Catholic Europe in the sixteenth century, was a student from 1507 to 1522; while it was in the ten years from 1508 to 1518 that the basic and most significant works of Renaissance jurisprudence were composed or published.[1] All of these developments were signs that the climate was no longer right for a theory of the Gersonian type, but the one which had probably the most substantial influence in the creation of the dominant ideologies of the sixteenth century was the last. The insights of the juridical humanists were taken up by Vitoria and his followers, but they were also taken up by the Reformed intellectuals of the mid-century, particularly the Calvinists. At some very deep level the attitude with which both Catholic and Calvinist faced the world at this period was the same, and at a much more superficial level some of their explicit arguments were almost identical. The Calvinist was generally, however, a much better humanist.

---

[1] For Luther's work at this time and his critique of Gerson, see S. E. Ozment, *Homo Spiritualis* (Leiden, 1969), *passim*. For Vitoria's education at Paris, see R. G. Villoslada, *La Universidad de Paris durante los estudios de Francisco de Vitoria O.P., 1507–22*, Analecta Gregoriana, 14 (Rome, 1938). For the humanist lawyers, the best study is D. Maffei, *Gli Inizi dell' Umanesimo Giuridico* (Milan, 1956). See also his study of an early humanist jurist, *Alessandro d'Alessandro. Giureconsulto Umanista (1461–1523)* (Milan, 1956), and Guido Kisch's study of the humanist lawyers at Basle, *Humanismus und Jurisprudenz*, Basler Studien zur Rechtswissenschaft, 42 (Basle, 1955). Kisch's study of the humanist lawyers' ideas on equity is also very useful: *Erasmus und die Jurisprudenz seiner Zeit*, Basler Studien zur Rechtswissenschaft, 56 (Basle, 1960). Some of the more important of the humanist legal works produced in these years were: G. Budé, *Annotationes in quattuor et viginti Pandectarum libros* (Paris, 1508); A. Alciato, *Annotatiunculae in tres posteriores Codicis Justiniani libros* (Strasbourg, 1515: preface dated 1513); M. Salamonio, *De Principatu*, finished in 1513 (see below, n. 6); A. Alciato, *Paradoxa Dispunctiones, Praetermissa* (Milan, 1518); and U. Zasius, *Lucubrationes* (Basle, 1518).

By virtue of their intellectual origins, humanist lawyers found it virtually impossible to talk about natural rights, and extremely difficult to talk about rights *tout court*. What was important to them was not natural law but humanly constructed law; not natural rights but civil remedies. This was bound up with what had been a central feature of Quattrocento culture in the cities of Italy: the contrast between civilisation, for which (it was believed) a city was essential, and the rude and barbaric life of a pre-civilised people. The *locus classicus* for the picture of the natural life of man which was to become a commonplace for the early sixteenth-century juridical humanists was the first pages of Cicero's *De Inventione*, in which he gave an account of the origin of eloquence:

There was a time when men wandered at large in the fields like animals and lived on wild fare; they did nothing by the guidance of reason, but relied chiefly on physical strength; there was as yet no ordered system of religious worship nor of social duties; no one had seen legitimate marriage nor had anyone looked upon children whom he knew to be his own nor had they learned the advantages of an equitable code of law ... At this juncture a man – great and wise I am sure – became aware of the power latent in man and the wide field offered by his mind for great achievements if once he could develop this power and improve it by instruction. Men were scattered in the fields and hidden in sylvan retreats when he assembled and gathered them in accordance with a plan; he introduced them to every useful and honourable occupation, though they cried out against it at first because of its novelty, and then when because of his reason and eloquence they had listened with greater attention, he transformed them into a kind and gentle folk.[2]

Eloquence, the main professional pursuit of the Quattrocento humanist, thus came to be seen as the means whereby man had moved from a naturally brutish life to one of civility. (Fortunately, the humanists did not have the manuscript of Cicero's *De Republica* in which a much more Aristotelian account of man's natural life was given.) Many humanists endorsed Cicero's judgement; thus Andrea Brenzi in an oration at Rome in 1480 quoted him on the power of eloquence to 'gather together men who originally like beasts wandered isolated in the fields and were bound by no laws, and to bring them from brutishness and barbarism to humanity and culture. Eloquence founds cities, arms people against their enemies, restrains the violent, pacifies the tumults and disorders of the citizens;

[2] 'Fuit quoddam tempus cum in agris homines passim bestiarum modo vagabantur et sibi victu fero vitam propagabant, nec ratione animi quicquam, sed pleraque viribus corporis administrabant; nondum divinae religionis, non humani officii ratio colebatur, nemo nuptias viderat legitimas, non certos quisquam aspexerat liberos, non ius aequabile quid utilitatis haberet, acceperat ... Quo tempore quidam magnus videlicet vir et sapiens cognovit quae materia esset et quanta ad maximas res opportunitas in animis inesset hominum, si quis eam posset elicere et praecipiendo meliorem reddere; qui dispersos homines in agros et in tectis silvestribus abditos ratione quadam compulit unum in locum et congregavit et eos in unam quamque rem inducens utilem atque honestam primo propter insolentiam reclamantes, deinde propter rationem atque orationem studiosius audientes ex feris et immanibus mites reddidit et mansuetos.' Cicero, *De Inventione*, 1.2 (Loeb edn, pp. 4–6). (Translation based on H. M. Hubbell's, *ibid.*, pp. 5–7.) See also his *De Oratore*, 1.33 for a similar and equally often-quoted account.

above all else, it safeguards justice and the laws of cities.' Many similar examples could be given.[3] Built into this picture was a contempt for untutored nature, and this contempt left little scope for any traditional theory of the natural law as revealing the necessary precepts of morality to all men (as in Aquinas, and indeed virtually all medieval theorists). Instead, the humanists were interested mainly in the laws which human societies imposed on themselves – the *ius gentium* or the *ius civile*, both bound up with civilisation. Hermogenianus had after all attributed the introduction of such central features of civil life as 'the grouping of houses, trade, buying and selling' to the *ius gentium* rather than the *ius naturale*. Ulpian's remarks in the Digest that the *ius naturale* was 'what nature teaches to all animals' fitted in with this view for it emphasised the *brutish* character of such a pre-civil man.

Valla indeed questioned whether such a state could properly be described in terms of *ius* at all. *Lex*, he said, was the decree of a ruler:

iura are more general. That is true of the *ius gentium* and the *ius civile*. For it is ridiculous to call *ius naturale* what nature teaches to all animals. Who will call the desire for association, and even more the desire to harm weaker animals, ravage and kill, a *ius*? So Cicero in his *De Officiis* is silent about the *ius naturale*, meaning that *ius* is only to be found among men, in the form of the *ius gentium* or the *ius civile*.[4]

This was going too far for most of his successors, who argued instead that man's natural promptings were a *ius naturale* in so far as they were morally permissible, but they agreed with him that it was the *ius gentium* which was really interesting.

The relationship of the *ius gentium* to the *ius naturale* had in fact been a constant problem for late medieval jurists, as many texts in the Digest supported the view that most phenomena of the moral world were post-

---

[3] 'qui primitus sicut ferae in agris dispersi vagabantur nullisque legibus tenebantur, in unum congregavit & a feritate & barbarie ad humanitatem & cultum convertit. haec civitates condere, haec populos in hostes armare, haec armatos reprimere, haec civium tumultus discordiasque sedare, haec iustitiam in civitatibus & leges servare omnium & prima potuit.' K. Muellner ed., *Reden und Briefe Italienischer Humanisten* (Vienna, 1899), p. 76. See *ibid.*, p. 110 for a similar oration delivered at Florence in 1421. For the general place of the study of eloquence in humanism, see above all P. O. Kristeller, 'Humanism and Scholasticism in the Italian Renaissance', reprinted in his *Renaissance Thought* (New York, 1961), J. E. Seigel, *Rhetoric and Philosophy in Renaissance Humanism* (Princeton, 1968), and the authorities cited by Seigel, p. 32 n. 3. As J. G. A. Pocock has pointed out (*The Machiavellian Moment* (Princeton, 1975), pp. 58–60), the views of Kristeller and Seigel are quite compatible with the interpretation of early Quattrocento humanism as 'active' and 'civic' put forward in the classic works of Hans Baron, *The Crisis of the Early Italian Renaissance*, 2nd edn (Princeton, 1966), and Eugenio Garin, *Italian Humanism*, trans. P. Munz (Oxford, 1965).

[4] 'Iura autem magis generalia sunt. Siquidem & ius gentium est, & ius civile. Nam ius naturale dicere, quod natura omnia animalia docuit, ridiculum est. Appetitum coeundi, atque adeo nocendi imbecilliori animali, spoliandi, occidendi, quis ius esse dixerit? Ideoque M. Tullius in libro Officiorum de iure naturali silentium egit, inter solos homines ius esse significans, idque gentium esse vel civile.' L. Valla, *Elegantiae*, IV.48, *Opera* (Basle, 1543), p. 139.

natural (including of course *dominium*, as we saw in the previous chapter). The jurists had somehow to square this with the commitment which they shared with the theologians to a distinction between the rights and duties possessed by natural man and those possessed by civilised man. In particular, they had got into a tremendous tangle over a particular passage of the Digest which spoke of the 'natural obligation' attached to a debt as arising from the *ius gentium*. By 'natural' obligation was meant an obligation which had no civil remedy other than through the equitable jurisdiction of the practor: thus a promise without consideration, made without the particular forms of Roman law contract, could not bind the promissor in a normal civil court, though it clearly had a moral force. The civil lawyers accepted this, unlike the canon lawyers, who insisted that any promise carried as much weight as any other; their problem was to explain it.

Bartolus provided the classic answer. He conceded to the ancient lawyers that the *ius naturale* was what was common to all animals, and could therefore not be the source of a promise's obligation; but he divided the *ius gentium* into two kinds. One was what *gentes* brought into being 'led by their natural reason, without any agreement, such as that a free man should keep faith or promises, etc. And under this primitive *ius gentium* the free status of a slave was not destroyed, indeed all men were free ... The other *ius gentium* was what all *gentes* used by agreement, not following natural reason ... such as wars, imprisonment, servitude and distinct *dominium*.' He thus rescued the basic late medieval theory, that there was a pre-conventional moral life, by dividing the *ius gentium* in this unclassical way. But as his sixteenth-century editor pointed out, there was no good reason why natural obligation should go in a primitive category of *ius gentium*, and distinct *dominia* in another.[5] The humanists instead simply accepted the classical Roman view: all real moral relationships belonged to the stage of civilisation.

This was particularly true of the greatest of the humanist jurists, Andrea Alciato and Mario Salamonio. Both came from a purely humanist culture, and were deeply influenced by Quattrocento ideas.[6] Thus Alciato, in a

---

[5] 'Debetis tamen scire, quod ius gentium est duplex. Quoddam est ius gentium, quod fuit eo ipso quodam gentes esse coeperunt, naturali ratione inductum, absque aliqua constitutione iuris gentium, ut fidem seu promissa servaret libertus, & si. Et isto iure gentium primevo status servi non annihilatus, imo omnes erant liberi ... Quoddam est ius gentium, quo omnes gentes utuntur ex constitutione earum, non secundum rationem naturalem ... ut bella, captivitates, servitus, distinctiones dominiorum.' Bartolus on the Digest XIII.6, *Si id quod. In Ius Universum Commentarii,* I (Basle, 1562), p. 640. The comment of his editor, Jacobus Concenatius, is *ibid.*

[6] For Alciato, see P. E. Viard, *André Alciat 1492–1550* (Paris, 1926), and R. Abbondanza, 'Premières considérations sur la méthodologie d'Alciat', *Pédagogues et Juristes, Congrès du Centre d'Etudes Supérieures de la Renaissance de Tours* (Paris, 1963), pp. 107–18, translated and abridged in E. Cochrane ed., *The Late Italian Renaissance 1525–1639* (London, 1970), pp. 77–90. A comprehensive modern study of Alciato is badly needed. For Salamonio, see the somewhat misleading study by Mario d'Addio, *L'Idea del Contratto Sociale dai Sofisti alla Riforma e il 'De Principatu' di Mario Salamonio*, Pubblicazioni dell'Istitut di Diritto Pubblico

notable oration in praise of the law, delivered at Avignon between 1518 and 1521, accepted the role of eloquence in drawing men together, though he also stressed that the law had an independent part to play:

ancient authors relate that in the first infancy of humankind men were unsociable, wandering through the mountains and fields in a brutish manner, unconscious of religion or of human duties, and solving every problem with bravery and bodily strength. Then either Mercury (as Plato and Aristides believed) or some other wise man, helped by his skill in eloquence, gathered them together with some suitable oration and urged mutually beneficial association and civil culture upon them ... And keeping faith, encouraging justice, suppressing deceit and respecting the law are of no greater concern to eloquence than to our profession.[7]

The role of the lawyer, as Alciato saw it, was to preserve that civilised and sociable life, just as earlier humanists had seen it to be the role of the rhetorician. This marked a shift from (say) Bruni, who compared the law unfavourably with literature (the concrete realisation of eloquence) and accused it of paying too much attention to evil men rather than good, and of being far too variable – 'things that are right in Florence are wrong in Ferrara'; but it was still recognisably a product of the same set of values.[8] The need for this shift to occur explains why legal humanism of this kind appeared only in the early sixteenth century: the actual and often barbarous law of fifteenth-century Europe had to be seen as worth defending in humanist terms. Alciato and his followers consistently defended lawyers such as Bartolus from the attacks of humanists such as Valla and Bruni, but they did so from a humanist standpoint themselves.

Elsewhere, Alciato gave a more precise account of his views in a discussion of natural obligation which reveals the shift from the late medieval

[7] 'Tradunt antiqui autores, in primaeva illa rerum humanarum infantia fuisse homines insociabiles, qui per montes agrosque passim, & bestiarum more vagarentur, non divinae religionis, nec humani officii memores, quique omnia sola fortitudine pro viribus corporis administrarent, donec sive Mercurius (ut Plato & Aristides credidit) sive quilibet alius vir sapiens eloquentiae artibus adiutus, accommodata oratione eos congregavit, quantumque in se utilitatis mutua conversatione, & studia civilia haberent, admonuit... Nec enim fidem servare, iustitiam colere, simultates abolere, sub legibus esse, eloquentiam magis, quam professionem hanc nostram respicit.' A. Alciato, *Omnia ... Opera,* II (Basle, 1546), col. 508.
[8] Garin, *Italian Humanism,* p. 34. See also his *La Disputa delle Arti nel Quattrocento* (Florence, 1948). An interesting (but undated) speech by Zasius at Freiburg makes the point that eloquence's claim to have rescued man from a brutish and unsociable life is one that the law should properly make instead – an example of just the shift we are concerned with. U. Zasius, *Opera,* V (Lyons, 1550), cols. 508–9.

dell' Università di Roma, Series IV, No. 4 (Milan, 1954), and his edition of the *De Principatu* and Salamonio's *Orationes ad Priores Florentinos,* in No. 5 of the same series (Milan, 1955). Salamonio's completely humanistic *In Librum Pandectarum Iur. Ci. Commentarioli* was first published at Rome in 1525. Alciato's esteem for Salamonio is recorded in a letter of 1521: 'Salamoni literas legi perhumanas, merentur tam boni mores et bonas literas.' (D'Addio, *L'Idea,* p. 13 n. 20.) He and Salamonio were linked together by the Basle humanist lawyer Chansonette (*De Officio Iudicis* in *Tractatuum e Variis Iuris Civilis Collectorum,* II (Lyons, 1549), p. 295r, and (along with Zasius) by Vives (*Opera Omnia,* VI (Valencia, 1785), I p. 234). See also Kisch, *Erasmus,* pp. 359–60.

position. He argued that the natural obligation of promises arose under the *ius gentium*, but so did the obligation between parent and child, and between master and slave. There was no distinction between two types of *ius gentium*. The move from the *ius gentium* to the *ius civile* came about because under the *ius gentium* recourse could only be had to the uncertain and arbitrary judgements of primitive kings. Under the *ius civile*, on the other hand, everything (including the magistrates) was regulated by settled law.[9] This emphasised that there was no categorical break between the *ius gentium* and the *ius civile*, and that both (unlike the *ius naturale* which Alciato virtually never mentions in the whole of his works) were the product of social and civilised man thinking about what was for his own convenience. There was no idea of any social contract involved in this, simply because promises took their force from their convenience to social man, just as property did. Natural man had nothing to contract about: no *dominium* and no rights to renounce or transfer.

Alciato's great pupil François Connan, in the commentaries on the civil law which he composed in the late 1540s, produced what was perhaps the best statement of this general theory:

The *ius naturale* relates properly to a solitary man, leading his life in the fields with a mate and children. But since he is led by nature itself to the society of other men and association with them, he gradually ventures out, and becomes involved in society first with close relatives, then with friends, with neighbours, and eventually through his commerce with them the whole human race ... And since each bit of the earth does not produce everything, nor can each person do everything, men sought advantages for themselves and an easier life by a division of labour and trade in commodities. It was necessary in this process for them to foster justice, to keep contracts, to harm no one by word or deed, and to use the same honesty with foreigners and strangers as they were accustomed to use with their mate and children ... Everyone thus very willingly embraced a *ius* which is called *gentium*; it is distinguished from the *ius naturale* in that the latter relates to man as an animal, prudent and cunning admittedly, but when at home not much different from the beasts. The former relates to man *qua* man, rational and wise, and fully involved with other men ... There are some people in our time who have divided the *ius gentium* into primary and secondary categories. But I think that they have not really divided it, but have wished to distinguish the periods when things appeared under it, and their development.[10]

---

[9] Alciato, *Opera*, III, col. 306.

[10] 'Ius itaque naturale proprium est hominis solitarii, vitam agentis in agro cum uxore & liberis. Sed cum ad hominum societates, & coetus suapte natura ferretur, paulatim exiit foras, cognationibus primum, tum affinitatibus, deinde amicitiis, postea vicinitatibus, & tandem commerciorum usu totum genus humanum societate complexus est ... Quia vero non omnis fert omnia tellus, ut dicitur, nec quilibet potest quod quisquam, mutuationibus officiorum & rerum commerciis utilitates sibi quaesiverunt ad vitam commodius degendam. In quo necesse fuit iustitiam colere, fidem servare contractuum, neminem dicto factove laedere, cum extraneis & sibi ignotis hominibus eadem probitate agere, qua soliti erant cum uxore & liberis ... Ius idem omnes magna voluntate amplectebantur, quod gentium dicitur, ab illo naturali diversum in eo, quod naturale est hominis qua animal est, providum quidem & sagax, caeterum inclusum domi, paulum admodum differens a brutis. Ius hoc gentium hominis est qua homo, plenus rationis & consilii, & iam hominum societate implicatus ... Sunt autem ex nostris, qui hoc ius gentium duplex fecerunt,

Given this general picture, it was inevitable that many humanists should have construed any civil law as necessarily socially beneficial, and arrived at through some sort of co-operative social action. Mario Salamonio's definition of civil law as a contract of the people in his *De principatu* and his *Commentarioli* is the most famous expression of this. It undoubtedly grew out of his humanistic legal studies, which led him in his remarkable commentary on the first few titles of the Digest to insist that the *ius naturale* was merely what nature taught all animals (including self-defence), and that moral relationships such as the obligation to keep promises came in with the *ius gentium*. Laws in the form of social compacts were necessary for the survival of a society, and it made no sense for someone to be in a position where he could threaten the society. Consequently any prince who stepped outside the agreed law became a tyrant, and (he remarks in his *Commentarioli*) can honourably be killed.[11] Salamonio's republicanism and stress on resistance are famous, but Alciato exhibits the same traits. In a late commentary on a title of canon law, he used what amounted to an argument about the mutual relationship between protection and obedience: 'I believe indeed that a prince ought of necessity to judge fairly, either in his own right or through magistrates, since otherwise he may be deprived of his kingdom ... This follows from the *ius gentium*, which the prince is not absolved from. And what Andrea de Isernia says is noteworthy, ... that a prince receives taxation and the profits of kingship in order to advance justice and protect his subjects from the attacks of evil-doers, otherwise he is making no return.'[12]

These early humanist lawyers had a very republican interpretation of the Empire: Salamonio is again the extreme case: he argued (not at all implausibly) that the desire of the early Emperors for offices such as the tribunate showed that they continued to work within the Republican constitution, and that their powers were simply an agglomeration of Republican magistracies.[13] But Alciato too claimed that the *lex regia* by which the Emperor

---

[11] M. Salamonio, *In Librum Pandectarum Iur. Ci. Commentarioli* (Basle, 1530), pp. 6r–13v for his discussion of the law of nature: 'Observa tripertitam iuris divisionem, quae a triplici de homine consideratione descendit. Consideratur primo ut animal, unde ius manat naturale: item ut homo, unde ius gentium sive humanum: tertio ut civis, a quo ius civile.' (13v). His remark about tyrannicide is *ibid.* p. 21r. See d'Addio's edition of *De Principatu*, particularly pp. 27–30, for his discussion of law as compact.

[12] 'Ego credo quod imo de necessitate debeat princeps ius dicere, vel per se, vel per magistratus, alias posset privari regno ... & istud videtur esse de iure gentium ... quo iure non est solutus princeps. & facit quod not. And. de Iser. ... ubi dicit, quod princeps habet vectigalia, & redditus regni, ut servet iustitiam, & teneatur subditos etiam ab incursibus latronum, aliter non facit fructus suos.' Alciato, *Opera*, IV, col. 388. Andrea de Isernia was a Neapolitan juridical historian and a younger contemporary of Alciato.

[13] Salamonio, *Commentarioli*, p, 41v.

---

primum, & secundum. In quo tamen mihi videntur non tam ipsum divisisse, quam aetatem rerum ab eo inventarum, progressumque notare voluisse.' F. Connan, *Commentariorum Iuris Civilis Libri* x (Paris, 1558), pp. 19v–20r. For a modern discussion of Connan, see C. Bergfeld, *Franciscus Connanus 1508–1551* (Cologne, 1968).

had received his power from the Roman people could not have superseded
the treaties which the Romans made with their allies (including the north
Italian cities) in the Republican period, and that consequently the Emperor
could have no more power over them than the Roman people had done.
He also praised the censors under the Republic for the way in which they
controlled public officers, and remarked that 'this old character is retained
only in the cities of Germany which they call "free", where they gladly
recognise the Emperor's dignity, but will not suffer themselves to be worn
down by tribute, goaded by violence or oppressed by tyranny'.[14]

In this as in most other respects, Connan was a true heir to Alciato: he
too held that a ruler who violates human law can be deposed.[15]

Not all of the early humanist lawyers were like this, the most notable
exception being Guillaume Budé (who perhaps significantly was not, as
Alciato sourly pointed out,[16] a professional jurist). Those that were not,
however, are explicable as coming from a rather different humanist tradition. While Bruni could praise rhetoric as the key to civil and republican
life, someone like Aeneo Silvio Piccolomini could see it as the key to the
enlightened counselling of an absolutist prince – the kind of prince that he
himself later became.[17] Both views of the role of eloquence in the modern
world were current at the end of the Quattrocento, and both were modified into theories of the comparable role of law. Budé, like Thomas More
and many other servants of the northern kings, was deeply involved with
the problem of counsel, and his absolutism goes along with that.[18] But

[14] 'Solum antiquam indolem retinuerunt in Germania civitates, quas illi francas vocant: ut
enim Imperatoris fastigium libenter agnoscunt, ita tributis se atteri, violentia urgeri,
tyrannide opprimi non patiuntur.' Alciato, *Opera*, I, col. 268.

[15] 'Ut si qui iusta haereditate rex est, tyrannicos mores induat, divina atque humana iura
pervertat, suorum non salutem petat, sed sanguinem, eiiciendus regno est: dum id fiat, rex
est: nec attentandus a quoquam est, nisi communi suorum decreto deliberatum sit &
constitutum.' Connan, *Commentarii*, p. 34r. Cf. Zasius's remarks on resistance, *Opera*, VI,
p. 245. A. J. Carlyle is one of the few people who have recognised this libertarian and
almost republican character of early sixteenth-century civil law studies – see R. W. and
A. J. Carlyle, *A History of Medieval Political Theory in the West*, VI (London, 1936), pp.
298–324. M. P. Gilmore has given a somewhat misleading account of Alciato's ideas about
rerum imperium in his *Argument from Roman law in Political Thought 1200–1600* (Cambridge,
Mass., 1941), pp. 49–56. Although (as he says) Alciato linked lesser magistrates' power to
the law and not the prince, he tends to see him as more of an absolutist than is fair. The same
tendency can be seen in D. R. Kelley's *Foundations of Modern Historical Scholarship* (New
York, 1970), p. 99.

[16] See Viard, *André Alciat*, pp. 53–5 for Alciato's controversies with Budé.

[17] The best guide to the voluminous writings of Piccolomini is the selection edited by B.
Widmer, *Enea Silvio Piccolomini* (Basle, 1960). Guido Kisch has provided an interesting
discussion of Piccolomini's (often critical) attitude to legal studies in his *Enea Silvio
Piccolomini und die Jurisprudenz* (Basle, 1967), especially pp. 67–86.

[18] The last part of Budé's *De Asse* (1513) is a dialogue on the problem of counsel, very
comparable to the first part of More's *Utopia*. See the discussion of it by D. O. McNeill in
his *Guillaume Budé and Humanism in the Reign of Francis I*, Travaux d'Humanisme et
Renaissance, 142 (Geneva, 1975), p. 35. (More's admiration for the *De Asse* is attested on p.
27.) For Budé's general ideas, L. Delaruelle, *Guillaume Budé. Les Origines, les Débuts, les
Idées Maîtresses* (Paris, 1907), is still useful.

Alciato and Salamonio came from a more truly *civic* tradition, in which eloquence was put to work by the citizen and not by the counsellor, and their legal theories differed from Budé's accordingly. Something of the tension between these two traditions may be glimpsed in More's *Utopia*, in which a discussion about the difficulties of counselling a prince is followed by the depiction of a civic republic.

Given the general attitude of the humanist lawyers, there was obviously no place in their thinking for natural rights of any kind. Man's natural life was simply not an appropriate setting for such things as *dominium*. This fitted in neatly with their observation, made very early on in the Renaissance study of the law, that the category of *dominium utile* was a postclassical development, for they were then able to show on two different grounds that there could be no natural *dominium*. Connan put this second point extremely well: it was true that in a state of nature men could use anything they needed, 'and that this use is very like *dominium*: but it is not *dominium*, as the classical jurists showed in "On usufruct". For nature did not give us *dominium* in anything, but rather use or possession for the sake of use.'[19]

All rights were thus civil rights: but by saying this, the humanist lawyers immediately diverted attention from the right to the remedy, the civil action which actually secured his objective for the possessor of a right. As Connan said (in a passage which among other things reveals how he took a natural obligation to be the product of settled law):

There is no *ius* to which is not given, either by nature or by law, some obligation as a companion and guide; so that if need be it can protect itself through a judgement in an action in front of judges. If I settle on vacant land, I become a possessor and a *dominus*: and although no one is bound to me by any definite obligation, nevertheless everyone is obliged to me thus far, that they do not dispossess me. And if they do, then immediately by virtue of an obligation which can now be termed definite and natural [*nata*, and not *naturalis*], an action lies, soliciting the aid of judges. Therefore *ius*, obligation, action and judgement do not differ if one regards the cause, the matter and the end, but they do differ in reason, role and scope. For a *ius* consists of a person, a possession, or the facts from which an obligation springs; from the obligation comes an action, which procures a judgement and finishes the matter.[20]

[19] 'Et in iis usus dominio est persimilis. non tamen dominium est: ut eleganter Iurisconsulti tradiderunt, De usufr. earum rerum quae usu consumuntur. at in nullis rebus ne in his etiam, natura nobis dominium dedit, sed usum tantum, aut usus nostri causa possessionem.' Connan, *Commentarii*, pp. 25v–26r.

[20] 'nullum ius est, cui non sit, aut a natura, aut a lege data quaedam obligatio tanquam comes & adiutrix: ut si opus sit, actionis ministerio iudiciorum se tueatur authoritate: velut si in vacua venerim, effectus sum possessor & dominus: & quamvis ulla certa obligatione nemo mihi teneatur, tamen omnes quodammodo mihi obligati sunt ad hoc, ut ne meam possessionem interpellent. quod si quis fecerit, statim obligationis beneficio, quae iam certa & nata dicitur, actio parata est, quae iudicum fidem imploret. Ergò ius, obligatio, actio, & iudicium, si causam, si materiam & finem spectes, non differunt: ratione, officio & ordine differunt. Nam in persona, rebus nostris, aut factis, ius consistit, a quo obligatio oritur: ab hac actio, quae iudicium procurat, & conficit.' Connan, *Commentarii*, p. 71r.

The humanists were thus able to explain the fact that the *Corpus Juris Civilis* does not talk about *iura in re* and *in personam*, but rather *actiones in rem* and *in personam*: the action was what really mattered, and their discussion of legal matters was always centred upon it.

Some of the later humanist lawyers, particularly in France, shied away from all this. Their tendency to return to older juridical ways has been termed (and rightly, in most cases) 'neo-Bartolism' – by which should be meant not that they began to read or even respect the medieval jurists, for that was true of all the humanists with the exception of Budé, but rather that certain substantive doctrines and distinctions of Bartolus were revived by them.[21] Even so, they were reluctant to go too far: the most famous of them, Charles du Moulin, rejected Bartolus's notion of *dominium utile* and replaced it with his own 'new and subtle distinction': the usufructuary had *dominium* in the role which he enjoyed, but not in the land itself, 'for there is no way in which one can be the *dominus* of something in which one has usufruct, indeed such a thing is impossible and repugnant'.[22]

François Hotman (who, though he deeply respected Connan and helped to edit his *Commentarii*, was too complex a character to be merely someone else's epigone) daringly reinstated a more Bartolist notion of *dominium utile* in his discussion of feudal law when he remarked that 'I think the opinion of the old commentators was quite sensible, when they said that both the lord and the vassal have a definite *dominium* in an estate – the former having *dominium directum* and the latter *dominium utile*.'[23] But it is significant that for Hotman at least the restoration of *dominium utile* did not lead back to a medieval rights theory. Although unlike Connan, he was prepared to use the *term* 'natural *dominium*', his understanding of what it meant was very different from that of a medieval theorist: '*Dominium* is either natural or civil. Natural *dominium* is common to all men (*gentes*): that is, it is acquired in those ways in which all peoples acquire things, such as occupation, seizure or cession. Civil *dominium* is unique to the Roman people ... It is acquired in three ways, mancipation, usucapion and *cessio in iure* ...'[24]

---

[21] The most sensitive discussion of this topic is in Kelley, *Foundations*, particularly Chapter IV, pp. 87–115. See also his remarks on du Moulin on p. 151, and his 'The Development and Context of Bodin's Method' in H. Denzer ed., *Jean Bodin. Verhandlungen der internationalen Bodin Tagung in München*, Münchener Studien zur Politik, 18 (Munich, 1973), pp. 123–50.

[22] 'nullo modo est dominus rei in qua habet usumfructum, imo hoc esset impossibile & repugnans.' C. du Moulin, *Opera*, 1 (Paris, 1681), p. 27. The description of his argument as a 'nova & subtilis distinctio' is a marginal note, *ibid.*

[23] 'Non omnino igitur incommode veterum Doctorum instituto statuemus, cum & senior & vasallus praedii dominium finitum habeant: tum vero illum esse dominium directum: hunc dominium utilem.' F. Hotman, *De Feudis Commentatio Tripertita* (Lyons, 1573), p. 97. For Hotman, see now above all D. R. Kelley, *François Hotman. A Revolutionary's Ordeal* (Princeton, 1973). His links with Alciato are discussed, pp. 24–7.

[24] '*Dominium* aliud est naturale, aliud civile. Naturale est, quod gentium omnium commune est: hoc est, quod iis modis acquiritur, quibus gentes omnes in acquirendis rebus utuntur: veluti occupatione, captivitate, traditione. Civile est, quod civium Romanorum proprium

Natural *dominium* was thus *dominium* under the *ius gentium*, the universal rules for the acquisition of private property as distinct from the particular rules of the city of Rome. It was not natural *dominium utile*, something different in *kind* from private property.

This reluctance to follow out the implications of his work on feudalism was absolutely characteristic of Hotman. He remained much closer to Connan in theoretical matters than he ever was to Bartolus, and despite his dabbling in the terminology of feudalism the basic categories of his thought remained those of the humanist Roman lawyer. Indeed, the interest (much investigated recently) of men like Hotman in the comparative science of law was a straightforward extension of their interest in the *ius gentium* rather than the *ius naturale*, for one obvious way of determining the nature of the *ius gentium* was to look at what all peoples had in common at the level of fairly complex and conventional social relationships. It is for this reason that it is misleading to make too definite a break between the activities of the early humanist civilians and those of their more 'anti-Roman' successors. A common attitude towards the difference between natural and human laws linked them both, as did (of course) a historical sense – a fundamental feature of humanist culture since its beginnings in the Quattrocento.[25]

Hotman is most famous in the general history of political thought for his contributions to the creation of a Calvinist resistance theory in the 1560s and 1570s. The relationship between the ideas of the humanist lawyers and those of the Huguenot propagandists is a complicated but important one. Many of the Calvinists (such as Beza) were trained in the law schools presided over by such men as Alciato, and their basic ideas were undoubtedly drawn from that environment. This explains, among other things, their noteworthy reluctance to talk about the law of nature as the foundation for their resistance theory – it occupies an extremely subsidiary place in all the major works – and their reiterated belief in pacts between king and people. It also explains the stress on the role of the lesser magistrates as the only people entitled to resist a prince, introduced by Lutheran thinkers of the 1540s and developed by Calvinists in the 1550s: for if what was important about a right or contract was the action attached to it, then the role of a judge as privileged executor of the law was indeed vital. It was after all a fundamental principle of Roman law that unilateral action to enforce a right entailed its loss: a plaintiff had to work through a judge.

[25] By taking Budé to be representative of the first generation of juridical humanists, Julian Franklin in his *Jean Bodin and the Sixteenth-Century Revolution in the Methodology of Law and History* (New York, 1963) has tended to exaggerate the break constituted by the new method of Hotman and François Baudouin. Kelley's *Foundations* is a rather better guide.

est ... Constat autem tribus modis: mancipatione, usucapione, in iure cessione.' F. Hotman, *Commentarius de Verbis Juris* (Lyons, 1569), col. 124.

But the Calvinists infused their humanism with a strong sense of the omnipotence of God and his part in human affairs, which men such as Alciato completely lacked. In what in many ways is the most interesting of all the Calvinist political pamphlets produced at this time, George Buchanan's dialogue *De Iure Regni apud Scotos* (written in 1567 though not published until 1579), we can see someone deeply imbued with humanism adjusting it to fit his religious sensibilities. Thus 'Buchanan', his spokesman, admits that the humanist picture of a time 'when men lived in huts and caves, and wandered around the place without laws or fixed habitations' is substantially true. But when 'Maitland', his interlocutor, proposes the two standard accounts of how men left this state, through the efforts of either an orator or a jurist, 'Buchanan' insists instead that they left it because God told them to.[26] The *De Iure Regni* denies that men construct political institutions for their own benefit: their political life is a direct gift from God, without being fully natural to them (i.e. coeval with them). This was to remain a fundamental feature of Calvinist political thinking, to recur in the great works of the seventeenth-century British Calvinists such as Rutherford.

Buchanan's work represents a synthesis between juridical humanism and the kind of religious arguments of an earlier generation of British Calvinists such as Knox, Goodman and Ponet. The keynote of their work (significantly in the vernacular, and derived stylistically from the sermon rather than the legal treatise) had been an exhortation to an oppressed people to rise against an heretical tyrant, and treat him as the Israelites had treated their oppressors. They had taken political life to be the direct creation of God after the Flood, through the ban on homicide in Genesis 8, and not the creation of fallen man; Buchanan accepted this but was not willing to accept all its basically anti-humanist implications: the rest of the dialogue, as J. W. Allen perceived, reads like a transcript of Salamonio.[27]

Much more could be said about the relationship between the Protestant resistance theories of the period 1540–80, and the humanist legal theories of the period 1510–30; but it is enough for my purposes to stress that the Calvinists were not putting forward a theory of natural rights, and indeed were not particularly concerned with the notion of a right at all. Like the humanists, specific constitutional remedies were at the focus of their concern. If we are to understand the developments in rights theories

[26] G. Buchanan, *De Iure Regni apud Scotos, Dialogos* (Edinburgh, 1579), pp. 8–11. For the circumstances of its composition, see H. R. Trevor-Roper, *George Buchanan and the Ancient Scottish Constitution*, English Historical Review, Supp. 3 (1966).

[27] See e.g. J. Ponet *A Shorte Treatise of Politike Power* (n.p. (Strasbourg?), 1556), sig. A4. Allen's observations about the similarity between Salamonio and Buchanan are in his *History of Political Thought in the Sixteenth Century* (London, 1928), pp. 336–42. Quentin Skinner has pointed out (*The Foundations of Modern Political Thought*, II (Cambridge, 1978), p. 320) that Goodman uses extensively the language of rights; these writers' anti-humanism may go further than I have acknowledged here.

during the sixteenth and early seventeenth centuries, then we must group
the Calvinist theorists with such men as Alciato, and see them all as
engaged in a retreat from the position where the natural law and natural
rights enjoyed primacy to one where the major concern was human law
designed by men for common utility either under their own initiative or
under the command of God.

In the last half of the century humanists brought up in this kind of
tradition, with its stress on the Ciceronian account of the divorce between
man's natural and civic, moral life, were increasingly faced with the task of
marrying it to an Aristotelian political and moral theory. This is a complex
subject, which badly needs a good treatment; but it is clear that by the
1570s and 1580s humanists and particularly Protestant humanists were
deeply interested in Aristotle. It is sometimes said that this led to a
Protestant scholasticism, the equivalent of the sixteenth-century Spanish
scholasticism which I shall be considering in the next section, and it can
similarly be seen as a continuation of late medieval trends.[28] To see it like
this is however to gravely misunderstand it: it was a *humanist*, a Renaissance Aristotelianism, with its roots in the Renaissance study of Aristotle
in Italy.

Its continuity with earlier humanism is brought out graphically in the
work of one of the first major popularisers of an Aristotelian political
attitude in northern Europe, Louis le Roy. In England by 1579 it could be
said that 'you can not steppe into a schollars studye but (ten to one) you
shall likely finde open either Bodin de Republica or Le Royes Exposition
uppon Aristoteles Politiques'.[29] Le Roy had grown up in just the intellectual environment we have been looking at, a friend of Budé and encomiast
of Connan; his approach to Aristotle's theory of the *zoon politikon* shows
how unwilling these humanists were to abandon the Ciceronian picture.
As a comment on the relevant passage in Book 1 of the *Politics*, le Roy
(however inconsistently) quoted Cicero's description of man's primitive
asocial life,[30] and the same theme recurs frequently elsewhere in the work.
Gundersheimer has indeed pointed to the frequency with which it occurs
in le Roy's other works also, and it must be reckoned as powerful an
element in le Roy's ideology as his explicit Aristotelianism.[31] Nowhere in
his work does le Roy ever deal with the traditional matters of late medieval
scholasticism, the natural law as a set of intuitive moral precepts or the
possibility of natural *dominium*.

[28] See e.g. H. Kearney, *Scholars and Gentlemen* (London, 1970), pp. 77 ff. A much better
account is given in H. Dreitzel, *Protestantischer Aristotelismus und absoluter Staat; die Politica
des H. Arnisaeus,* Veroft. d. Inst. f. Europaische Geschichte, Mainz, LV (Wiesbaden, 1970).
[29] Gabriel Harvey quoted in W. L. Gundersheimer, *The Life and Works of Louis Le Roy*
(Geneva, 1966), p. 47. Le Roy's *Politiques* was first published at Paris in 1568.
[30] See the English translation, *Aristotles Politiques* (London, 1598), pp. 16–17.
[31] Gundersheimer, *Louis Le Roy,* pp. 103–5. It is not unreasonable to see Bodin in the same
light.

The same divergence from medieval traditions can be seen in the later, more systematic works produced by humanist and Protestant Aristotelians. When medieval scholastics considered Aristotle's ideas on justice, they generally assumed that one fundamental issue was the question of the distribution and exchange of *dominium*, property rights. The sixteenth-century Spanish scholastics were at least partially faithful to this tradition; they accepted that commutative justice – in Aristotle's terms the branch of justice which deals with contracts and exchange – had *dominium* as its basic subject-matter. As one of them, Domingo de Soto, said, '*dominium* of things and their division is the basis and foundation of all contracts, agreements and pacts which are dealt with by commutative justice'.[32] They insisted on this, despite the fact that (as we shall see) their discussion of the other Aristotelian category, distributive justice, did not involve any concept of property or rights.

The Protestant Aristotelians, on the other hand, treated both branches of justice in the same way, and with greater fidelity to the historical Aristotle. In their treatises (called, often, *Ethica* or *Politica* rather than the scholastic *De Justitia et Jure*) we find that commutative justice is handled as an extension of distributive justice: it consisted of the principles whereby a fair distribution of possessions could be arrived at through exchange without one section of the human race ultimately being denuded of everything.[33] There was no question of rights being primary, or of *dominium* being something basic about which the rules of justice had to be framed: all was a matter of social convenience, just as it had been for the humanist Roman lawyers of an earlier generation. Aristotle, in their eyes, had provided guidance for the prudent politician, the political scientist (to use a term that came into vogue in the later part of the century) who wished to organise a society along beneficial lines. The medieval marriage between Aristotle and a theory of rights was terminated.

II

While these writers were trying to come to terms with the insights of the Renaissance, Catholic theologians (in particular) were evolving a rival

---

[32] 'dominium huiusmodi rerum, earumque divisio, basis fundamentumque est omnium contractuum conventorumque & pactorum, quae per commutativam iustitiam celebrantur.' D. de Soto, *De Iustitia et Iure* (2nd edn, Lyons, 1582), f. 99r.

[33] A particularly good example of this is Johannes Magirus's *Corona Virtutum Moralium, Universam Aristotelis Summi Philosophi Ethicen, exacte enucleans* (Frankfurt, 1601), pp. 466–78 for commutative justice and pp. 446–9 for the distinction between the two kinds of justice and some general remarks. A very early example is provided by Melancthon's *Moralis Philosophiae Epitome. Item in Quintum Librum Ethicorum Arist: Commentarius* (Strasbourg, 1539). The roots of this movement have yet to be investigated, but presumably they lie in early sixteenth-century Italy, among the humanist Aristotelians of whom Benedetto Varchi is an example. See U. Pirotti, 'Aristotelian Philosophy and the Popularization of Learning: Benedetto Varchi and Renaissance Aristotelianism' in *The Late Italian Renaissance 1525–1630*, ed. E. Cochrane (London, 1970), pp. 187–90.

theory of the natural life of men. But in the process they ran into a set of problems to do with the incompatibility between their medieval inheritance and their Renaissance understanding of such notions as *dominium*. If we can characterise the humanist attitude as one of greater interest in objective law than subjective rights, then we can detect broadly the same phenomenon among the theologians; but in their case it was a much more complex and compromised development.

The founder of this new school of theology, which was to flower so brilliantly in sixteenth-century Spain, was the Dominican theologian Francisco de Vitoria. He had been a student at Paris in the critical years between 1507 and 1522, and had been exposed both to the last advocates of the Gersonian theory and to the first productions of the juridical humanists. After his return to take up a teaching post at Salamanca, he announced his programme in a course of lectures on the *Secunda Secundae* of Aquinas which he gave to his students in the last part of 1535. His choice of subject, a commentary on Aquinas, in itself reveals a change from the fifteenth-century pattern – Vitoria was following the lead of such people as Cajetan in the revival of Thomism as an alternative to nominalism. His lectures were enormously influential, although they were never published; notes from them were the basis of practically all the works on legal theory produced by Vitoria's followers until the end of the century.[34] Presumably there was no need for the originals to be published after a particularly comprehensive version of them had been given by Vitoria's pupil Domingo de Soto in *De Iustitia et Iure*, published in 1553.

The fact that it was a new style of discussion was signalled by Vitoria's beginning his investigation with the question of whether *dominium* was an authentically classical term. He had to re-assure himself that it was not just to be found in the 'jurisconsults and scholastic doctors' before he could proceed with his enquiries. Having done so, he suggested as a definition of *ius* simply 'what is allowed under a law' – an *objective* definition, which meant that he had to deal with the extreme subjectivism of Gerson and Summenhart, and their assimilation of *ius* and *dominium*. He did so by using two main arguments. One was the point about *iura ad rem* which Summenhart had faced and had believed he had dealt with. Vitoria however insisted that 'a son has a *ius* to food against his father, since he can sue him if he is denied food, but he does not have *dominium* since he is not the *dominus* of his father'.[35] It was characteristic of Vitoria, and a revealing

[34] Examples of this are: D. de Soto, *De Iustitia et Iure* (Salamanca, 1553); M. de Ledesma, *Secunda Quartae* (Coimbra, 1560) (this contained transcripts of Vitoria's notes without acknowledgement – see V. B. de Heredia in *Ciencia tomista*, 49 (1934), pp. 5–26); M. B. Salon, *Controversiae de Iustitia et Iure* (Valencia, 1591); D. Bañez, *Decisiones de Jure et Justitia* (Venice, 1595); P. de Aragon, *Commentarii in Secundam Secundae* (Venice, 1595).

[35] 'filius habet jus in patrem quantum ad alimenta, quia posset illum convenire coram judice si ei negaret alimenta, et tamen non habet dominium quia non est dominus patris.' F. de Vitoria, *Comentarios a la Secunda Secundae de Santo Tomas*, III, ed. V. B. de Heredia (Salamanca, 1934), p. 65.

indication of his affinity with his humanist contemporaries, that he should interpret such a *ius ad rem* in terms of a possible court action: any right had somehow to be related to a remedy.

The other argument which he used was completely derived from the discoveries of the legal humanists. *Dominium* could not be *ius*, as in the Digest 'it is said that *dominium* is one thing, and *ius* another: for those who have legitimate possession, use or usufruct have a *ius* of a kind, but they are not *domini*'. He used this to refute Summenhart's casuistic argument that because theft is the removal of something from the control of a *dominus*, and any *ius* can be stolen, therefore *ius* and *dominium* are the same. Vitoria simply pointed out that

if someone takes something from a usuary or a usufructuary or a possessor, that is described as a theft, and they are bound to restore it, but such people are not true *domini*; just as if I am the proprietor of a horse which I have hired to Peter, and I then take it from him, I am guilty of theft, ... but it is not taken against the will of the proprietor, for I *am* the proprietor, but against his will who has legitimate possession of it.[36]

In place of a Gersonian active rights theory, the Spanish Dominicans in general put the objective sense of *ius* at the centre of their concern. De Soto followed Vitoria in this, as in so much else:

ius is the same as *what is just* (as Isidore says in Book v). It is the object of justice, the equity which justice establishes between men; *dominium* is the *facultas* of a lord (as its name implies) in servants or objects which he can use as he likes for his own benefit. *Ius* must therefore not be confused with *dominium*, as it is superior to it, and of wider reference.[37]

Another of Vitoria's later followers, Domingo Bañez, simply outlined the possible meanings of *ius* in a very classical way, as follows:

It first and principally means what comes about as a result of the workings of justice and what it tends to. Secondly it can be taken to mean the law which is the rule for doing justice. Thirdly it can mean knowledge of the laws. Fourthly the decision of judges, ordering justice to be done. Lastly it can mean the public setting where such decisions are made.[38]

[36] 'dicitur quod omnino aliud est dominium, et aliud est jus; quia qui habet legitimam possessionem, et usuarius, et usufructuarius, habent aliquo modo jus, et tamen non sunt domini ... Si aliquis subriperet rem ab usurario vel usufructuario vel possessionario, diceretur fur, et teneretur illis restituere, dato quod non sint vere domini; ut si ego essem proprietarius hujus equi quem locavi Petro, et illum ab eo subriperem, essem fur, quia diceretur contractatio rei alienae invito domino, et tamen non invito proprietario, quia ego sum proprietarius, sed invito eo qui legitimam possessionem habet in eum.' *ibid.*
[37] 'Ius namque idem est (ut ait lib. 5. Isid.) quod iustum. Est enim obiectum iustitiae: puta aequitas quam iustitia inter homines constituit: dominium autem facultas est domini (uti nomen sonat) in servos vel in res, quibus suo arbitratu, ob suumque commodum utitur. Fit ergo, ut ius non convertatur cum dominio, sed sit illi superius & latius patens.' De Soto, *De Iustitia et Iure* f. 99r.
[38] 'Primo & principaliter, ut nominet illud quod fit per actionem iustitiae & ad quod terminatur. Secundo accipiatur pro lege quae est regula faciendi ipsum ius seu iustum. Tertio accipitur pro ipsa peritia legum. Quarto pro sententia iudicis, qui praecepit iustum fieri. Denique accipitur pro ipsomet loco publico ubi istae sententiae feruntur.' Bañez, *Decisiones*, p. 3.

This objectivism was in part a result of their attempt to restore Aquinas's theories to an intellectual primacy, for (as we have seen) Aquinas was reluctant to talk about *ius* as subjective when he formally analysed the concept, though he undoubtedly did understand subjective *iura*. But it was also of course a result of their sensitivity towards the achievements of the humanists.

However, their programme for a syncretic Thomism and humanism ran into a number of problems when it came to the discussion of natural *dominium*. Aquinas's theory of natural *dominium* relied on the concept of *dominium utile*, and without such an unclassical notion he could not have generated his account of the natural life of man. But it was precisely this notion which the Spanish Dominicans had abandoned, and whose abandonment was the basis for their attack on Gerson. The tangles which they got themselves into as a result of this are well illustrated by de Soto. He defined *dominium* as 'someone's *facultas* and *ius* in something, by which he can take possession of it for his own benefit and use it in any way allowed by law'. The dangers of this definition quickly emerged:

I said 'in any way' in order to distinguish *dominium* from use and usufruct. For *dominium* is not simply the ability to use something and take its produce, but to alienate it, give it away, sell it, neglect it, &c. However, I added the phrase 'allowed by law', to meet any objection which might undermine the definition. For a minor before coming of age is physically capable of giving away his property. But he does not have the right to give away his goods or sell them, since he is prevented by human law from doing so.[39]

But of course, as the medieval theorists had perceived, with a definition of *dominium* of that kind, usufruct was obviously a kind of *dominium*, for it was simply a legally permitted way of possessing and using land.

It was virtually impossible to combine a Renaissance concept of property, with its strict distinction between *dominium* and usufruct, with Thomism. The Renaissance concept belonged to a theory in which the natural life of man was right-less and therefore property-less, while the Thomist believed that by nature man did possess certain limited rights, particularly the right to use material objects for his own benefit. Nevertheless, the Spanish Dominicans continued to attempt such a combination. But they insisted all the time on the *limited* character of men's natural rights, and their subordination to the laws of nature and God. By doing so

[39] 'Dominium ergo, si secundum artem describas, est propria cuiusque facultas & ius in rem quamlibet, quam in suum ipsius commodum usurpare potest quocunque usu lege permisso... At dictum est universaliter, quemcunque usum, ut distinguatur dominium ab usu & usufructu. Est enim dominium facultas non solum utendi fruendique re, verum & ipsam distrahendi, donandi, vendendi, negligendi. &c. Veruntamen adhibitus est modus, ut usus ille sit lege permissus, ad dissoluendam obiectionem, qua quis tentaret infirmare definitionem. Enimvero pupillus ante aetatem legitimam donatio rerum suarum pollet: quarum tamen potiundi liberam facultatem non habet, cum talia bona neque donare valeat, neque vendere: quoniam lege humana prohibetur ea dilapidare.' De Soto, *De Iustitia et Iure*, p. 99v.

they hoped in part to refute the post-Aquinas theory of grace as the source of property, which they took (rightly) to have produced Wycliffe and even Luther. Property was a right given by God's laws, not his grace; it was limited by those laws and was not a replica of the kind of all-inclusive right which God himself enjoyed outside the bounds of any law.

This stress in a Thomist context on the limitations of what men were free to do was the central feature of the Spanish Dominican theory. It found expression in their views on what was fast becoming a key issue in political thought, the problem of slavery. The Gersonians such as Mazzolini had argued that free men were free (among other things) to enslave themselves *ad libitum* and unconditionally.[40] For them, this was to some extent an academic or historical issue, of interest because of Roman or Hebrew practices rather than because of the practices of their own society. But for the Spaniards, slavery of both black and red men was of immediate concern. The Dominicans' response to it fitted both their response to other problems of colonisation and their general political theory: men were not, they argued, in general free to enslave themselves, and they could not rightfully be traded as slaves if the grounds for their servitude were unclear.[41]

Thus Vitoria remarked that 'liberty cannot rightfully be traded for all the gold in the world: it can be traded for life, which is more precious than any gold'.[42] Only in *extremis* could men enslave themselves; they were not masters of their own destiny, and it was not up to them to fix the exchange-value of their liberty. That was given by the law of God, and it was fixed at more than anything except life itself. For a Gersonian, liberty was property and could therefore be exchanged in the same way and under the same terms as any other property; for a Vitorian it was not and could not be. Once again (and this is a recurrent, perhaps *the* recurrent theme in the history of rights theories) a theory of rights permitted practices which an anti-subjectivist theory prohibited. This theoretical difficulty was important given the murky character of the events in their own countries which led to the Africans being enslaved. The white men generally found them already traded as slaves at the coast, and had merely to be confident that a fairly wide variety of slaveries was in principle permissible in order to be able to trade them themselves with a clear conscience. Any theory which radically limited the circumstances under which men could rightfully become slaves, as the Dominicans did, could therefore help to undermine the trade.

[40] S. Mazzolini da Prierio, *Summa Summarum quae Silvestrina nuncupatur*, 1 (Lyons, 1539) p. 256v.

[41] On their attitude to slavery and colonialisation, see L. U. Hanke, *Aristotle and the American Indians* (Chicago, 1959), and D. B. Davis, *The Problem of Slavery in Western Culture* (Ithaca N.Y., 1967).

[42] 'licet non bene libertas pro toto vendatur auro, licite tamen venditur pro vita quae praestantior est omni auro.' See V. B de Heredia in *Ciencia Tomista*, 43, 1931, pp. 173–5, and *ibid.*, 49, 1934, pp. 25–8.

The concern for the welfare of men rather than their liberty which this reveals was eminently characteristic of the Dominican school. In general, they concentrated far more on questions of distributive justice than their late medieval predecessors had done, putting at the centre of their discussions questions about fair distributions and the claims of the needy on the well-off. In many ways they had returned to a claims-right theory, and their interest in this aspect of political theory was so marked that a modern scholar has been able to devote a whole book to it alone.[43]

Another area in which, it is possible to argue, the Dominicans' emphasis on the limited character of human freedom played an important part was their general theory of free will. This is a difficult matter, as certainly Vitoria and his early followers never came near to denying the freedom of the will. But it is suggestive that Bañez, his follower, became famous for his allegedly 'Calvinist' treatment of the problems of grace, free will and predestination. He insisted that God was *causally* responsible for all human acts, including those which won the agent divine approval or disapproval, though he caused free agents to act freely while unfree agents acted necessarily. The notion of *cause* here is, to say the least, unclear; but it is clear that Bañez was trying to stress the causal character of predestination in a way which was not unnaturally taken to be Calvinist. Bañez himself believed that his position was a reasonable development of the ideas of Vitoria and de Soto, though de Soto at any rate wanted to say that our own free decision is in some way the material cause of our justification or reprobation.[44]

III

If the 1520s were the moment at which European thought swung away from a radical rights theory and towards either a humanist or a Thomist objectivism, the 1580s were the moment at which those theories themselves faltered. Coming out of Portugal and the Netherlands (the main centres of the slave trade), a new generation of theorists revived the late medieval ideas and began to construct a modern rights theory. It was their work on which Francisco Suarez and Hugo Grotius were to build in their own attempts to perfect such a rights theory, and not until the generation after Hobbes was this new movement to lose its momentum.

Elements of the late medieval rights theory had of course been able to survive in the interstices of Vitorian Thomism or humanism throughout the sixteenth century. Their main rescue centre was the University of Louvain in the Netherlands, where a succession of teachers contrived to provide an alternative to the Thomism of the Spaniards. The most impor-

[43] K. Deuringer, *Probleme der Caritas in der Schule von Salamanca*, Freiburger theol. Studien, 75 (Freiburg, 1959).
[44] The best and most accessible account of these issues is still the article 'Molinisme' by E. Vansteenberghe in the *Dictionnaire de Théologie Catholique*, x (Paris, 1928), cols. 2093 ff. The discussion of Bañez and the school of Salamanca is in cols. 2097–8.

tant figure among them was Johannes Driedo, whose work neatly shows the relationship suggested above between ideas about free will and rights theories. In 1537 he published his *De Concordia Liberi Arbitrii et Praedestinationis Divinae* in which he argued very clearly for a genuine freedom of the will: God precognised but did not strictly predetermine the free actions of men. He followed that up eleven years later with his *De Libertate Christiana*, in which he gave a remarkably Gersonian definition of *ius*: '*ius* is to be taken in two ways. One is for law, as when we say that the law of the Decalogue is the *ius divinum*, etc. The other is for *dominium*, as when we say that someone has a *ius* in his possession or his field.'[45] He thus had no scruples about making precisely the identification of *ius* with *dominium* which Vitoria and his pupils were attacking.

A similarly intersticial figure was the Spanish lawyer Fernando Vazquez y Menchaca. In 1559 he published a survey of knotty problems in jurisprudence, the *Controversiarum Illustrium*. It includes a definition of *dominium* in terms of liberty which could have come straight from Gerson: *dominium* is

a natural *facultas* which allows someone to do something, unless prohibited by force or law. I extracted this definition from the *Institutes*, where it is said that liberty is a natural *facultas* allowing someone to do something unless prohibited by force or law. For I ask what is it to have *dominium* in something, other than to have a free and uncontrolled *facultas* in it? Thus parents can kill or give away children which they have in their power ...[46]

This is both a highly unclassical account – the humanists, for example, would have been amazed at the claim that parents have *dominium* over their children, with its implications of *ownership*; and a highly un-Thomist one – the Dominicans would have been horrified at the implication that human beings have *dominium* over themselves.

Although Vazquez's book was popular, his views and those of the Louvain professors would have remained peripheral if a new institutional development had not intervened. In the 1580s the Jesuit movement began to be interested in the Louvain ideas, and to throw its immense influence behind their development and deployment against the Dominicans. We can see in this a sign of the deep-rooted suspicion of the Jesuits about Dominican theology: many Dominicans had earlier become Protestants,

[45] 'Ius bifariam accipitur, Nunc pro lege, veluti cum dicimus legem decalogi esse ius divinum, &c. Nunc pro dominio, veluti quum dicimus aliquem habere ius in possessionem, vel in agrum.' J. Driedo, *De Libertate Christiana* (Louvain, 1548), p. 33v. See Vansteenberghe, 'Molinisme', col. 2096 for a discussion of the Louvanists' ideas about free will.

[46] 'Est enim naturalis facultas eius, quod facere libet, nisi vi aut iure prohibeatur, quam definitionem colligo ex ... Inst. ... ubi dicitur libertas est naturalis facultas eius, quod cuique facere libet, nisi quid vi aut iure prohibeatur, dominium enim in rebus habere quid obsecro aliud est, quam eam liberrimam ad libitumque facultatem habere circa illam rem? Hinc parentes liberos, quos in potestate haberant, occidere et perdere poterant.' F. Vazquez y Menchaca, *Controversiarum Illustrium ... libri tres* (Frankfurt, 1572), p. 48v. An extreme statement of Vazquez's importance in the development of a modern natural rights theory is E. Reibstein, *Die Anfaenge des neuren Natur- und Voelkerrechts: Studien zu den 'Controversiae Illustres' des Fernandus Vasquius* (Bern, 1949).

and the kind of theology espoused by Bañez looked too much like Calvinism to be a secure foundation for the Counter-Reformation. Although Aquinas enjoyed a position of hegemony in the Jesuits' studies, they were also prepared to consider (under the wishes of their founder) the adoption of a guide 'more appropriate to our time'; this intellectual openness, combined with their determination to clarify the difference between Protestant and Catholic, led them naturally to consider the possibilities represented by Louvain and therefore ultimately by Gerson.

The debate between the orders which was to last intermittently from 1585 to 1607 began when a Jesuit, Leonard Lessius, arrived from Douai to teach theology at Louvain. He proclaimed as his intention the recovery of the ideas of the old Louvain teachers, and proceeded to launch an attack on Catholic crypto-Calvinists and to expound the doctrine of free will. In a work of juridical philosophy apparently written before 1592 though not published until 1606, Lessius also talked about *iura* as *potestates* or *facultates*, and tried to interpret passive rights as *potentiae passivae*,[47] but in most ways the book was still not disengaged from a Vitorian framework. That was true also, to some extent, of his psychology: despite his claims, Lessius could do little more than act as a publicist for the new movement. The real work was done by a Portuguese, Luis de Molina, after whom the psychological doctrine has often been termed 'Molinism'.

He put forward his ideas about free will, including the famous concept of *scientia media*, the precognition God possesses about what free human beings are going to do in the context of his grace, in a work published in 1589. He immediately found himself locked in a controversy with Bañez, and the debate between the orders eventually got so bitter that a special Congregation, *De Auxiliis*, was called from 1598 to 1607 to discuss the matter – a kind of Catholic Synod of Dort. More or less its only conclusion was that the Jesuits should stop calling the Dominicans Calvinists, and that the Dominicans should stop calling the Jesuits Pelagians.

But at the height of the argument Molina launched a further attack, this time on the political theory of the Dominicans, in his *De Iustitia et Iure* of 1592. He began with what must have seemed a dramatic return to a late medieval claim: *ius* may be defined as a

facultas of doing something, or getting something, or holding onto something, or being in some position where to be impeded without legitimate reason would be an injury … *The facultas* which in the nature of things everyone has to use their possessions, eat their own food, wear their own clothes, pick fruit from their own

---

[47] See L. Lessius, *De Iustitia et Iure* (Paris, 1606), p. 19. See Vansteenberghe, 'Molinisme', cols. 2099–100 for Lessius's activities at Louvain.

[48] 'facultas aliquid faciendi, sive obtinendi, aut in eo insistendi, vel aliquo modo se habendi, cui si sine legitima causa contraveniatur, iniuria fit eam habenti … Facultas, quam ex natura rei habet unusquisque ad utendum rebus suis, ad comedendum proprium cibum, ad induendam propriam vestem, ad decerpenda ex arboribus suis poma, ad ambulandum in

fruit-trees and walk round their own house or on the public highway, is a *ius* of the kind under discussion.[48]

He did not go as far as Gerson in claiming that all possible agents had such *iura*, but made the more reasonable point that only certain kinds of being suffered from the deprivation of their *facultates*:

We must exclude from the area of *ius* those *facultates* by the contravention of which, for whatever reason, no injury could be done to their possessors. Of this kind are *facultates* of all beings deprived of reason and free will by their very nature, such as the *facultas* of animals to graze and to use their limbs, or of stones to fall downwards, etc. Anything which is not endowed with free will is not capable of injury, so that anything which goes against their *facultates* for any reason is no injury to them, nor can their *facultates* be regarded as *iura*.

But like Gerson, he saw a *ius* entirely in terms of the dispositional characteristics of its possessor: 'if anyone asks what actually is this *ius* or *facultas* I have been talking about, I would reply that it is nothing other than a disposition, or relation of the person who has it to the thing to which he has the *facultas*'.[49]

But perhaps the most remarkable feature of his exposition is the explicit attack which he launched on any idea of passive rights.

We divide *ius* into *ius in re* and *ius ad rem*. When we say in this second way that someone has a *ius* to something, we do not mean that anything is owed to him, but that he has a *facultas* to it, whose contravention would cause him injury. In this way we say that someone has a *ius* to use his own things, such as consuming his own food – that is, if he is impeded, injury and injustice will be done to him. In the same way we say that a pauper has the *ius* to beg alms, a merchant has the *ius* to sell his wares, (etc.).[50]

Just as Mazzolini had done eighty years earlier, Molina insisted that all rights must be active, and that apparently passive rights are really rights to do things. But of course, a right to beg is not the same as a right to be given alms: Molina's intensely active rights theory turned out unsurprisingly to be less interested in human welfare than in human liberty.

propria domo, aut in via publica, est ius, de quo modo loquimur.' L. de Molina, *De Iustitia et Iure*, 1 (Mainz, 1614), col. 27.

---

[49] 'Rejiciuntur a ratione iuris, facultates, quibus, quacunque ratione contraveniatur, nulla habentibus eas facultates iniuria infertur: cuiusmodi sunt facultates rerum omnium ratione & libero arbitrio suapte natura carentium, ut brutorum, ad pastum, & ad utendum propriis membris, lapidum ad descendum deorsum, & caeterae aliae. Cum enim eiusmodi res eo ipso, quod libero arbitrio praeditae non sint iniuriae non sint capaces, sane ut in eo, quod earum facultatibus quacumque ratione contraveniatur, nulla eis fit iniuria, sic nec facultates illae iuris rationem habent ... Quod si quis petat, quidnam sit ius, seu facultas hactenus explicata? Respondeo, non esse aliud, quam habitudinem, seu relationem personae, a quo habent, ad id quod est talis facultas.' *ibid.*, 1, cols. 28–9.

[50] 'Ius ... divisimus in ius in re, & in ius ad rem. Altero modo dicitur aliquis habere ius ad aliquid, non quod sit ei aliquid debitum, sed quod facultatem habeat ad aliquid, cui si contraveniatur, fit ei iniuria. Hoc modo dicimus, unumquemque habere ius utendi suis rebus propriis, ut concedendi suum proprium cibum; ita ut, si impediatur, iniuria ac iniustitia ei fiat. Dicimus etiam, pauperum habere ius petendi eleemosynam, mercenarium habere ius locandi operas suas, ...' *ibid.*, III, col. 399.

This was a feature of his remarks about slavery also:

Man is *dominus* not only of his external goods, but also of his own honour and fame; he is also *dominus* of his own liberty, and in the context of the natural law can alienate it and enslave himself. [The Roman law imposed conditions for voluntary servitude, but they only applied to Rome.] It follows ... that if a man who is not subject to that law sells himself unconditionally in some place where the relevant laws allow him, then that sale is valid.[51]

According to Molina the 'Aethiopians', that is the blacks, were in that position: there was no reason to suppose that they were not voluntary slaves, and they could have made themselves such for any sort of return, ranging from their lives to a string of beads.

Molina's book was a dramatic incursion into the settled territory of political theory. It was a consistent and comprehensive alternative to everything which Vitoria and his followers had been saying, and it paid little or no attention to the niceties of humanism. Coming from a country with a deep involvement in the slave trade and in colonial rivalry with other powers, his revival of a Gersonian rights theory looks very much like an attempt to produce an ideology of mercantile capitalism. But its undoubted connexion with his general ideas about free will suggests also a much wider ideological scope: it was a theory which involved a picture of man as a free and independent being, making his own decisions and being held to them, on matters to do with both his physical and his spiritual welfare.

Why such a picture should have had the appeal it did at the end of the sixteenth century is as difficult a question to answer as any similar question about ideological change, but there is no doubt of its popularity, particularly in the Spanish Netherlands.[52] The most famous person to develop Molina's ideas was however a Spaniard, Francisco Suarez. His great achievement was to produce a kind of synthesis of Molinism and Vitorian Thomism, though with the emphasis very much on Molina. This was true of his ideas on human free will, as Vansteenberghe pointed out.[53] Believing as he did in the complete contingency of all created beings, he could not take human freedom to be conceptually equivalent to God's freedom; but it was possible, he thought, for a being which was essentially contingent to be free in its particular actions. And the same was true of his rights theory.

[51] 'Ponendumque in primis est, hominem, sicut non solum externorum suorum bonorum, sed etiam proprii honoris et famae est dominus, ... sic etiam dominium [sic] esse suae libertatis, atque adeo stando in solo iure naturali, posse eam alienare, seque in servitutem redigere ... Efficitur ... ut si homo, legibus illis non subiectus, seipsum sine illis conditionibus vendat in loco, ubi huiusmodi leges vigent, emptio sit valida.' *ibid.*, I, cols. 162–3.

[52] See for example Johannes Malderus, *De Virtutibus Theologicis et Iustitia et Religione Commentaria ad Secundam Secundae* (Antwerp, 1616) for a totally Molinist discussion of these matters.

[53] Vansteenberghe, 'Molinisme', col. 2170.

In his *De Legibus ac Deo Legislatore* (1612) he gave a famous analysis of the concept of a *ius*:

This name is properly wont to be bestowed upon a certain moral *facultas* which every man has, either over his own property or with respect to that which is due to him. For it is thus that the owner of a thing is said to have a *ius* in that thing, and the labourer is said to have that *ius* to (*ad*) his wages by reason of which he is declared worthy of his hire. Indeed, this acceptation of the term is frequent, not only in law, but also in Scripture; for the law distinguishes in this wise between a *ius* in a thing and a *ius* to a thing ... And in Scripture, we read that Abraham said to the sons of Heth, 'Give me the *ius* of a burying-place', that is, the *facultas* of burying ... Again, it would seem that *ius* is so understood in the Digest in the passage where justice is said to be the virtue that renders to every man his own *ius*, that is to say, the virtue that renders to every man that which belongs to him. Accordingly, this *actio* or moral *facultas* which every man possesses with respect to his own property or with respect to a thing which in some way pertains to him, is called *ius*; and appears to be the true object of justice ...[54]

He thus allied himself firmly with those like Gerson and Molina who analysed a right as a *facultas*. But the important move which he made was then to reinterpret the Thomist theory of the natural life of men in those terms. He was aware (indeed, it had been pointed out by an early sixteenth-century jurist, Fortunius Garcia)[55] that Aquinas's theory of the *ius naturale* implied merely that it was neutral with regard to most features of man's natural life, and not that men had any *prima facie* natural rights other than the natural right to use necessary commodities. But Suarez argued that in fact under the *ius naturale* men had natural *dominium* in a wide variety of things, including their own liberty, and this in no way conflicted with Aquinas's ideas. He thus returned to a late medieval position on the matter, conscious that only thus could he escape the morass into which Vitorian Thomism had blundered:

We have said that *ius* sometimes signifies *lex*; while at times it means *dominium* over a thing, that is, a claim to its use. At present, then, we make the same statement with respect to natural law.

Accordingly, the distinction laid down by St. Thomas and commonly agreed upon should be understood as relating to the preceptive natural law, and with reference to the subject-matter under discussion. From this point of view, it is

---

[54] 'Solet proprie ius vocari facultas quaedam moralis, quam unusquisque habet, vel circa rem suam, vel ad rem sibi debitam; sic enim dominus rei dicitur habere ius in re, & operarius dicitur habere ius ad stipendium ratione cuius dicitur dignus mercede sua. Et haec significatio vocis huius frequens est non solum in iure, sed etiam in scriptura. Nam in iure hoc modo distinguuntur ius in re, vel ad rem: ... In Scriptura vero legimus, dixisse Abraham ad filios Heth, Gen. 23. *Date mihi ius sepulchri*, id est, facultatem sepuliendi ... Illa ergo actio, seu moralis facultas, quam unusquisque habet ad rem suam, vel ad rem ad se aliquam modo pertinentem vocatur ius, & illud proprie videtur esse obiectum iustitiae ...' F. Suarez, *De Legibus ac Deo Legislatore* (Coimbra, 1612); reproduced as Vol. I of the Carnegie Endowment edition (Oxford, 1944), p. 11. Translation by G. L. Williams *et al.*, Vol. II of this edition, pp. 30–1.

[55] See F. Garcia in *Repetitionum seu Commentariorum in Varia Jurisconsultorum Responsa*, I (Lyons, 1553), p. 62r.

manifest that a division of property is not opposed to natural law in the sense that the latter absolutely and without qualification forbids such division. The same is true with respect to slavery and other, similar matters.

If, however, we are speaking of the natural right of *dominium* (*iure naturali dominativo*), it is then true that liberty is a matter of the *ius naturale* in a positive and not merely a negative sense, since nature itself confers upon man the true *dominium* of his liberty. Community of things would also pertain in some sense to the *dominium* held by men under the *ius naturale*, if no division of them had been made, since men would have a positive *ius* and claim to use the common stock ...[56]

This *dominium* over things in common was a genuine *dominium*, though it would in practice involve only the appropriation of consumables rather than durables. Potentially, things could be exchanged among the commoners and eventually settled rules of private property could be introduced and a transition made from the state of nature. Like Richard Fitzralph, Suarez was prepared to allow a use-right which was not *dominium*, when an owner permitted someone else to use his possessions for his own benefit (like an ostler), and he thought that Franciscan poverty came into that category, but it was a marginal case.[57] The right to use commodities in the state of nature was more like usufruct, and it was a genuine and transferable property right. This applied to man's liberty also: 'nature, although it has granted liberty and *dominium* over that liberty, has nevertheless not absolutely forbidden that it should be taken away. For, ... for the very reason that man is *dominus* of his own liberty, it is possible for him to sell or alienate the same.'[58]

Suarez drew the obvious conclusions from this when he came to discuss political authority. If voluntary slavery was possible for an individual, so it was for an entire people. Such a people could count as an individual in the sense that it had a common purpose distinct from those of its members *qua* individuals, and was an agent in the world in the same way as they were; it therefore had *dominium* over its own liberty and could transfer it wholly to a master.[59] A natural rights theory defence of slavery became in Suarez's hands a similar defence of absolutism: if natural men possess property

[56] 'Diximus enim ius aliquando significare legem; aliquando vero significare dominium, vel quasi dominium alicuius rei, seu actionem ad utendum illa: nunc ergo idem dicimus de iure naturali. Atque ita distinctio D. Thomae, & communis intelligitur de iure naturali praeceptivo, & in ordine ad materiam, de qua sermo est. Quo sensu manifestum est, divisionem rerum non esse contra ius naturale, quod illam prohibeat absolute, & simpliciter. Et idem est de servitute, & aliis similibus. At vero sic loquamur de iure naturali dominativo, sic veram est libertatem esse de iure naturali positive, & non tantum negative, quia ipsa natura verum dominium contulit homini suae libertatis. Communitas etiam rerum aliquo modo pertineret ad dominium hominum ex vi iuris naturae, si nulla esset facta rerum divisio, quia homines haberent positivum ius, & actionem ad usum rerum communium.' Suarez, *De Legibus*, p. 159, trans., p. 278.
[57] See Suarez, *Opera*, xv (Paris, 1859), pp. 563–4 (*Opus de Religione*).
[58] 'quamvis natura dederit libertatem, & dominium eius, non tamen absolute prohibuisse, ne auferri possit. Nam ... eo ipso, quod homo est dominus suae libertatis, potest eam vendere, seu alienare.' Suarez, *De Legibus*, p. 160; trans., p. 279.
[59] See *ibid.*, p. 205; trans., p. 381.

rights over their liberty and the material world, then they may trade away that property for any return they themselves might think fit; a bad bargain has to be kept to by virtue of the general law of nature that we must keep our promises. Suarez's view of this preceptive law of nature was fundamentally the same as that of his medieval predecessors, and of the Renaissance scholastics, and was of course utterly unhumanistic. He took it to be the body of general moral principles which were intuitively obvious to a human being. It included a set of principles about distributive justice, which allowed him to incorporate many of the welfare ideas of the Vitorians into his general theory; but it included other principles of expletive justice, in particular a rule about the keeping of contracts, by virtue of which men could find themselves committed both in their personal and in their public lives to a total and mistaken loss of liberty. His work in this area is a graphic illustration of the ambiguous character of a natural rights theory.

3

Hugo Grotius

Hugo Grotius was born into the humanist, Calvinist and Aristotelian world surveyed in the previous chapter. Its humanism stayed with him throughout his life, but he died under bitter attack for his desertion from its Calvinism and Aristotelianism. Yet it was this desertion which (as the eighteenth-century historians of the Enlightenment realised) transformed Protestant culture and made the political theories of the later seventeenth and eighteenth centuries possible. He is the most important figure in the history which we are tracing, and the origins of his treachery (as it seemed to contemporaries) need to be carefully eucidated.

Born in 1583, and a precocious student at Leiden University from 1594 to 1597, he was educated in the heyday of Protestant Aristotelianism and counted distinguished Aristotelian scholars such as Daniel Heinsius among his close friends. He was also exposed there to the older Protestant tradition of juristic humanism, an exposure continued in the law faculty of the University of Orleans where he studied from 1597 to 1599, and in the training for advocacy on which he embarked when he returned from France. His family and friends had long expected heroic achievements from him: their adulation and his own brilliant career combined to make him a sharp, confident, fast-talking intellectual of a recognisably modern kind, capable (for example) of immediately disrupting the restrained dinner tables of England on his visit there in 1613.[1] His knowledge of contemporary scholastic writers was slight: as late as March 1618 he could write to G. J. Vossius asking for a loan of works by Suarez and Bañez, and remarking that 'I have read scarcely any of the Dominicans.' The only writer in the medieval tradition that he was at all familiar with as a young

---

[1] For this story and for his biography generally, see W. S. M. Knight, *The Life and Works of Hugo Grotius*, Grotius Society Publications, IV (London, 1925); pp. 144–6 for the disastrous dinner party. For his early works, see also F. de Michelis, *Le Origini Storiche e Culturali del Pensiero di Ugo Grozio*, Pubb. della Fac. di Lettere e Filosofia dell'Univ. di Milano, XLV (Florence, 1967). The old life of Grotius by Kaspar Brandt, *Historie van het Leven des Heeren Huig de Groot* (Dordrecht, 1727), is still useful. His Aristotelianism may have been weakened by his father's friendship with Simon Stevin, the well-known anti-Aristotelian physicist, whom he helped with his gravitational experiments; see Knight, *Grotius*, p. 22.

man was Vazquez, though through him he was aware of the later medieval rights theories.[2]

The first work of political theory which he produced reflected these influences, and was in no way a challenge to orthodox attitudes. It was his manuscript *Parallelon Rerumpublicarum* of 1602, in which he compared the 'mores ingeniumque' of the Athenians, Romans and Dutch. It emphasised in a traditional humanist way the similarity between the mixed constitutions of the three states, and the way in which they all safeguarded liberty – though in the eloquence with which he defended the ideal of liberty, and the centrality which it enjoyed in his account, we can see something of the roots of his later theory.

But it was in a work written only five years later, when he was still only twenty-four, that Grotius began to break away decisively from his intellectual environment. In some ways this work, the *De Iure Praedae*, is the most impressive and remarkable of all Grotius's writings, though it remained in manuscript (except for one chapter, printed as the famous *Mare Liberum* in 1609) until it was discovered in a sale of his manuscripts in 1864. It was designed as a discussion of the problems raised by colonial conflict, particularly on the high seas, but it allowed Grotius to range freely through the territory of natural law and political relationships. Its first editors thought that it was substantially the same as his later and central work, the *De Iure Belli ac Pacis* of 1625;[3] this is true to some extent, but the differences between the two works are important. Roughly, we can say that two of the ideas which were to strike contemporaries as most original in the *De Iure Belli* were first put forward in the *De Iure Praedae*, but that their overall theoretical framework still belonged more to the late sixteenth century – though with strong signs of the breach that was to come.

Thus Grotius put forward a theory of justice that was avowedly Aristotelian and accommodated to the assumptions of Protestant political thinkers. Its basic premiss was that 'what God has shown to be his will, that is law'[4] – Grotius could not yet disengage himself from the divine voluntarism inevitably associated with Protestantism. But he explained what God wants in terms of man's innate sociability, to which all further

[2] 'Dominicanorum vix legi quemquam.' *Briefwisseling*, I, ed. P. C. Molhuysen (The Hague, 1928), p. 611. His knowledge of Vazquez is shown in *De Iure Praedae* (1607); see below.
[3] See for example the comments by R. Fruin in 'An Unpublished Work of Hugo Grotius', *Bibliotheca Visseriana*, v (Leiden, 1925), pp. 3–71, a translation of an essay originally written to accompany Hanaker's edition and published in *De Gids*, IV (1868). See also G. Finch's preface to the Carnegie Endowment edition (below).
[4] 'Quod Deus se velle significavit, id jus est.' *De Jure Praedae Commentarius* ed. H. G. Hanaker (The Hague, 1868), p. 7. I have used this legible though in some ways incomplete edition in preference to the facsimile of the manuscript published by the Carnegie Endowment; the translation however is theirs: *De Iure Praedae Commentarius*, I, trans. G. L. Williams (Oxford, 1950), p. 8.

natural laws were to be related, and in that explanation we can see the first indications of what was to be his eventual untheistic theory, with man's sociability becoming the sole premiss. Chief among the rules which conduced to a stable and worthwhile society were its principles of justice, and here Grotius accepted the validity of the distinction between distributive and commutative justice, giving a straightforwardly Aristotelian account of the former. But his interpretation of commutative justice at once revealed the kinship between him and the contemporary scholastics (indeed, he explicitly referred to Vazquez): for to explain the powers of a creditor in an exchange relationship, he argued that

there is one kind of good that is so called in an absolute sense, and there is another that is good from the standpoint of a particular individual. Indeed, to borrow Aristotle's admirable explanation, 'Whatever each person's understanding has ruled for him regarding a given matter, that to him is good.' For God created man αὐτεξούσιον, 'free and *sui iuris*', so that the actions of each individual and the use of his possessions were made subject not to another's will but to his own. Moreover, this view is sanctioned by the common consent of all nations. For what is that well-known concept 'natural liberty', other than the power of the individual to act in accordance with his own will? And liberty in regard to actions is equivalent to *dominium* in material things.[5]

Grotius was thus much more willing to explain relationships in terms of the transfer of *dominium*, and to treat liberty as a piece of property, than anyone in the Protestant Aristotelian tradition. And it was his willingness to think in this kind of way which led him to the first of his original ideas (of whose originality he was himself well aware). It was in some ways the central theme of the work, for it enabled him to justify his claims for free competition on the high seas; the chapter in which it was put forward was the one published in 1609 as *Mare Liberum*. What he said was that

it must be understood that, during the earliest epoch of man's history, *dominium* and common possession (*communio*) were concepts whose significance differed from that now ascribed to them. For in the present age, the term *dominium* connotes possession of something peculiarly one's own, that is to say, something belonging to a given party in such a way that it cannot be similarly possessed by any other party; whereas the expression 'common property' is applied to that which has been assigned to several parties, to be possessed by them in partnership (so to speak) and in mutual concord, to the exclusion of other parties. Owing to the poverty of human speech, however, it has become necessary to employ identical terms for concepts which are not identical. Consequently, because of a certain degree of similitude and by analogy, the above-mentioned expressions descriptive of our modern customs are applied to another right, which existed in early times. Thus

---

[5] 'Bonum enim aliud simpliciter dicitur, aliud quod alicui bonum est: et ut rectissime Aristoteles esponit . . . *quod de re unaquaque mens unicuique dictavit id unicuique bonum est.* Fecit enim Deus Hominem αὐτεξούσιον, liberum, suique iuris, ita ut actiones uniuscuiusque et rerum suarum usus ipsius non alieno arbitrio subjacerent. Idemque gentium omnium consensu approbatur. Quid enim est aliud naturalis illa libertas, quam id quod cuique libitum est faciendi facultas? Et quod libertas in actionibus idem est dominium in rebus.' Grotius, *De Iure Praedae*, p. 18; trans., p. 18.

with reference to that early age, the term 'common' is nothing more nor less than the simple antonym of 'private' (*proprium*); and the word *dominium* denotes the power to make use rightfully of common property.[6]

He thus ingeniously linked together both the scholastic and the humanist theories. It was true that there was no private property in the later sense in a state of nature: the scholastics were wrong in thinking that there was a natural *dominium* identical in character to civil *dominium*. But the humanists were also wrong in denying man any rights under a natural order: there was a unique kind of right, which might be termed *dominium* by similitude or analogy. Natural man *was* the subject of rights. Moreover the rights he possessed, though not strictly property rights, were not categorically dissimilar. Grotius made this point clearer when he went on to argue that there need have been no abrupt transition from such a state of nature into civil society with its familiar property relationships. Certain goods had to be uniquely apportioned – how else could food or clothing be consumed? But other goods would also tend to be so apportioned, on the basis of occupation: 'just as the right to use [consumables] was originally acquired through a physical act of attachment, the very source ... of the institution of private property, so it was deemed desirable that each individual's private possessions should be acquired, as such, through similar acts of attachment'.[7] And the example he gave, famously, of this process was the classical one of the acquisition of seats in a theatre. They must be claimed by physical occupancy, yet once claimed they are regarded as private property, and cannot be taken by latecomers even though they may temporarily be left vacant.

It was an important feature of Grotius's theory at this point that the general principle of occupation was not taken to be conventional. It is true that the principle was an established 'law', but he stressed that 'this law was patterned after nature's plan'.[8] There was something natural in the development into the institution of private property of the basic and inherent human right to use the material world, and no agreement was ever necessary. Rather, all that was necessary was labour or some kind. Men had physically to take possession of the material object, or to alter or define it in some way: 'with respect to moveables, occupancy implies

---

[6] 'Sciendum est igitur in primordiis vitae humanae aliud quam nunc est dominium, aliud communionem fuisse. Nam dominium nunc proprium quid significat, quod scilicet ita est alicuius ut alterius non sit eodem modo. Commune autem dicimus, cuius proprietas inter plures consortio quodam aut consensu collata est exclusis aliis. Linguarum paupertas coegit voces easdem in re non eadem usurpare. Et sic ista nostri moris nomina ad ius illud pristinum similitudine quadam et imagine referuntur. Commune igitur tunc non aliud fuit quam quod simpliciter proprio opponitur: Dominium autem facultas non iniusta utendi re communi ...' Grotius, *De Iure Praedae*, p. 214; trans., pp. 226–7.

[7] 'Sicut enim initio per applicationem corporalem usus ille habetur, unde proprietatem primum ortam diximus, ita simili applicatione res proprias cujusque fieri placuit.' Grotius, *De Iure Praedae*, p. 216; trans., p. 229.

[8] 'lex ... quae naturam imitaretur.' Grotius, *De Iure Praedae*, p. 216; trans., p. 229.

physical seizure; with respect to immoveables, it implies some activity involving construction or the definition of boundaries'.[9]

It is easy to see how Grotius was able to argue from these premisses that the sea was not yet private property in the modern sense, but equally that men did have rights of a kind over it and on it. What they enjoyed were the original rights of (analogical) *dominium*; they could take what they wanted, knowing that they had a definite right to do so. This right was also something which they had the further right to protect against threats: by putting forward this theory of property, Grotius had provided a useful ideology for competition over material resources in the non-European world, and had clearly begun the intellectual process that was to culminate in the competitive rights of the Hobbesian state of nature. But he had also (as the extensive quotations from Vazquez in this chapter reveal) moved away from a humanist and Aristotelian moral theory to something which, despite the differences, was substantially closer to the late medieval scholastic tradition.

This was true also of the second of his major original ideas, which however made less impact as it was not incorporated in the *Mare Liberum*. Not only did Grotius concede to natural man a natural right of (a kind of) *dominium*, he also conceded to him a natural right of punishment. This was of course to play an important part in his developed political theory, and he adumbrated it in full consciousness of his originality. 'Since a great many persons maintain that the power to punish has been granted to the state alone ... it might seem that private application of force is ruled out entirely. The best method we can adopt for the discussion of this point will be found, however, in the consideration of what was permissible for individuals prior to the establishment of states.'[10] He proceeded to do so, quoting Cicero on the naturalness of vengeance, which he took to be the infliction of punishment for wrongdoing, and Biblical examples of justified individual retribution.

But he also established his case on *a priori* grounds:

Is not the power to punish essentially a power that pertains to the state? Not at all! On the contrary, just as every right of the magistrate comes to him from the state, so has the same right come to the state from private individuals ... Therefore, since no one is able to transfer a thing that he never possessed, it is evident that the right of chastisement was held by private persons before it was held by the state. The following argument, too, has great force in this connexion: the state inflicts punishment for wrongs against itself, not only upon its own subjects, but also upon foreigners; yet it derives no power over the latter from civil law, which is binding

[9] 'Occupatio in mobilibus est apprehensio, in immobilibus instructio aut limitatio.' Grotius, *De Iure Praedae*, p. 217; trans., p. 229.

[10] 'Cum enim doceant plerique puniendi potestatem soli reipublicae concessam, ... videri potest privata manus omnino excludi. Sed hoc commodius expediri non potest quam si videamus, quid licuerit unicuique ante respublicas ordinatas.' Grotius, *De Iure Praedae*, p. 89; trans., p. 89.

upon citizens only because they have given their consent; and therefore, the law of nature, or law of nations, is the source from which the state receives the power in question.[11]

This is of course identical to John Locke's 'very strange doctrine' of punishment which he presented as highly original in the *Second Treatise*.

Having taken this view of punishment, Grotius was committed to a much more individualistic theory of the state than any of his Protestant contemporaries. The rights enjoyed by the atomic individuals in the Grotian state of nature filled out the moral world: the state possessed no rights which those individuals had not formerly possessed, and was the same kind of moral entity as them. This was true too of his theory of property: private individuals and states were interchangeable with respect to property, and a state's boundaries were the same kind of thing as the boundaries of a private estate. In some ways, such an assimilation of the private and public realms was characteristic of all rights theorists from Gerson onwards; for by attributing rights of *dominium* or a kind of sovereignty to individuals in a state of nature, they immediately made the distinction between the two realms fluid and in effect purely a question of numbers.

Grotius recognised the unAristotelian character of all this, and of his general claim that 'human society does indeed have its origin in nature, but civil society as such is derived from deliberate design' – by which he meant that there is a natural obligation to mankind as such, and natural moral rules for men, but no such obligation to a state. He felt obliged to find some quotation from 'Aristotle himself, the author chiefly relied upon by those who hold the contrary view' in order to justify his position, thereby revealing his schizophrenia at this time.[12] On the one hand he was still avowedly an Aristotelian, but on the other the content of his theory had moved him well away from any genuine Aristotelianism.

The same schizophrenia is perhaps evidenced by his ideas on resistance. It was characteristic of the liberal Protestant humanist tradition, as we have seen, to allow a high degree of resistance to established authority, while it was characteristic of the major rights theorists such as Mazzolini or Molina to allow the complete subordination of individuals either to a master in the case of a slave or to a sovereign in the case of a subject. Grotius was to become notorious after the publication of the *De Iure Belli* for his permissive attitude towards absolutism, but at the time of writing

---

[11] 'Quid ergo, nonne puniendi potestas reipublicae propria est? Imo vero ut a republica ad magistratum, jus omne a singulis devenit ... Quare cum transferre nemo possit, quod non habuit, jus illud antiquius penes privatos fuisse quam penes rempublicam necesse videtur. Est et hoc argumentum in eam rem efficacissimum. Respublica non tantum subditos sibi ob maleficium punit, sed etiam extraneos. In hos autem potestatem non habet jure civili, ut quod cives tantum ex consensu obliget. Habet igitur ex jure naturae seu gentium.' Grotius, *De Iure Praedae*, p. 91; trans., pp. 91–2.

[12] Grotius, *De Iure Praedae*, p. 92; trans., p. 92.

the *De Iure Praedae* he was not prepared to abandon his inheritance. There is no adequate discussion of slavery in the work, a striking omission in view of the implications of his theory; what discussion there is, is based entirely on the Aristotelian category of the natural slave, a very different entity from the voluntary slave of the natural rights tradition. In the political sphere, moreover, Grotius eloquently attacked 'that detestable practice of adulation which is unworthy of freeborn men and characteristic of persons who seem to have been created for the express purpose of corrupting the finest princely spirits. For such flatterers maintain that there is no such thing as a just cause for rebellion ...'[13]

He put forward two arguments against this 'practice of adulation'. One, the more straightforward, was that it did not apply to princes whose sovereignty was restricted by law, and the implication of his discussion was that the authority of the King of Spain over the Netherlands had been of this limited kind. Even in the *De Iure Belli* Grotius continued to believe this: he never became an absolutist of the Bodinian type, but was always prepared to accept a high degree of variety in constitutional norms. This allowed him throughout his life to justify the revolt of the Netherlands, whatever his feelings about the principle of absolutism might be. But the other argument was more important, for he said that 'even if it were in some way possible for a whole state to sin against its prince, the state that sinned thus still could not be called rebellious. For the prince exists through and for the state; the latter does not exist through or for the prince.'[14] Grotius in the *De Iure Praedae* thus ruled out the complete renunciation of liberty by a subject people as *in principle* impossible. It was here that the great change was to come.

We can date Grotius's abandonment of a liberal position reasonably precisely, and get a clear idea of its occasion. In the years following the completion of the *De Iure Praedae*, Grotius found himself heavily involved in the conflict between Remonstrant and Counter-Remonstrant, Arminian and Calvinist, which split the Dutch Church and which culminated in the Synod of Dort in 1618. The issues involved were in many ways those which had split the Catholic Church twenty years earlier, with the doctrines of predestination and free will at the heart of the dispute.[15]

---

[13] 'Res ipsa poscit hic reprimi foedam et ingenuis hominibus indignam adulationem eorum, qui nati in hoc videntur, ut optima etiam Principum ingenia corrumpant. Ita enim docent, nullam justam esse causam rebellandi.' Grotius, *De Iure Praedae*, p. 282; trans., p. 298.

[14] 'rempublicam universam, etiamsi posset aliquo modo in Principem peccare, rebellem tamen dici non posse. Princeps enim est per et propter rempublicam, non respublica per aut propter Principem.' Grotius, *De Iure Praedae*, p. 283; trans., p. 299. This kind of political point is the object of his *De Antiquitate Reipublicae Batavicae* (1610), formerly taken to be a spin-off from the *Parallelon*, but shown by Michelis to belong to this period in his life (Michelis, *Ugo Grozio*, pp. 104–5).

[15] The resemblance between the two was noted by contemporaries. See A. W. Harrison, *The Beginnings of Arminianism* (London, 1926), p. 123. On the movement in Holland generally, see D. Nobbs, *Theocracy and Toleration: a Study of the Disputes in Dutch Calvinism from 1600 to*

And just as Grotius had found himself in 1607 coming close to the Catholic rights theorists, so in the religious conflict he found himself close to the Protestant equivalent of the Molinists, the Arminians.

The result of his involvement in this conflict, apart from a certain amount of more limited controversial literature, was another unpublished manuscript, the *De Imperio Summarum Potestatum Circa Sacra*. Though it was published posthumously in 1647, it is generally agreed that it was composed in the period 1614 to 1617, when Grotius's letters to his friends (especially G. J. Vossius) are full of progress reports on it. The work's main importance for us is that in it we can see very clearly Grotius abandoning his earlier liberal stance on state power, and adopting a much more rigid attitude towards resistance. In this, he was to some extent merely following the example of other Remonstrants (particularly Vossius and Johannes Uytenbogaert) in an ideological move which was entirely comprehensible in the circumstances. The Arminians in the years before the Synod consistently appealed to the States of Holland for protection from the orthodox Church, and found a degree of sympathy there: in 1611, for example, the States forbade the Church from censuring Arminians or rejecting ordinands solely on the grounds of their Arminianism. Political support for them dwindled just before and during the Synod, with the Stadholder throwing his weight behind the orthodox, but it remained true that the Arminians reasonably anticipated more help from the secular authorities than they could hope to win from the ecclesiastical ones.

Where Grotius's work differs from his fellow Remonstrants' is that he was not content to rely upon the Protestant non-resistance theories to which they turned. Just as a liberal humanist political theory could be easily married to an Aristotelian ethic, so could the standard Protestant theory of non-resistance, as the example of writers such as Henning Arnisaeus (or, in England, Robert Filmer) shows;[16] but Grotius looked elsewhere for the basis of his theory. He was prepared to cite the usual scriptural examples of non-resistance, but at the centre of the *De Imperio* is a very different though highly elusive kind of argument.

Essentially, his discussion of sovereignty rested on a distinction between two kinds of association. One was kept in being by the continuous assent of its members, and though it might have disciplinary powers (just like any club or society) it could not be regarded as strictly *sovereign*. Sovereignty emerged at the point at which dissent was no longer possible: membership of the association committed its members to obedience to its constituted leader even though he might be acting against the rules of equity or

[16] For a discussion of this, see H. Dreitzel, *Protestantischer Aristotelismus und absoluter Staat; die Politica des H. Arnisaeus*, Veroft, d. Inst. f. Europaische Geschicte Mainz, LV (Wiesbaden, 1970).

1650 (Cambridge, 1938), and R. L. Colie, *Light and Enlightenment: a Study of the Cambridge Platonists and the Dutch Arminians* (Cambridge, 1957).

justice.[17] Unfortunately, the discussion of these two kinds of association is
not enlarged on: we cannot tell what the source of the obligation in the
latter kind might be. For reasons that will emerge presently, I doubt if it is
the voluntary cession of liberty postulated by Grotius in the *De Iure Belli*; it
is likely that Grotius's silence on the matter betokens a genuine uncertainty
at this stage in his life about the nature of political obligation (an evasive-
ness which remained characteristic of his own remarks about obligation of
any kind). But the distinction, necessary to his general argument because it
explained elegantly the difference between the disciplinary powers
enjoyed by any church and the political power possessed by the state, had
forced him away from the liberal position of the *De Iure Praedae*. The
power of the state in that work had been elucidated in terms very comparable to those with which he now elucidated the inferior power of a *church*.
State power was something different and by its nature irresistible, though
Grotius could not yet provide a theoretical explanation of this, and was to
have (as we shall see) considerable difficulty in doing so.

It is ironic that Grotius should have argued in this way in 1614–17, for
two years later the power of one part of the state (though Grotius denied
that it was in this context a legitimate power), the Stadholdership, was
used to crush the Arminians, and he himself was imprisoned for two years
in the Castle of Lowenstein. His imprisonment and his romantic escape to
France in a clothes-basket were dramatic and famous events, but as so
often happened in the sixteenth or seventeenth century the relatively loose
supervision and normal way of life enjoyed by a political prisoner enabled
him to produce some major intellectual works. (It is, incidentally, a
curious coincidence that the two men whom the eighteenth century
thought had created the Enlightenment, Grotius and Descartes, both
produced some of their seminal work out of conditions of enforced
idleness in the years 1619 and 1620, Descartes in army winter quarters and
Grotius in prison.)

Two of Grotius's works written at this time achieved a lasting fame: the
De Veritate Religionis Christianae and the *Introduction to the Jurisprudence of
Holland* (*Inleidinghe tot de Hollandsche Rechts-gheleertheydt*). Both represented a significant break with previous ways of thinking in their respective fields of theology and jurisprudence, but it is with the second that we
are chiefly concerned. Although it has always been seen as a major work by
Dutch and South African lawyers, its importance in general political
theory and in the genesis of the *De Iure Belli* has only rarely been recognised. But it constitutes the decisive move away from an Aristotelian
theory of justice, and is in fact the first reconstruction of an actual legal
system in terms of rights rather than laws. Consequently it is the true
ancestor of all the modern codes which have rights of various kinds at their
centre.

[17] *Opera Theologica*, III (London, 1679), pp. 212–16.

The fundamental principles of the work are adumbrated in the first chapter. Grotius distinguished between two senses of *recht*: the wide sense ('what is right') and the narrower sense, a right proper. It was with this narrower sense that he was to be concerned, and he defined it as follows:

Right, narrowly understood, is the relation which exists between a reasonable being and something appropriate to him by merit or property.

Merit is the fitness of a reasonable being for any object of desire.

Property means that something is called ours: it consists, as will be seen, in real rights (*jus reale*) and in personal rights (*jus personale*) ...

Of the justice which has regard to right, narrowly understood, the kind which takes account of merit is called 'distributive justice'; the other kind which gives heed to property is called 'commutative justice': the first commonly employs the rule of proportion, the second the rule of simple equality.[18]

Although Grotius was still talking about two kinds of justice, distributive and commutative, he had nevertheless moved definitively away from the Aristotelian structure of the *De Iure Praedae*. Now rights are the necessary subject-matter of justice, and for there to be a category of distributive justice, there must be a category of 'distributive rights', the rights of merit or desert. This is of course the antithesis of a Renaissance Aristotelian theory of justice, and even the Spanish Dominicans had not sought to assimilate distributive to commutative justice in this way. In effect, as we shall see, the only change that now had to occur in order to produce the notoriously anti-Aristotelian theory of the *De Iure Belli* was for Grotius to become more sceptical about whether there could in fact be such a thing as distributive justice, given that the category of distributive rights was difficult to handle.

Grotius was now able to treat the law of nature as totally to do with the maintenance of other people's rights, whether of property or merit. Thus he divided what he called 'the duty which regards another' into three: 'the duty of benevolence, the duty of keeping faith, the duty of making amends for wrongdoing', the last two being entirely to do with property while the former was broadly equivalent to respect for merit or desert.[19] Rights have come to usurp the whole of natural law theory, for the law of nature is simply, respect one another's rights.

In some ways this fits uneasily with Grotius's general account of the

---

[18] 'Eng genomen recht is het opzicht dat daer is tusschen een redelick wezen ende yet dat op het zelve past, door waerdigheid ofte toebehooren. Waerdigheid is de bequamheid van een redelick wezen tot yet dat begeert werd. Toebehoren is waer door yet het onze werd genoemt, ende bestaet (als hier nae zal werden verklaert) in begering (L. Jus reale) ende in inschuld (L. Jus personale) ... Van de rechtvaerdigheid die op 't eng genomen recht zie werd die soorte die op de waerdigheid acht neemt ghenoemt begevende (L. Justitia distributiva): de andere die op het toebehoren let, de vergeldende (L. Justitia commutativa): waer van die, de evenredenheid, deze, de slechte evenheid meest gebruickt.' *The Jurisprudence of Holland*, I, ed. and trans. R. W. Lee (Oxford, 1926), pp. 2–3.

[19] 'De schuld ziende op een ander bestaet meest in drie hoofdstucken in weldaed-schuld, in trouw-schuld ende misdaed-schuld.' Grotius, *Jurisprudence*, pp. 292–3.

logical character of the law of nature. He defined the natural law, in terms which pointed towards the famous discussion in the *Prolegomena* to the *De Iure Belli*, as 'an intuitive judgement, making known what things from their own nature are honourable or dishonourable, involving a duty to follow the same imposed by God'.[20] This was close to the scholastic tradition, with its emphasis on the intrinsic moral character of situations, and it was a clear break with the Protestant voluntarist tradition. God's will is no longer the unique source of moral qualities: things are good or bad *from their own nature*, and that is logically prior to God commanding or forbidding them. But the unease comes when Grotius further argues that the things which are intrinsically good are those which are associated with the natural, social character of men. For example,

just as every thing that is seeks the common good, and therefore its own, particularly its self-preservation; and just as animals by union of male and female seek the propagation of their species and provide for their young; so it is that man, doing the same, is conscious of doing what is right ...[21]

One feature of this passage, as of the comparable passages in the *De Iure Belli*, is that the reflective and rational character of men plays a relatively small part in the argument. Grotius stipulated that only rational beings are genuinely subject to *law* – but their obligation is to perform reflectively those actions which they would if not rational perform unreflectively. The natural psychological facts about men (and about comparable animals) are the crucial elements: if men wanted different things, then the laws of their nature would be different. But Grotius was not putting forward a prudential theory of obligation; he ruled that out elsewhere when he argued that punishment is logically distinct from obligation. He simply assumed that men want to be responsible and social beings even though they may suffer as individuals for those wants in the short term, and that the law of nature obliges them to follow their natural bent. No special explanation of why it is rational for individuals to do so seemed necessary to Grotius, and it was an important point in the history of natural right theories (marked, as we shall see, by the work of Selden) when such an explanation did become necessary.

The problem with this account of the law of nature in the *Inleidinghe* is how a principle of community (*gemeenschap*, as he calls it) can lead to a strong theory of rights. If we consider those theories which have traditionally stressed communitarian principles (such as classical utilitarian-

[20] 'het oordeel des verstands, te kennen ghevende wat zaken uit haer eighen aerd zijn eerlick ofte oneerlick, met verbintenisse van God wegen om 't zelve te volgen'. Grotius, *Jurisprudence*, pp. 4–5.

[21] 'Want gelijck al wat daer is zoeckt het gemeene goed ende voorts sijn eigen, ende namentlick sijne behoudenisse, gelijck oock de dieren door gajing van man ende wijf zoecken haers geslachts voorteeling ende 't gheboren onderhouden, zoo is 't dat een mensch oock sulcks doende, in sijn ghemoed bevind dat hy doet dat recht is.' Grotius, *Jurisprudence*, pp. 6–7.

ism), we can see that they have been precisely the theories which placed rights in a subsidiary position. The inconsistency remains unexplored in the *Inleidinghe*, but in the *De Iure Belli* Grotius (as we shall see presently) was able to reconcile the two aspects of his theory in a convincing way.

Having set up his theory in this way, Grotius proceeded to analyse the contemporary law of Holland in terms of the real and personal rights which it assigned to its citizens. The theory of real rights, rights of property in the modern sense, was substantially the same as that put forward in 1607 and as that which he was to put forward in the *De Iure Belli*; indeed, there is a long disquisition on the concept of private ownership and its historical genesis which is more or less a literal translation of the relevant passage in the *De Iure Praedae*.[22] But Grotius was now capable of producing a much more coherent and structured account of personal rights, though he was still in some difficulties over them.

Essentially, what he argued was that men were naturally free to contract and bargain in all kinds of ways over all their property, and that it was only the civil law which stepped in to prevent certain kinds of bad bargain. Personal liberty was a part of a man's property and in fact it was only because it was such a part that contracts were possible. As he said:

'Contract' is something more than promise. Promise has indeed the consequence that it is improper not to perform what is promised, but does not give another party any right to accept the same.
    The reason for this consists in a man's free disposal of his acts: for just as the power which a man has over his own property, whether in complete or incomplete ownership, enables him by delivery or sufferance to make another person owner, ... so too a man may make over to another who accepts the same, a portion, or rather a consequence, of his own freedom, so that the other acquires a right over it, which right is termed a personal right ...[23]

An important feature of Grotius's argument at this point is that he explicated the general obligation to keep a promise, of which a contract was a special case, in terms some distance removed from traditional natural law thinking. What he said was that

The duty of keeping faith arises from speech or anything that resembles speech. Speech is given to men alone amongst animals for the better furtherance of their common interest in order to make known what is hidden in the mind; the fitness whereof consists in the correspondence of the sign with the thing signified, which is called 'truth'. But since truth considered in itself implies nothing further than the

---

[22] Grotius, *Jurisprudence*, pp. 78–83.
[23] 'Toezegging is iet meer dan belofte: want de belofte maeckt wel dat het onbehoorlick is zulcks te laten als belooft is, maer geeft een ander gheen recht om zulcks te mogen aenneemen. Den grond hier van bestaet in des mensches vrije macht over sijne daden: want ghelijckerwijs de macht die iemand heeft over sijn eighen goed, 't zy in vollen ofte gebreckelick en eigendom, zoo veel werckt dat hy door levering ofte toelating een ander mag eigenaer maecken, ... alzoo oock vermag een mensch een deel, ofte veel eer een gevolg, sijns vrijheids aen een ander zulcks aenneemende over te draghen, zoo dat die andere eenig recht daer over werd geboren, welck recht inschuld werd gemoemt.' Grotius, *Jurisprudence*, pp. 294–5.

correspondence of the language with the mind at the actual moment when the language is used, and since man's will is from its nature changeable, means had to be found to fix that will for time to come, and such means are called 'promise'.[24]

Intimations of this position are to be found in the *De Iure Praedae*, but it is much clearer and more precise here. And of course, its thrust was to direct attention once again away from a *law* towards the individual's *will*; the binding character of a promise is part of a co-operative human attempt to substantiate an act of will, and it is part of the law of nature precisely because of the usefulness of such co-operation.

Grotius's general claim that men are naturally free to strike bargains in all kinds of ways over their property, and that developed social relationships grow up as a result of this, had however certain important qualifications in the *Inleidinghe*. In particular, there is something of a contradiction over the central question of a man's *liberty*. On the one hand, he argued that 'although by the law of nature everyone is master of his own property and of his own actions, nevertheless the civil law has not thought fit that people should use their freedom to their own damage, without advantage to the commonwealth' – restraints on self-injury are civil and not natural in character.[25] But on the other hand, he argued earlier in the book that

Things belonging to individuals are by nature inalienable or alienable.

Inalienable things are things which belong so essentially to one man that they could not belong to another, as a man's life, body, freedom, honour.

A man's life is so far his own that he may defend it even at the cost of injury to an aggressor; may forfeit it for crime; may sacrifice it in the service of his country.

But no one has unlimited right over his life; therefore in Holland punishment has always attached to persons who deliberately made away with themselves ...

Likewise no one may pledge his life by contract.

A man's body is so far his own that he may defend it as he may defend his life ... But no one may bind his body by contract except to marriage ...

A man's freedom belongs to him, so that he may protect and use it. A man may also forfeit his freedom for crime, as those who are banished to the galleys or to houses of correction. With us no one may entirely dispose of their freedom by contract, though a man may well bind himself to certain defined acts.

A man's honour belongs to him; first to protect it: it may also be forfeited for crime, as in the case of persons who are pronounced infamous: but it cannot,

[24] 'Trouw-schuld ontstaet uit de spraecke ofte iet dat spraecksghelijck is: welcke spraeck den menschen alleen onder alle dieren tot beter betrachtinghe van de onderlinghe ghemeenschap is gegeven, om daer mede bekent te maken 't gunt in 't gemoed is verholen: waer van de behoorlickheid bestaet in de over-een-kominghe van het teicken met het beteickende, 't welck waerheid werd genoemt. Maer alzoo de waerheid alleen inghezien zijnde niet anders medebrengt als een over-een-koming van de tael met het ghemoed voor die tijd als de tael werd gebruickt, zijnde des mensches wil uit haer eigen aerd veranderlick, zoo heeft een middel moeten gevonden werden om die wille voor het toekomende vast te stellen, welcke middle is belofte.' Grotius, *Jurisprudence*, pp. 292–3.

[25] 'Want hoe wel een ider nae 't aenghebooren recht meester is van sijn goed ende daden, nochtans heeft de burgher-wet niet ghewilt dat de luiden zulcks zouden ghebruicken tot haer eigen schade, zonder voordeel van het ghemeene beste.' Grotius, *Jurisprudence*, pp. 452–3.

properly speaking, be bound by contract, although dishonour is a consequence of breach of faith: however, a man may renounce something that belongs to him as part of his honour.[26]

It is clear from these remarks that in fact Grotius had certain doubts about the inalienable character of all these four properties (with the exception, perhaps, of life); but in the *Inleidinghe* he was still not prepared to allow liberty, in particular, to be traded away. It is for this reason that I was inclined earlier to rule out voluntary slavery as a basis for political sovereignty in the *De Imperio*: Grotius seems to have found it extremely difficult to come to terms with the possibility, so alien to the whole Protestant and humanist tradition, that men may freely and totally renounce their liberty. But despite these contradictions and hesitations, Grotius's use of the notion of inalienable property in the *Inleidinghe* is extremely important.[27] The *De Iure Belli* exhibits something of the same kind of attempt to clear a small liberal space within a theory which strictly speaking implies the possibility of absolutism: Grotius was both the first conservative rights theorist in Protestant Europe and also, in a sense, the first radical rights theorist.

With this exception about the possibility of voluntary slavery, the theory of the *Inleidinghe* was substantially the same as the theory of the *De Iure Belli*. Grotius recognised it as such when in the 1630s he made manuscript notes on a copy of the earlier work, pointing out the similarities.[28] But it was of course far less accessible to a general audience: it circulated only in manuscript until 1631, six years after the publication of

[26] 'Bysondere luiden toe-komende zaken zijn of uit haer eigen aerd onwandelbaer (L. Inalienabiles) ofte wandelbaer (L. Alienabiles). Onwandelbare zaken sijn, die iemand zoo toebehooren dat de zelve een ander niet en zoude konnen toe-behooren, als een yder sijn leven, lighaem, vryheid, eer. 't Leven behoort yder mensch zoo verre toe, dat hy 't mag beschermen, oock met schade van den aenvaller: dat hy 't mag verbeuren, met misdoen: dat hy 't oock mag ten beste geven voor 's lands dienst. Maer vol-recht heeft niemand over sijn leven: oversulcks zijn altijd in Holland strafbaer gheweest, die haer zelve door opzet verdeden, ... Insgelijcx en vermag niemand by eenige handeling sijn leven te verbinden. 't Lichaem behoort yder een zoo verre toe, dat hy 't zelve mag beschermen, zulcks als van 't leven is ghezeit ... maer niemand mag door handeling sijn lichaem verbinden, anders als tot den echt ... De vrijheid behoort yder een mede toe, zulcks dat hy die mag beschermen ende gebruicken. Iemand kan oock de selve door misdaed verbeuren, also die tot de roei-schepen ofte in tuchthuizen werden verbannen: maer niemandt en mag by ons door handeling hem zelve sijns vrijheids in 't gheheel weerloos maecken: dan wel vermag yder een hem tot zeeckere daden te verbinden. De eer behoort mede een yder toe: eerst om te beschermen: kan oock door misdaed verbeurt werden, als by den ghenen die eerloos werden verklaert: maer en is mede eigentlick door handeling niet verbindelick: hoewel uit ontrouw oneer volgt: dan iemand kan afstand doen van iet dat hem als een deel van syn eer behoort.' Grotius, *Jurisprudence*, pp. 70–3.

[27] A comparable equivocation marks his discussion of usury: men are free to make whatever bargains they choose, but it is also the case that interest is independently fair. See Grotius, *Jurisprudence*, pp. 348–9.

[28] For an account of these notes, see the most recent Dutch edition of the *Inleidinghe*, ed. F. Dovring, H. F. W. D. Fischer and E. M. Meijers (Leiden, 1952), p. xx. For an example of them, see *ibid.*, p. 3 n. 2.

the *De Iure Belli*, and it was in the largely incomprehensible Dutch language. It was the *De Iure Belli* that gave Grotius his European reputation,
and it is to the rights theory set out in that work that we must turn.

We know that in the first years at Paris after his escape from Lowenstein,
he was engaged in going over the work he had done in prison and
preparing it for publication. The *De Veritate Religionis Christianae* was
published (in its original Dutch) in 1622, and in the same year Grotius
wrote to his brother William that he was engaged on some juridical
work.[29] Two years later, in November 1624, he delivered the manuscript
of the *De Iure Belli* to the printer, most of it having been composed in the
relative seclusion of the county house belonging to the legal dynasty of the
de Mesmes at Balagny-sur-Therain. It was not actually published until
June 1625.[30] It would have been surprising, in view of the speed with
which he produced it after his escape, if it had represented a substantial
break with his thoughts as they had developed at Lowenstein. What he did
do was to clarify his opinions and put a more arresting edge on them, and
nowhere is this more the case than in his open rejection of the Aristotelian
theory of justice.

Once again, as in the *De Iure Praedae*, Grotius began by expounding the
principle of sociability: the law of nature was rooted in man's sociable
character. But the content of the law was no longer (in part) the observation of Aristotelian principles of justice. Instead, it was openly what it had
become by implication in the *Inleidinghe*, the injunction to respect
another's rights.

This Sociability, . . . or this Care of maintaining Society in a Manner conformable
to the Light of human Understanding, is the Fountain of Right, properly so called;
to which belongs the Abstaining from that which is another's, and the Restitution
of what we have of another's, or of the Profit we have made by it, the Obligation of
fulfilling Promises, the Reparation of a Damage done through our own Default,
and the Merit of Punishment among Men.
  From this Signification of Right arose another of larger Extent. For by reason
that Man above all other Creatures is endued not only with this *Social* Faculty of
which we have spoken, but likewise with Judgement to discern Things pleasant or
hurtful, and those not only present but future, and such as may prove to be so in
their Consequences; it must therefore be agreeable to human Nature, that according to the Measure of our Understanding we should in these Things follow the
Dictates of a right and sound Judgement, and not be corrupted either by Fear, or the
Allurements of present Pleasure, nor be carried away by blind Passion. And
whatsoever is contrary to such a Judgement, is likewise understood to be contrary
to Natural Right, that is, the Laws of our Nature.
  And to this belongs a prudent Management in the gratuitous Distribution of
Things that properly belong to each particular Person or Society, so as to prefer
sometimes one of greater before one of less Merit, a Relation before a Stranger, a
poor Man before one that is rich, and that according as each Man's Actions, and the

---

[29] *Briefwisseling*, II, ed. P. C. Molhuysen (The Hague, 1936), p. 254.
[30] For these details, see Knight, *Grotius*, pp. 192–3.

Nature of the Thing require: which many both of the Ancients and Moderns take to be a part of Right properly and strictly so called; when notwithstanding that Right, properly speaking, has a quite different Nature, since it consists in leaving others in quiet Possession of what is already their own, or in doing for them what in Strictness they may demand.[31]

Grotius was now able to argue that the law of nature was in effect the obligation men are under to preserve social peace, and that the principal condition for a peaceful community is respect for one another's rights. He thus solved the contradiction left unresolved in the *Inleidinghe*. Indeed not only is such respect a principal condition, it is also one of the chief points of leading a social existence:

Right Reason, and the Nature of Society, ... does not prohibit all Manner of Violence, but only that which is repugnant to Society, that is, which invades another's Right: For the Design of Society is, that every one should quietly enjoy his own, with the Help, and by the united Force of the whole Community. It may be easily conceived, that the Necessity of having Recourse to violent Means for Self-Defence, might have taken Place, even tho' what we call *Property* (*dominium*) had never been introduced. For our Lives, Limbs, and Liberties, had still been properly our own, and could not have been, (without manifest Injustice) invaded.

---

[31] 'Haec vero, societatis custodia humano intellectui conveniens, fons est ejus juris quod proprie tali nomine appellatur: quo pertinet alieni abstinentia, & si quid alieni habeamus aut lucri inde fecerimus restitutio, promissorum implendorum obligatio, damni culpa dati reparatio, & poenae inter homines meritum. Ab hac juris significatione fluxit altera largior: quia enim homo supra caeteras animantes non tantum vim obtinet socialem de qua diximus, sed & judicium ad aestimanda quae delectant aut nocent, non praesentia tantum, sed & futura, & quae in utrumvis possunt ducere, pro humani intellectus modo etiam in his judicium recte conformatum sequi, neque metu, aut voluptatis praesentis illecebra corrumpi, aut temerario rapi impetu, conveniens esse humanae naturae; & quod tali judicio plane repugnat, etiam contra ius naturae, humanae scilicet, esse intelligitur. Atque huc etiam pertinet in his quae cuique homini aut coetui propria sunt elargiendis prudens dispensatio, ut quae nunc sapientiorem minus sapienti, nunc propinquum extraneo, nunc pauperem diviti, prout actus cujusque & rei natura fert, praeponit: quam juris proprie stricteque dicti partem jam olim multi faciunt, cum tamen ius illud proprie nominatum diversam longe naturam habeat, in eo positam ut quae jam sunt alterius alteri permittantur, aut impleantur.' Grotius, *De Iure Belli ac Pacis* (Paris, 1625), sig. abv. (Prolegomena, 8–10). The translation is *The Rights of War and Peace*, ed. J. Barbeyrac, trans. anon. (London, 1738), pp. xvii–xviii. Regrettably, the commonly available texts and English translations of Grotius leave a great deal to be desired. The standard texts (e.g. Whewell's of 1853 or the Carnegie Endowment edition of 1913–27) are all based ultimately on the quite extensively revised edition of *De Iure Belli* which Grotius published in 1631. To understand his original intentions, it is far better to work with the first edition. A variorum edition of *De Iure Belli* was published at Leiden in 1939, ed. B. J. A. de Kanter-van Hettinga-Tromp, but it is probably less generally available than copies of the 1625 edition. A list of variants between the 1625 edition and subsequent texts was published by P. C. Molhuysen, 'The First Edition of Grotius's *De Iure Belli ac Pacis'*, *Bibliotheca Visseriane*, v (Leiden, 1925), pp. 103–49. No subsequent editor has ever equipped Grotius with anything like the remarkable notes attached to Barbeyrac's edition, first published at Amsterdam in 1720. For that reason, and because of its importance in the intellectual history of eighteenth-century England, I have chosen to use the English translation of his great edition. For the bibliography of Grotius generally, see J. ter. Meulen and P. J. J. Diermanse, *Bibliographie des écrits imprimés de H. Grotius* (The Hague, 1950).

So also, to have made use of Things that were then in common, and to have consumed them, as far as Nature required, had been the Right of the first Possessor: And if any one had attempted to hinder him from so doing, he had been guilty of a real Injury ...[32]

The passionate desire for peace (both between states and between individuals) which informs the *De Iure Belli*, and for which Grotius was famous, was thus intimately connected with his rights theory: peace required respect for and protection of property, and disputes over rights were the prime cause of war.

Grotius made the non-Aristotelian character of his theory of justice and rights clear in a more technical way in his discussion of the meaning of *ius* in Book I. In addition to the objective sense of the word,

there is another Signification of the Word *Right* ... which relates directly to the *Person*: In which Sense *Right* is a *moral Quality* annexed to the Person, *enabling him to have, or do, something justly* ... This moral Quality when perfect, is called by us a *Faculty*; when imperfect, an *Aptitude*: The former answers to the *Act*, and the latter to the *Power*, when we speak of natural Things.

Civilians call a *Faculty* that Right which a Man has to his *own*; but we shall hereafter call it a *Right properly, and strictly taken.* Under which are contained, 1. A Power either over our selves, which is term'd *Liberty*; or over others, such as that of a *Father over his Children*, or a *Lord over* his Slave. 2. Property, which is either *compleat*, or *imperfect*. The last obtains in the Case of *Farms*, for Instance, or *Pledges*. 3. *The Faculty of demanding what is due,* and to this *answers the Obligation of rendering what is owing* ...

'Tis expletive Justice, Justice properly and strictly taken, which respects the *Faculty*, or *perfect Right*, and is called by *Aristotle* συναλλακτικὴ, *Justice of Contracts*, but this does not give us an adequate Idea of that Sort of Justice. For, if I have a Right to demand Restitution of my Goods, which are in the Possession of another, it is not by vertue of any *Contract*, and yet it is the Justice in question that gives me such a Right. Wherefore he also calls it more properly ἐπανορθωτικὴν, *corrective* Justice. *Attributive Justice,* stiled by *Aristotle* διανεμητική, *Distributive*, respects Aptitude or *imperfect* Right, the attendant of those Virtues that are beneficial to others, as Liberality, Mercy, and prudent Administration of Government ...[33]

---

[32] 'Recta autem ratio ac natura societatis, ... non omnem vim inhibet, sed eam demum quae societati repugnat, id est quae ius alienum tollit. Nam societas eo tendit ut suum cuique salvum sit communi ope ac conspiratione. Quod facile intellegi potest locum habiturum, etiamsi dominium quod nunc ita vocamus introductum non esset. nam vita, membra, libertas sic quoque propria cuique essent, ac proinde non sine iniuria ab alio impeterentur. sic & rebus in medio positis uti, & quantum natura desiderat eas absumere ius esset occupantis: quod ius qui ei eriperet faceret injuriam.' Grotius, *De Iure Belli*, p. 18 (I.II.I.5); trans., pp. 25–6.

[33] 'Ab hac iuris significatione diversa est altera, sed ab hac ipsa veniens, quae ad personam refertur; quo sensu ius est Qualitas moralis personae competens ad aliquid juste habendum vel agendum. Personae competit hoc ius, etiamsi rem interdum sequatur, ut servitutes praediorum quae iura realia dicuntur comparatione facta ad alia mere personalia: non quia non ipsa quoque personae competant, sed quia non alii competunt quam qui rem certam habeat. Qualitas autem moralis perfecta, Facultas nobis dicitur; minus perfecta, Aptitudo: quibus respondent in naturalibus, illi quidem actus, huic autem potentia. Facultatem Iurisconsulti nomine Sui appellant: nos posthac ius proprie aut stricte dictum appellabimus: sub quo continentur Potestas, tum in se, quae libertas dicitur, tum in alios, ut

He proceeded to criticise Aristotle not only for not seeing that justice proper was to do with active rights, and that there could be no true distributive justice, but also for talking about arithmetical and geometrical principles of distribution.

Grotius's open attack on the basis of Aristotelian ethics immediately aroused his Protestant contemporaries. They rallied to the defence both of their reading of Aristotle, and of the Renaissance juridical insights which they had long ago blended with their Aristotelianism. The first major critique of the *De Iure Belli*, by a German lawyer, Johannes Felden, contained both a long defence of Aristotle from Grotius's strictures, and an attack on the whole notion of a right as Grotius was employing it. He accused him of imitating 'the ineptitudes of the scholastics, who confounded everything with their petty distinctions and removed all correct meaning from words'.

He says that 'Civilians call a *Faculty* that *Right properly, and strictly taken*'; I do not understand why. For no one will readily describe liberty as a *ius* over themselves, nor can *dominium* properly be termed a *ius* in something; nor is a father properly said to have a *ius* in his children, or a master in his slaves ... The Roman jurists agree with me – see [Digest] 13.1 and 19 *de damn. inf.*, which distinguishes *dominium* from a *ius*; and they never term liberty a *ius* in ourselves.[34]

He could not have put better the point which the Renaissance jurists had made about the language of rights, and which Grotius had quite deliberately repudiated: in the response of conservative Aristotelians to the *De Iure Belli* we can see precisely the significance of the move which Grotius had made. Felden was inclined to be a liberal in his views on state power, and criticised Grotius's defence of absolutism,[35] but Aristotelians who were themselves absolutists were also hostile to the book: the best example

---

[34] 'Imitatur hic Autor ineptias scholasticorum, qui distinctiunculis suis res ipsas contundentes vocum proprietates tollunt ... Facultatem nomine sui venire Jetis, seque Jus stricte appellaturum ait, nescio an satis bene. Nam libertatem nemo facile Jus in se vocabit, nec dominium Jus in res [sic] videtur proprie dici posse; nec fortasse pater in liberos, aut dominus in servos ius proprie habere dicitur ... Consentiunt mecum U. Romanae 13.§1. & 19. de damn. inf. quae Dominum [sic] juri contradistinguunt, liberalitatem vero nuspiam Jus aliquod in nos metipsos appellitant.' J. Felden, *Annotata in Hug. Grotium. De Iure Belli et Pacis* (Amsterdam, 1653), pp. 6, 8–9. ('U. Romanae' is an obscure phrase, but clearly refers to Ulpian and Gaius in the Digest XXXIX.2.13 and 19.)
[35] See e.g. *ibid.*, p. 35.

---

patria, dominica: Dominium, plenum sive minus pleno, ut ususfructus, ius pignoris: & creditum cui ex adverso respondet debitum ... Facultatem respicit justitia Expletrix, quae proprie aut stricte iustitiae nomen obtinet, συναλλακτικὴ Aristoteli, nimis arcto vocabulo: nam ut possessor meae rei eam mihi reddat, non est συναλλάγματος, & tamen ad eandem hanc iustitiam pertinet: itaque ἐπανορθωτικὴν idem felicius dixit: Aptitudinem respicit Attributrix quae Aristoteli διανεμητικὴ, comes earum virtutum quae aliis hominibus utilitatem adferunt, ut liberalitatis, misericordiae, providentiae rectricis ...' Grotius, *De Iure Belli*, pp. 4–5 (I.I.IV–VIII); trans., pp. 3–6.

of this is the Englishman Robert Filmer's attack on Grotius in his *Patriarcha.*

Grotius not only made the anti-Aristotelian thrust of his rights theory more apparent, he also made its untheistic character obvious, and thereby stirred up as much criticism from the same kind of source. What he said, notoriously, was that his theory about the natural law maintaining human society and therefore human rights 'would take place, though we should even grant, what without the greatest Wickedness cannot be granted, that there is no God, or that he takes no Care of human Affairs'.[36] This was because the law of nature was *logically* necessary:

tho' the Power of God be infinite, yet we may say, that there are some Things to which this infinite Power does not extend, because they cannot be expressed by Propositions that contain any Sense, but manifestly imply a Contradiction. For Instance then, as God himself cannot effect, that twice two should not be four; so neither can he, that what is intrinsically Evil should not be Evil.[37]

These remarks occasioned a great deal of argument among Protestants, and many people who were otherwise very sympathetic to Grotius, such as Salmasius or Pufendorf, felt obliged to criticise him for them.[38] But they were simply an expansion of the ideas put forward in the *Inleidinghe*, and were very close to what Suarez had argued. Grotius clarified the matter in a letter to his brother some years later:

God was at full Liberty not to create Man. The Moment he is determined to create Man, that is, a Nature endowed with Reason, and formed for a Society of an excellent Kind, he necessarily approves of such Actions as are suitable to that Nature, and as necessarily disapproves of those which are contrary to it. But there are several other Things which he commands or prohibits, because he thought fit to do so, and not because he could not act otherwise.[39]

In other words, it is not *conceptually* possible to envisage a rational social being to whom the laws of nature do not apply. The Protestants were right to be worried by this, however, for it undeniably limited the point of talking about God in a moral context. Given the natural facts about men,

---

[36] 'Et haec quidem quae jam diximus, locum haberent, etiamsi daremus, quod sine summo scelere dari nequit, non esse Deum, aut non curari ab eo negotia humana.' Grotius, *De Iure Belli*, sig. el (Prolegomena, 11); trans., p. xix.

[37] 'Quanquam enim immensa est Dei potentia, dici tamen quaedam possunt ad quae se illa non extendit, quia ita dicuntur, dicuntur tantum, sensum autem qui rem exprimat nullum habent; sed sibi ipsis repugnant: Sicut ergo ut bis duo non sint quatuor ne a Deo quidem potest effici, ita ne hoc quidem, ut quod intrinsica ratione malum est malum non sit.' Grotius *De Iure Belli*, p. 7 (I.I.x.5); trans., p. 11–12.

[38] See C. Salmasius, *De Usuris* (Leiden, 1638), pp. 588–9; S. Pufendorf, *The Law of Nature and Nations*, ed. J. Barbeyrac, trans. B. Kennet (London, 1749), pp. 117–18.

[39] 'Deo liberum erat hominem non condere. Condito homine, id est natura ratione utente et ad societatem eximiam conformata necessario probat actiones tali naturae consentaneas, contrarias improbat. At multa alia non necessario, aut jubet aut punit, sed quia ita ipsi visum.' *Briefwisseling*, IX, ed. B. L. Meulenbroek (The Hague, 1973), p. 301. For the translation see the English translation of *De Iure Belli*, p. 16 n.1.

the laws of nature followed by (allegedly) strict entailment without any mediating premisses about God's will (though his will might still be an explanation of those natural facts). It was this which Pufendorf denied, holding that *in addition* to the facts some theory about what God wanted his creation to do was still necessary.

Given these general principles, Grotius proceeded to fill in the substantive theory. A lot remained unchanged from *De Iure Praedae* and the *Inleidinghe* – for example his ideas on punishment – but in two important areas he provided some new ideas. One area was the question of the origin of private property. While the theory of the *Inleidinghe* was entirely the same as that of *De Iure Belli* Grotius remarked that the transition from a common use-right to private property, while prompted by natural requirements, 'resulted from a certain Compact and Agreement, either expressly, as by a Division; or else tacitly, as by Seizure. For as soon as living in common was no longer approved of, all Men were supposed, and ought to be supposed to have consented, that each should appropriate to himself, by Right of first Possession, what could not have been divided.'[40] By introducing the idea of a *contract*, which he had been careful to exclude at this point in *De Iure Praedae*, Grotius gave a hostage to fortune, for Selden was to use this idea against him in his attack on *Mare Liberum*. In fact, Grotius's theory in *De Iure Belli* is not radically different from his earlier view: the tacit agreement, to which all men are *supposed* to have consented, is a very weak condition, for it would in principle be impossible to say that men could not have made such an agreement; and as we shall see, it must always be supposed to be rescinded in emergencies. As he presents it, it is still rather the *recognition* of a right (as it had been in the original theory) than what *constitutes* it.

The one feature of the work which was completely new was his discussion of the state. As Felden said, he 'touched here on the weightiest controversy'.[41] The picture of a political society or state which Grotius presented was of a group of individuals with a 'Community of Rights and Sovereignty' (*consociatio iuris atque imperii*) that is to say, a group who had in some way defined themselves as separate from the rest of human society by particular transfers of rights.[42] One such transfer which he now took to be possible was the total alienation of all their original liberty by the members of a society to one ruler. If that ruler was himself a member of the society, then it had an independent existence; if not, then it had ceased to

---

[40] 'pacto quodam aut expresso, ut per divisionem, aut tacito, ut per occupationem. simulatque enim communio displicuit, nec instituta est divisio, censeri debet inter omnes convenisse, ut quod quisque occupasset id proprium haberet.' Grotius, *De Iure Belli*, p. 141 (II.II.II.5); trans., pp. 145–6. The translation is rather loose, but I have allowed it to stand.
[41] 'Attingit hic gravissimam controversiam.' Felden, *Annotata*, p. 34.
[42] Grotius, *De Iure Belli*, p. 248 (II.IX.VIII.2); trans., p. 266. See also his remarks on p. 202 (II.VI.IV); trans., p. 215.

exist, and had become merged with the other individuals or societies dependent on that ruler.

What Grotius said, in one of the most famous passages of the book, was that he had to

reject their Opinion, who will have the Supreme Power to be always, and without Exception, in the People; so that they may restrain or punish their Kings, as often as they abuse their Power. What Mischiefs this Opinion has occasioned, and may yet occasion, if once the Minds of People are fully possessed with it, every wise Man sees. I shall refute it with these Arguments. It is lawful for any Man to engage himself as a Slave to whom he pleases; as appears both by the *Hebrew* and *Roman* Laws. Why should it not therefore be as lawful for a People that are at their own Disposal, to deliver up themselves to any one or more Persons, and transfer the Right of governing them upon him or them, without recovering any Share of that Right to themselves? Neither should you say this is not to be presumed: For the Question here is not, what may be presumed in a Doubt, but what may be lawfully done? In vain do some alledge the Inconveniences which arise from hence, or may arise; for you can frame no Form of Government in your Mind, which will be without Inconveniences and Dangers ... A people may choose what Form of Government they please: Neither is the Right which the Sovereign has over his Subjects to be measured by this or that Form, of which divers Men have divers Opinions, but by the Extent of the Will of those who conferred it upon him.[43]

Central among the rights which people renounce when they set up a sovereign, or submit to a conqueror (which is the same kind of transfer), is the right of self-defence. As Grotius said,

all Men have naturally a Right to secure themselves from Injuries by Resistance ... But civil Society being instituted for the Preservation of Peace, there immediately arises a superior Right in the State over us and ours, so far as is necessary for that End. Therefore the State has a Power to prohibit the unlimited Use of the Right towards every other Person, for maintaining publick Peace and good Order, which doubtless it does, since otherwise it cannot obtain the End proposed; for if that

[43] 'Atque hoc loco primum rejicienda est eorum opinio, qui ubique & sine exceptione summam potestatem esse volunt populi, ita ut si reges quoties imperio suo male utuntur, & coercere & punire liceat; quae sententia quot malis causam dederit, & dare etiamnum possit penitus animis recepta, nemo sapiens non videt. Nos his argumentis eam refutamus. Licet homini cuique se in privatum servitutem cui velit addicere, ut & ex lege Hebraea & Romana apparet. quidni ergo populo sui iuris liceat se uni cuipiam, aut pluribus ita addicere, ut regendi sui ius in eum plane transcribat nulla ejus iuris parte retenta? Neque dixeris minime id praesumi: non enim iam quaerimus quid in dubio praesumendum sit: sed quid iure fieri possit. Frustra quoque afferentur incommoda quae hinc sequantur, aut sequi possint. nam qualemcumque formam gubernationis animo finxeris, nunquam incommodis aut periculis carebis ... populus eligere potest qualem vult gubernationis formam: neque ex praestantia huius aut illius formae, qua de re diversa diversorum sunt iudicia, sed ex voluntate ius metiendum est.' Grotius, *De Iure Belli*, pp. 67–8 (I.III.VIII.1–2); trans., p. 64.

[44] 'Naturaliter quidem omnes ad arcendam a se iniuriam ius habent resistendi ... Sed civili societate ad tuendam tranquillitatem instituta, statim civitati ius quoddam maius in nos & nostra nascitur, quatenus ad finem illum id necessarium est. Potest igitur civitas ius illud resistendi promiscuum publicae pacis & ordinis causa prohibere: Et quin voluerit, dubitandum non est, cum aliter non posset finem suum consequi. Nam si maneat promiscuum illud resistendi ius, non iam civitas erit, sed dissociata multitudo ...' Grotius, *De Iure Belli*, pp. 95–6 (I.IV.II.1); trans., pp. 102–3.

promiscuous Right of Resistance should be allowed, there would be *no longer a State*, but a Multitude without Union ...[44]

In particular, men no longer have a right to defend themselves against the person of the sovereign; Grotius defended this elsewhere on the more general grounds that even in a state of nature, a man who is attacked by someone whose continued life would be more utile than his own ought not to resist – 'because the *Aggressor's* life may be serviceable to *many*, it would be *criminal* to take it from him'.[45] As John Locke (though virtually only John Locke) was to perceive, in the context of Grotius's general theory this renunciation of liberty and the right of self-defence was quite unnecessary.[46] Grotius accepted in *De Iure Belli*, just as he had in *De Iure Praedae*, a natural right to punish: the only thing necessary to create civil society successfully would thus be a transfer of that right to some common authority. The underdetermined character of Grotius's absolutism is striking, once it is looked at in this way.

Reading the *De Iure Belli* in this way, we can easily see why it should have been taken up by theoreticians of absolutism, why Felden should have said that it 'destroys civil society, which is a community of free men, and makes it an aggregation of slaves',[47] and why Rousseau should have attacked it so bitterly. And yet there are also in the *De Iure Belli*, as in the *Inleidinghe*, arguments of a different kind, which were to be taken up by much more radical political theorists. The book is Janus-faced, and its two mouths speak the language of both absolutism and liberty. The libertarian arguments are of a simple kind; they merely require that we consider what kind of agreements reasonable people might have made in the past. While it remains true that our rights and duties are always to be understood as formed by anterior agreements, it is nevertheless the case that we must be generous in our interpretation of those agreements. There were two areas where these kinds of argument were particularly important. One was a modification of the principle of non-resistance, and the other was a modification of the principle of private property.

Thus Grotius raised the question of 'whether the Law of Non-resistance obliges us in the most extreme and inevitable danger', and replied,

this Law (of which we now treat) seems to depend upon the Intention of those who first entered into civil Society, from whom the Power of Sovereigns is originally derived. Suppose then they had been asked, Whether they pretended to impose on all Citizens the hard Necessity of dying, rather than to take up Arms in any Case, to defend themselves against the higher Powers; I do not know, whether they would have answered in the affirmative: It may be presumed, on the contrary, they would have declared that one ought not to bear with every Thing, unless the Resistance

---

[45] 'quia invasoris vita multis sit utilis, occidi is sine peccato nequeat.' Grotius, *De Iure Belli*, p. 128 (II.I.IX.I.); trans., p. 134.
[46] See below, pp. 172–3.
[47] 'Destruit societatem civilem, quae coetus liberorum hominum est, facitque ex ea conflugem servorum.' Felden, *Annotata*, p. 35.

would infallibly occasion great Disturbance in the State, or prove the Destruction of many Innocents. For what Charity recommends in such a Case to be done, may, I doubt not, be prescribed by a human Law.[48]

In principle, Grotius was arguing, all our rights *could* be renounced; but interpretive charity[49] requires that we assume that all were not *in fact* renounced.

Similarly, he raised the question of 'whether Men may not have a Right to enjoy those Things that are already become the Properties of other Persons', and used the same kind of argument.

We are to consider the Intention of those who first introduced the Property of Goods. There is all the Reason in the World to suppose that they designed to deviate as little as possible from the Rules of natural Equity; and so it is with this Restriction, that the Rights of Proprietors have been established: For if even written Laws ought to be thus explained, as far as possible; much more ought we to put that favourable Construction on Things introduced by a Custom not written, and whose Extent therefore is not determined by the Signification of Terms. From whence it follows, first, that in a Case of absolute Necessity, that ancient Right of using Things, as if they still remained common, must revive, and be in full Force ...[50]

It is significant that the first major public expression of a strong rights theory to be read in Protestant Europe should have contained both a defence of slavery and absolutism and a defence of resistance and common property *in extremis*; for the following generation was to be deeply split over which of these two features of a rights theory was the more important. The *De Iure Belli* contained in an embryonic form most of the political theory of the following fifty years, though the developed offspring had to live in a world where the principle of sociability, so important to Grotius, was under fierce attack.

Grotius himself lived on into that world. For the last twenty years of his life, he was content that his political philosophy should be that of the *De Iure Belli*. He spent some of his time showing the consistency between his

[48] 'Haec autem lex de qua agimus pendere videtur a voluntate eorum, qui se primum in societatem civilem consociant, a quibus ius porro ad imperantes manat. Hi vero si interrogarentur an velint omnibus hoc onus imponere, ut mori praeoptent, quam ullo casu vim superiorum armis arcere, nescio an velle se sint responsuri, nisi forte cum hoc additamento, si resisti nequeat, nisi cum maxima reipublicae perturbatione, aut exitio plurimorum innocentium. Quod enim tali circumstantia caritas commendaret, id in legem quoque humanam deduci posse non dubito.' Grotius, *De Iure Belli*, p. 105 (I.IV.VII.2); trans., p. 112.
[49] To adapt a phrase used most notably in another context by Quine; see e.g. *Word and Object* (Cambridge, Mass., 1960), p. 59.
[50] 'Spectandum enim est quae mens eorum fuerit qui primi dominia singularia introduxerunt: quae credenda est talis fuisse, ut quam minimum ab aequitate naturali recesserit. Nam si scriptae etiam leges in eum censum trahendae sunt quatenus fieri potest, multo magis mores, qui scriptorum vinculis non tenentur. Hinc primo sequitur in gravissima necessitate reviviscere ius illud pristinum rebus utendi tanquam si communes mansissent.' Grotius, *De Iure Belli*, p. 144 (II.II.VI.1); trans., p. 149. A similar principle governs Grotius's rejection of the idea that a sovereign can alienate his state without his people's consent; see p. 202 (II.VI.IV); trans., p. 215.

ideas in it and the law of Holland, and some of it doing the same for the *Corpus Juris Civilis*.[51] He remained wedded to the principle of sociability, and when he read Hobbes's *De Cive* shortly before his death he selected the idea of a *bellum omnium contra omnes* as his main grounds for objecting to it.[52] Indeed, a set of observations on Campanella's *Politica in Aphorismos Digesta* which he composed in the 1640s contains a notable defence of the principle.[53] But already by the time he read Hobbes the tradition which he had helped to develop (and which he had almost single-handedly created in Protestant Europe) had split into two rival camps which in the English civil war were to be literally at one another's throats. The two groups can be characterised as the conservative and the radical rights theorists, the first sceptical about the principle of sociability but condoning slavery and absolutism, dominated by Selden (with Hobbes a somewhat deviant member), while the second held fast to the principle of interpretive charity, and was dominated by the radical English pamphleteers of the 1640s. England, not Holland, was indeed to be the scene of all the important developments in the next twenty years, in which ideological and military conflict went hand in hand.

[51] For his notes on Dutch law, see above, n. 28; the comparison with the Corpus Juris Civilis composed in these years was published as *Florum Sparsio ad Ius Iustinianeum* (Paris, 1642).
[52] *Epistolae* (Amsterdam, 1687), pp. 951–2. (The relevant volume of the *Briefwisseling* has not yet been published.)
[53] T. Campanella, *Aforismi Politici* ... *integrati* ... *dal commento di Ugo Grozio*, ed. L. Firpo, Istituto Giuridico della R. Univ. di Torino Testi Inediti o Rari, v (Turin, 1941), pp. 229–30.

John Selden

Although, as we have seen, Grotius's achievement was a remarkable one, and his theory provided a formidable and exciting ideology for his mid-seventeenth-century audience, it was nevertheless incomplete in a number of important respects. In particular, it stressed individuality in the area of rights, but communality in the area of obligation, and though that might be logically coherent there was a certain psychological implausibility in it. Grotius's men were fiercely defensive of their original rights, and capable of so far controlling their own lives that they could commit themselves to slavery; and yet their moral world was informed by the principle of sociability with its distributive and unindividualistic implications, and *in extremis* their more harmful commitments could be disregarded. We have seen that Grotius reconciled these two sides of his theory with the claim that sociability necessitates respect for individual rights, but the psychology required to make this work was unconvincing. The history of natural rights theories during the next fifty years is indeed a story of argument over precisely this issue: does a natural rights theory require a strongly individualistic psychology and ethical theory? The most famous figure to answer this question in the affirmative was of course Hobbes, but the first person to do so was John Selden, and his contribution to the development of natural rights theories needs to receive more attention than it has hitherto enjoyed.

Only a year younger than Grotius, Selden was brought up in the same kind of world as the Dutchman, with its dominant modes of thought being Protestant, humanist and Aristotelian. He too exhibited the same kind of precocious intellectual control over it, and the same capacity to change it from within; like Grotius, also, he was a modern kind of intellectual, learned in a Renaissance way but also extremely quick-witted and provocative. We are able to see this better in his case than in Grotius's, for his conversation was fully and fascinatingly recorded in the justly famous *Table Talk*, whereas the record of Grotius's conversation is far less interesting.[1] Indeed, it is the case that Selden's conversation was often much clearer than his written work, a fact obvious to contemporaries such

[1] For Grotius's conversation (mainly on religious matters) as recorded by Guy Patin in 1643, see R. Pintard, *La Mothe le Vayer, Gassendi, Guy Patin* (Paris, 1943), pp. 69–86.

as Clarendon or Aubrey, and we will have frequent occasion to elucidate the obscure and complicated arguments of his published works with his crisp remarks at the dinner-table.[2]

Selden belonged to the generation of English humanist scholars who realised that it was possible to give an historical account of the English law in terms of the gradual accretion of new laws and loss of old ones. They had absorbed the theoretical ideas of men like Alciato and Connan, according to which (as we have seen) the laws operating in human societies were to be construed in terms of developing social utility, and they applied that insight to their own society. This was not the revolutionary development that Pocock thought it to be in *The Ancient Constitution and the Feudal Law*: a number of practising English lawyers in the period (such as Lord Ellesmere) were perfectly capable of contemplating historical change in the English law, and in a way the real puzzle is why men like Edward Coke did not do so (particularly given the criticism which contemporaries levelled at him precisely on this ground).[3] But it was a development which inspired a remarkable series of major works in a few years.

Selden gave one of the first clear expressions of the attitude in a substantial context in his *Jani Anglorum Facies Altera* (1610) when he remarked that 'the times on this side the *Normans* entrance, are so full of new Laws, especially such as belong to the rights of Tenancy or Vassalage; though other laws have been carefully enough kept up from the time of the *Saxons*, and perhaps from an earlier date ...'[4] This passage might almost stand as the epigraph to the works of his methodical though less inspired senior Sir Henry Spelman. Six years later Selden provided the general theory underlying such a view in his critical notes to Sir John Fortescue's *De Laudibus Legum Angliae*, a classic of the opposite school:

---

[2] Aubrey commented that 'in his younger years he affected obscurity of style' (*Brief Lives*, II, ed. A. Clark (Oxford, 1898), p. 224), while Clarendon (who knew him well) said that 'his style in all his writings seems harsh and sometimes obscure ... but in his conversation he was the most clear discourser, and had the best faculty of making hard things easy, and presenting them to the understanding, of any man that hath been known': *The History of the Rebellion ... Also his Life* (Oxford, 1843), p. 923. We still lack a full treatment of Selden; the D.N.B. article by Edward Fry is still the best guide to his biography.

[3] As Ellesmere said in the second case of the *post-nati*, 'Some lawes, as well statute lawe as common law, are obsolete and worne out of use: for, all humane lawes are but *leges temporis*; and the wisedome of the iudjes found them to bee unmeete for the time wherein they were made. And therefore it is saide, "leges humanae nascuntur, vigent, et moriuntur, et habent ortum, statum, et occasum".' *A Complete Collection of State Trials*, II, ed. T. B. Howell (London, 1809), p. 674. For the early criticisms of Coke, see the papers read to the Society of Antiquaries almost as soon as Coke's Third Report was published, particularly that by William Hakewill. *A Collection of Curious Discourses*, I, ed. T. Hearne (London, 1771), pp. 2, 8.

[4] 'Nam ita novis scatent, praecipue ad jus spectantibus clientelare, citeriora a Normannis tempora; aliis hucusque satis assiduo ab aevo Saxonico receptis, & forte a superiori.' *Opera Omnia*, II, ed. D. Wilkins (London, 1726), p. 964. The translation is *The Reverse or Back-face of the English Janus*, trans. R. Westcot (London, 1682), sig. a3v–a4.

In truth, and to speak without perverse affection, all laws in general are originally equally antient. All were grounded upon nature, and no nation was, that out of it took not their grounds; and nature being the same in all, the beginning of all laws must be the same . . . [But] although the law of nature be truly said immutable, yet it is as true, that it is limitable, and limited law of nature is the law now used in every state. All the same may be affirmed of our *British* laws, or *English*, or other whatsoever. But the divers opinions of interpreters proceeding from the weakness of man's reason, and the several conveniences of divers states, have made those limitations, which the law of Nature hath suffered, very different. And hence it is, that those customs which have come all out of one fountain, *nature*, thus vary from and cross one another in several commonwealths. Had the *Britons* received the ten or twelve tables from *Greece* . . . clearly the interpretations, and additions which by this time would have been put to them here, must not be thought on as if they would have fell out like the body of the *Roman* civil law . . . Infinite laws we have now that were not thought on D. years since. Then were many that D. years before had no being, and less time forward always produced divers new; the beginning of all here being in the first peopling of the land, when men, by nature being civil creatures, grew to plant a common society. This rationally considered, might end that obvious question of those, who would say something against the laws of *England* if they could. 'Tis their trivial demand, *When and how began your common laws?* Questionless it is fittest answered by affirming, when and in like kind as the laws of all other states, that is, *When there was first a state in that land, which the common law now governs:* Then were natural laws limited for the conveniency of civil society here, and those limitations have been from thence, increased, altered, interpreted, and brought to what now they are; although perhaps, saving the meerly immutable part of nature, now, in regard of their first being, they are not otherwise than a ship, that by often mending had no piece of the first materials, or as the house that's so often repaired, *ut nihil ex pristina materia supersit,* which yet, by the civil law, is to be accounted the same still . . .[5]

This was in fact already the Burkean theory of English law, and its influence (as we shall see) can be traced directly on to Matthew Hale, Selden's friend and executor, and thence to Blackstone and the mainstream of eighteenth-century English legal thinking.

But its implications are much wider. Although Selden talked about a 'meerly immutable' core to civil laws, in practice this core shrank to very little. The wide variety of human laws on almost every topic made the obligatory rather than the permissive dimension of the law of nature (as he was to term them later) almost nugatory. This became clear – and notorious – in a work which appeared the following year, the *History of Tythes*. The purpose of the history was to show that the institution of tithes was not part of the divine or natural law, by demonstrating that all over the known world (and particularly in England) tithes had been the subject of civil laws, and had been appropriated or not paid as it suited the different societies. The fact of appropriation he made a central part of his argument: tithes due to the priesthood had been treated by the monasteries and their lay successors just like any other rent-charges. 'No man can doubt that any kind of persons may enjoy a profit under the name of tythe or tenth, as well

[5] Selden, *Opera*, III, cols. 1891–2.

as a rent of the ninth part or of the eleventh.'[6] He was careful not to draw
the conclusion that it was all right just to treat them as rent-charges:

it is a gross error to make it clear, as many do, that if tythes be not due to the
priesthood *jure divino morali*, then appropriated tythes may be still possessed with
good conscience by laymen; and that if otherwise, then they may not. For though
they be not so; yet is the consecration of them in the appropriation, nothing? For if
they be not due so, then it will be clear, I think, to all, that they might pass in the
appropriation, as other things, subject to the titles of humane and positive law.[7]

But consecration was now viewed as a human act, producing effects
comparable to the restrictions with which many heritable properties are
burdened (e.g. against the cutting down of trees).

In all this, Selden differed strikingly from many of his contemporaries.
One interesting comparison is with Spelman: in his various works on
tithes, Spelman always insisted that they must be due *iure divino*, and
operated with a very traditional concept of divine and natural law.[8] The
same can be said of Selden's direct opponents in the controversy his *History*
opened up, such as Richard Mountagu and Sir James Sempel. Mountagu
realised what was at issue:

Some particular aberration of some men, doth not annihilate or make void an
universall Sanction ... [Many men might be mentioned who killed their parents]
and some Nations that counted it no sinne to doe so: and others that thought it
lawfull, nay, piety for to eate them afterward ... But such as presume to transgresse
that Law (men, or Nations, upon Custome, or howsoever) are punished therefore,
even as those are that violate humane Lawes ... Particular Lawes, made to command a thing done in some one state, do not take away that generall tye, and
precept, and inforcement from reason, and nature: for then, even *Deos colere*, and
Parentes venerari, were not naturall.[9]

Selden replied in tones of mock innocence to similar criticisms made by
Sempel, 'We [i.e. Selden and Scaliger, another participant in the con-
troversy] write of what *was* in use *settled*, he [i.e. Sempel] what (*he thinks*)
should have been. Why could he not have done so, and let us alone?'[10] There
was of course much more of a normative point which his critics could not
understand. In effect he was denying that there was any use in talking
about *ius divinum* in this very general way at all, or in hoping to establish its
positive precepts from dubious sources (among which, he later included
the Ten Commandments). If human laws permitted a particular practice
on a widespread scale, the presumption was that neither the natural nor the
divine law forbade it. And if that was right, then it followed that there was

[6] Selden, *Opera*, III, col. 1322. (*A Review* of the History, published with the first edition.)
[7] *ibid*.
[8] H. Spelman, *The English Works* (London, 1727), pp. 110–11.
[9] R. Mountagu, *Diatribae upon the first part of the late History of Tithes* (London, 1621), pp. 572–3.
[10] Selden, *Opera*, III, col. 1361.

no point in talking about the *ius divinum*: at any stage the argument was collapsible to a discussion of *civil* laws. He put the matter succinctly, as usual, when talking to his friends later:

All things are held by *jus divinum*, either immediately or mediately. Nothing has lost the pope so much in his supremacy, as not acknowledging what princes gave him. 'Tis a scorn upon the civil power, and an unthankfulness in the priest; But the church runs to *jus divinum*, lest if they should acknowledge what they have, they have by positive law, it might be as well taken from them, as given to them.[11]

We have in the argument of the *History* one of the roots of Selden's notorious Erastianism, but it appears in that work as part of a general move away from the traditional way of talking about natural and divine laws to one where the civil law is paramount.

So far, Selden was by no means a natural rights theorist, precisely because he lacked any way of talking about the moral or jural relations of men outside the civil laws of their society. The fascinating and important feature of his work, however, is that he was able to do what the sixteenth-century juristic humanists had found impossible: he was able to transform their theory into one of natural rights while maintaining the open-ended and almost anarchic character of the pre-civil state. His thinking about natural rights began under the influence of Grotius: in 1618 he was asked by the king to prepare a defence of the English claims to sovereignty over the North Sea and the North Atlantic as a reply to Grotius's *Mare Liberum* (published nine years earlier). This first draft was never published, but in 1635 the fishing dispute between England and Holland by which it had been occasioned broke out again (and led, incidentally, to Ship Money; the fleet for which the tax was intended was designed to protect English fishing). Selden was once more approached, this time by Charles and Laud, and he revised his earlier work for publication in the following year. It is difficult to sort out what is left in the final work from the 1618 draft: substantial portions certainly date from 1635, as they include references to the *De Iure Belli et Pacis*.[12] In general, we must treat the *Mare Clausum* as a reply to Grotius's later work as much as to his earlier, and we can see in it how far Selden had absorbed ideas from his great contemporary.

In many ways, as the Enlightenment historians of natural law theories (and Grotius himself) realised, the difference between Selden and Grotius over the juridical status of the oceans was more apparent than real. Selden began by accepting Grotius's ideas about the original community of *dominium* and its later division; as a necessary condition of this position, he accepted a non-humanist account of *dominium* itself, which allowed a wide variety of different property rights to be classed as cases of *dominium*.

Dominion, which is a Right of Using, Enjoying, Alienating, and free Disposing, is either Common to all men as Possessors without Distinction, or *Private* and

[11] Selden, *Opera*, III, col. 2037.
[12] (e.g.) Selden, *Opera*, II, cols. 1198, 1227 etc.

peculiar onely to som; that is to say, distributed and set apart by any particular
States, Princes, or persons whatsoever, in such a manner that others are excluded,
or at least in som sort barred from a Libertie of Use and Enjoiment.[13]

Where he differed from Grotius, in this part of his argument, was simply
over the question of whether the oceans had been apportioned as private
property along with the land. As his claim that this was so involved in part
a dense set of historical references, he was led to be more specific about
when the division of common property had taken place than Grotius had
ever been. Thus he asserted that initially the earth had been given in
common to Adam and his descendants, and that they had divided it
between them. After the Flood, the world was once again (literally) a *tabula
rasa*, and was given in common to Noah and his children to divide between
themselves. Here Selden relied mainly on non-Biblical Hebrew traditions,
based ultimately on the Talmud, a reliance which was to prove increasingly central in his natural law thinking.

However, although the basic structure of his argument was very similar
to Grotius's, with this proviso about the seas being included along with the
land in the division, he emphasised far more than Grotius had done in *Mare
Liberum* both the contractual nature of the partition and the independent
status of contract within a natural law framework. In that work, after all,
Grotius had suggested a definite continuum between private property and
an original individualised 'quasi dominium'. It was this aspect of Selden's
theory which was to be developed into his mature position in the *De Iure
Naturali et Gentium iuxta disciplinam Ebraeorum*. In the *Mare Clausum*, he
first rehearsed the difference between a permissive and an obligatory *ius* –
the Thomist or Suarezian distinction, already implicit in his *History of
Tythes* and notes on Fortescue: *ius*

(as it is the rule, measure, and pointing out of things lawful or unlawful) falls under
a twofold consideration ... As *Obligatorie*, it is known by such things as are
commended or forbidden, as *to give every man his due, not to forswear*, and the like. As
Permissive, it is set forth by things whose use is neither commanded nor forbidden,
but permitted; as in the very Act of buying, selling, infranchisement, framing
conditions of contract according to the will of the contractors, and many more of
the same nature.[14]

---

[13] 'Dominium, quod est jus utendi fruendi, alienandi, libere disponendi, aut omnium
hominum, pro indiviso possidentium, commune est, aut aliquorum tantum privatum, id
est, inter universitates singulares, principes, personas qualescunque, privatim ita tributum,
ut libertas utendi fruendi aliis aut intercludatur aut saltem minuatur.' Selden, *Opera*, II, col.
1195; The translation is *Of the Dominion, or, Ownership of the Sea*, trans. M. Nedham
(London, 1652), p. 16.
[14] '*Jus* autem (quod est liciti atque illiciti norma, mensura, ac index) consideratur bifariam: ...
Qua obligativum est, in quae vel jubentur vel vetantur, ut, suum cuique tribuere, non
perjerare, caeteris similibus, cernitur; qua permissivum, in eis quorum nec jubetur usus nec
vetatur, sed permittitur tamen; quemadmodum in ipso emtionis, venditionis, manumis-
sionis actu, in contrahentium conditionibus pro eorum arbitratu contractui adjici solitis, id
genus aliis.' Selden, *Opera*, II, col. 1192; trans., p. 12.

Property relationships belonged to the second category of *ius*; the original community had existed until

> there intervened, as it were, a consent of the whole bodie or universalitie of mankinde (by the mediation of something like a compact, which might binde their posteritie) for quitting of the common interest or antient right in those things that were made over thus by distribution to particular Proprietors; in the same manner as when Partners or Co-heirs do share between themselves any portion of those things which they hold in common . . .[15]

This was a sufficient explanation of the settled descents of title, but Selden also had to explain the convention that now the vacant spaces of the earth can be possessed by the first occupier. To provide an explanation, he once again postulated a contract, rather than taking it (as Grotius had done) to be the relic of a primitive pre-contractual right. According to Selden, it was agreed

> that any persons whatsoever might become particular masters of those places which should remain vacant or undisposed, who should first corporally seiz them . . . Therefore (I suppose) it must be yielded, that som such Compact or Covenant was passed in the very first beginnings of private Dominion or possession, and that it was in full force and virtue transmitted to posteritie by the Fathers, who had the power of distributing possessions after the flood . . .[16]

Selden summed up his theory of property, and related it to the diversity of actual property rules (such as, we may assume, those of feudalism) as follows:

> From this Original sprang every Dominion or Proprietie of things, which either by Alienation, or any other kinds of Cession, is transferr'd upon others, or held by a continued possession; respect beeing alwaies had to those particular Forms and Qualifications, which usually relate unto Dominion, either by Law, Custom, or compact, according to the various institutions of several people: For by these, the free and absolute power of the Proprietor, in what hee enjoies, is lesned and restrained; but when this Reason wholy ceaseth, then what the Proprietor possesseth is so his own, that it cannot lawfully in any wise, without his consent, becom another man's. And all these things are derived from the alteration of that *Universal* or *Natural Law of nations* which is *Permissive*: For thence came in private Dominion or Possession, to wit from the *Positive Law*. But in the mean while it is established by the *Universal Obligatorie Law*, which provides for the due observation of Compacts and Covenants.[17]

---

[15] 'In territoriis ita distribuendis, consensus veluti humani generis corporis seu universitatis (interposita fide, quae etiam posteros obligaret) intervenit, ut a communione seu pristino jure eorum, quae ita distributim singulis dominis cederunt, plane discederetur: non aliter ac ubi socii seu cohaeredes partes aliquas rerum pro indiviso possessarum inter se dividunt.' Selden, *Opera*, II, col. 1197; trans., p. 21.

[16] 'ut deinceps eorum, quae vacua manerent, seu in distributionem non venirent, domini fierent singulares quicunque . . . corporaliter occuparent . . . Itaque pactum ejusmodi primariis dominii privati initiis intercessisse, ejusque vim a primis, quorum post diluvium intererat res distributim possidere, ad posteros transmissam esse, puto, est statuendum.' Selden, *Opera*, II, col. 1198; trans., pp. 22–3.

[17] 'Atque ab hac origine manavit omnis rerum proprietas seu dominium, quod sive alienatione, seu quacunque alia cessione, in alios transfertur, sive possessione continua

In all this, Selden was ingeniously using the later Grotius to attack the earlier. As we have seen, Grotius avoided committing himself to such a definite use of the notion of a covenant in his *Mare Liberum*. His object in depicting the growth of private property gradually, through the increasing allocation of goods to individuals that only they could use, was precisely to deny that the sea could ever be so allocated: 'All those things which have been so constituted by nature that, even when used by a specific individual, they nevertheless suffice for general use by other persons without discrimination, retain to-day and should retain for all time that status which characterized them when first they sprang from nature.'[18] But in *De Iure Belli*, as Selden pointed out, Grotius *did* talk about private property as founded on contract. As we have seen, Grotius's theory in the later work did not differ radically from his earlier position – it was a very weak notion of contract with which he operated. For Selden, on the other hand, it was a very strong notion of contract: the agreement need not have been made, and if it had not then the original state of affairs would have continued; moreover it could have been made about anything, including the oceans. Natural suitability or necessity was irrelevant.

Grotius himself did not reply to Selden, but his pupil and friend Dirck Graswinckel (who had seen the *De Iure Belli et Pacis* through the press) 'took the burden on himself', in Grotius's words.[19] His response was very quick, and by the end of 1635 Selden had received an extensive manuscript critique of the *Mare Clausum* from him. It was never published in its original form, though minor parts of it appeared in a later work of Graswinckel's, the *Maris Liberi Vindiciae* of 1652. The manuscript is very revealing, as it shows the difficulties a Grotian had in rebutting Selden while at the same time preserving Grotius's original position on property. Graswinckel in fact abandoned Grotius: in order to rule out the possibility of *dominium* over the sea, he provided a far more stringent definition of *dominium* than Grotius himself had ever done – 'a harmless *facultas* to use and dispose of a corporeal object belonging to oneself in whatever way one

---

[18] 'eas res omnes, quae ita a natura comparatae sunt, ut aliquo utente nihilominus aliis quibusvis ad usum promiscue sufficiant, eius hodieque conditionis esse, et perpetuo esse debere cuius fuerant cum primum a natura proditae sunt.' Grotius, *De Iure Praedae*, ed. H. G. Hanaker (The Hague, 1868), p. 218; trans. G. C. Williams (Oxford, 1950), pp. 230–1.

[19] This is from a letter of Grotius, May 12 1636, in his *Briefwisseling*, VII, ed. B. L. Meulenbroek (The Hague, 1969), pp. 143–5.

---

retinetur; habita semper ratione specialium modorum ac temperamentorum, quae, sive ex legibus moribusque, sive ex pacto, dominio solent, pro variis populorum institutis, accedere. Nam hisce restringitur & minuitur libera, in re, domini potestas. Quae ubi prorsus definit, ita suum est, quod privatim possidet dominus, ut alius esse, ejus injussu, omnino jure esse nequeat. Atque haec omnia ex mutatione juris gentium universalis seu naturalis, quod permissivum est, orta sunt. Inde enim introductum dominium privatum, ex jure nempe positivo. Sed interea stabilitum est ex jure universali obligativo, quo pactis standum est & servanda fides.' Selden, *Opera*, II, cols. 1198–9; trans., pp. 24–5.

chooses'.[20] With such a definition, he quickly ruled out the sea as a suitable object of *dominium*, but he also ruled out many of the types of *dominium* which Grotius had been trying to include in his theory. Selden never seriously replied to Graswinckel, though he did respond to various arguments *ad hominen* put forward in the later work.[21]

Although Selden had been obliged to develop the theory of the *Mare Clausum* for polemical purposes, it was a reasonable development from his earlier ideas. The objective natural law with which he was concerned had been very largely reduced to the simple precept, 'Keep your covenants' – which allowed the widest possible variety of civil laws to be compatible with the law of nature. The freedom men were under apart from that law was now described in terms of their natural rights, and to that extent he had become a Grotian. But unlike Grotius he remained puzzled by the relationship between the law of nature and the rights of nature; and the source of his puzzlement seems to have been precisely the issue which we isolated as unconvincing in the *De Iure Belli*. Why should rational individuals possessed of a full complement of natural rights be under laws at all? What sort of mechanism was it by which men moved from their extensive state of natural freedom to their present state of obedience to law? For Selden, coming to this problem from a humanistic position, the problem presented itself as an historical one, with its solution to be found in an event in real time; and it was his attempt to work out this solution which led him to compose his most original and influential work, the *De Iure Naturali et Gentium iuxta disciplinam Ebraeorum*, published in 1640. In particular, the *De Iure Naturali* constitutes the first example of the English interest in the nature of moral obligation, and of the scepticism found in many later seventeenth-century English philosophers over whether there can be an account of obligation distinct from one of motivation.

The basic structure of the theory was given by Selden's analysis of the central concepts of liberty, obligation and punishment in Chapter Four. He first postulated a state of absolute liberty, on which obligations were supervenient – a move of the greatest importance, as he was the first modern natural law thinker to put such a notion of *complete* freedom at the beginning of his account. What he said was that

The idea of liberty is either absolute and simple, or restricted and complex. It is absolute in the first part of the definition of liberty, [in the *Digest*, which I have already quoted several times] 'the natural *facultas* of doing what one wants' . . . With such a conception, liberty can be thought of equally well among both animals and men, if there is no relevant law which in any way restrains either a man's will or an animal's appetite (which can be taken to be the same kind of thing as a will). But I want to stress that it can be *thought of* in this way: we hypothesise such a state of

[20] 'facultas nulli obnoxia de quacunque re corporali sibi propria in quicumlibet usum libere ac perfecte disponendi.' Bodleian MS Selden Supra 128, f. 1. The manuscript is discussed in D. M. Barratt, 'The Library of John Selden and its later history', *Bodleian Library Record*, III (1950–1), p. 210.

[21] See his *Vindiciae . . . Maris Clausi*, published in 1653 (Selden, *Opera*, II, cols. 1415–38).

boundless liberty for the purpose of our argument, just as a line is often extended infinitely to demonstrate something in geometry. The idea of restricted liberty comes about when there is added to the absolute liberty which we have postulated the modification which follows in the *Digest* definition, 'as long as it is not prevented by force or law', although in this context force, in so far as it means *injury*, is irrelevant ...[22]

Once law is introduced into this state of absolute liberty, he said later in the work,

the actions of those who for the sake of argument we supposed were originally free in every way, released from every kind of command or prohibition and in a condition of absolute liberty, are now restricted, and they can now be regarded as culpable or dishonest according to the criteria laid down by whoever decreed the law.[23]

Such a state of total freedom was logically prior to everything else because the obligations which he held to supervene upon such a state had to be seen in terms of *punishment*. 'The idea of a law carrying obligation irrespective of any punishment annexed to the violation of it ... is no more comprehensible to the human mind than the idea of a father without a child'[24] – i.e. it is a logical and not contingent connexion. This might be clear enough in the case of human laws, but the natural law was more of a problem. Selden began by accepting the reality of natural obligations: examples would be the obligations to pay incurred by a ward who had run up debts without his guardian's authority, or by a child to his brother while they were both under the control of their father. In neither case was there any legal obligation to repay the debt (any more than there is in the modern cases of bookmakers' or barristers' clients), and no legal punishment could be incurred. But there was undoubtedly some kind of obligation, which could be termed natural; but where did the punishment come from?

This in no way contradicts what I have said about a prospective punishment from some source being a necessary correlative of obligation. For jurisprudence is defined [in the *Institutes*] as 'the knowledge of divine as well as human matters, and

---

[22] 'Libertatis nempe his notio aut absoluta est ac simplex, aut restricta & temperata. Absoluta; velut in priore illa ... libertatis definitionis parte, qua dicitur *naturalis facultas ejus quod cuique facere lubet* ... Hac quidem notione libertas pariter in brutis atque hominibus concipi potest; nullo nimirum accedente jure quod sive horum voluntatem sive illorum appetitum ac propensionem, quod voluntatis plane instar satis agit, omnino cohibeat. Concipi, dico: Nam necessariam de interminata utrisque hujusmodi libertate atque dissertationi inservientem conceptionem tantum ejusmodi supponimus; ut fere geometrae demonstraturi quid, lineam saepius in infinitum excurrentem. Restrictae autem libertatis notio est, cum libertati quam ita supponimus adjicitur id quod in memorata definitione sequitur temperamentum, *nisi si quid vi aut jure prohibetur*. Ad hunc locum vis, quatenus injuria in ea contineatur, non spectat.' Selden, *Opera*, i, col. 105.

[23] 'actus quotquot eorum quos antea omnino liberos seu omnimodo & jussu & interdicto solutos, in libertate absoluta, notionis causa, supposuimus, nunc restricti sunt, in malum culpae seu turpe juxta constituentis, quisquis ille fuerit, mentem transeunt.' Selden, *Opera*, i, col. 109.

[24] 'Neque sane juris obligatio sine poenae alicujus violationi imminentis ratione ... mortalibus magis potest fingi quam in relatis paternitas sine filio.' Selden, *Opera*, i, col. 106.

the study of justice and injustice'. It once even flourished in colleges of priests, who gave judicial opinions, as Livy and Pomponius record. [The priests] taught of the *ius* and duties which must be followed towards God and man, naturally and civilly, and warned of the punishment which follows any violation of them, either from God, the father and governor of nature, or from men . . .[25]

Even pagans recognised the force of such divine punishments, which could be incurred either in this world or in the next – Selden quoted Virgil's description of Jupiter sending 'an alarm of war into cities which have sinned' (*Aeneid* XII.852).

For Selden, then, a necessary correlative of any obligation was a punishment, and the punishment in the case of the law of nature came from God. This led him, interestingly, to a very clear statement of a modified retributivist position against both Plato and Grotius. Plato had commented that no sensible person punishes someone because he has done wrong, but rather to prevent him doing wrong again; but if such a claim made any sense, it followed that one could have obligation without punishment. Punishment was simply an effective way of preventing people from breaking their obligations, which could be independently specified, instead of something the prospective incurring of which *constituted* being in a state of obligation. Grotius accepted this position, both in the *Inleidinghe* and in the *De Iure Belli*, and it is obvious that it does not contradict his view of the obligation to obey the law of nature. But Selden had to deny it, and insist that all punishment is retributive, because what was wrong about a particular course of action was precisely that it was the sort of thing which led to suffering being inflicted by God or man.[26] It is clear that by arguing in this way, Selden had solved the Grotian dilemma and had moved to a completely individualistic and hedonist view of moral obligation, the development of which in later English moral philosophy was to be of central importance.

His position was summarised pungently in *Table Talk*:

I cannot fancy to myself what the law of nature means, but the law of God. How should I know I ought not to steal, I ought not to commit adultery, unless some body had told me so? Surely 'tis because I have been told so. 'Tis not because I think I ought not to do them, nor because you think I ought not; if so, our minds might change: Whence then comes the restraint? From a higher power, nothing else can bind. I cannot bind myself, for I may untie one another. It must be a superior power, even God Almighty.[27]

---

[25] 'Sed haec, inquam, nihil adversantur eis quae de obligatione & qualicunque simul & perpetua ejus comite poena alicunde imminente diximus. Etenim jurisprudentia definiebatur *tam divinarum quam humanarum rerum notitia, justi atque injusti scientia.* Ea autem olim viguit maxime in pontificum collegio quod de jure respondebat, ut ex Livio, & Pomponio scimus ... de jure ac officiis tam erga Numen quam erga homines sive naturaliter sive civiliter observandis, ac de poena quae violationi immineret sive a Numine, ut naturae totius parente & rectore, sive ab hominibus infligenda monerent.' Selden, *Opera*, I, col. 107.

[26] *ibid.*, cols. 109–10.

[27] Selden, *Opera*, III, col. 2041.

This position must of course be distinguished from the divine voluntarism of (for example) Grotius's *De Iure Praedae*. The voluntarists, including most Protestant thinkers in the sixteenth and early seventeenth centuries, believed that the 'formal cause' of a law's obligation is the command of a superior, that is, a law to be binding must be promulgated by someone in authority, and cannot be simply a rational principle. But it does not follow that the obligation is *constituted* by fear of a prospective punishment administered by such a superior, and most voluntarists were at pains to deny this.[28]

It followed that before God's punishments came to be known, either through observation of the world or through God's pronouncements to an already created mankind, men were under no obligation: the historicity of natural law *entailed* a state of total freedom, as the traditional theory of natural law in terms of an innate human reason did not. To show that the law of nature was only to be known in that fashion, Selden had to show that its equation with the law of 'right reason', the necessity to follow which was intuitively obvious (the view of Suarez, among others), was false. After refuting the classical idea that the *ius naturale* was the *ius* common to men and animals, he turned to refute the traditional theory. He did so in the first place simply by making relativistic empirical points: even the most sophisticated philosophers have differed about fundamental moral issues, and no precepts of the law of nature can actually be shown to be intuitively obvious.[29] But his second point was more subtle and more important: it was a development of the thought expressed in the passage of *Table Talk* quoted above.

He postulated (along with most sixteenth-century juridical humanists, as we have already seen) that 'there was once a time when men wandered through the countryside like animals, sustaining a bestial existence and managing their lives by brute force rather than reason'.[30] His use of this classical picture shows very neatly the way in which he transformed the humanist theory into one of natural rights. In these conditions, men were all free and equal in rationality; but they had somehow come to be grouped into societies with laws and subordination of one man to another. This could not have come about simply through the exercise of their reason and their intuitions about what they ought morally to do: 'For pure, unaided reason merely persuades or demonstrates; it does not order, nor bind anyone to their duty, unless it is accompanied by the authority of someone

---

[28] Locke is a good example of this: in his voluntarist period, he argued explicitly that 'not fear of punishment, but a rational apprehension of what is right, puts us under an obligation'. J. Locke, *Essays on the Law of Nature*, ed. W. von Leyden (Oxford, 1954), p. 185. For Grotius in *De Iure Praedae*, see above, p. 59.

[29] Selden, *Opera*, I, cols. 137 ff.

[30] 'tempus quoddam fuisse cum in agris homines passim bestiarum more vagabantur, & sibi victu ferino vitam propagabant, nec ratione animi quidquam sed pleraque viribus corporis administrabant.' Selden, *Opera*, I, col. 139.

who is superior to the man in question ... And where is such a disparity necessary for obligation to be found when everyone, as we have said, has the same rights as everyone else, and there was no civil society?'[31] In other words, even if there is, empirically, consistency in people's opinions, there is no way of bridging the gap between our opinion about what we ought to do and being *obliged* to do it without the introduction of a superior with powers of punishment. Once again, he put it neatly in conversation.

When the school-men talk of *recta ratio* in morals, either they understand reason, as it is governed by a command from above; or else they say no more than a woman, when she says a thing is so, because it is so; that is, her reason perswades her it is so. The other reason has sense in it. As take a law of the land. I must not depopulate, my reason tells me so. Why? because if I do, I incur the detriment.[32]

This extreme scepticism about the possibility of moral obligation independent of an egotistical motivation, in which the moral 'ought' simply becomes the prudential 'ought', makes Selden the clear forerunner of Hobbes. We shall see in Chapter Six how Hobbes altered this position by the simple expedient of dropping information about an after-life out of the prudent egotist's calculations about the ways in which he will 'incur the detriment'. But information about what will happen to us in this life is important in Selden's theory also: in some ways, his account of God's punishment looks rather like a Puritan account of providence (and Cud- worth famously made a similar point about Hobbes). The difference was essentially that the Puritan regarded providential punishments as contingently linked to the sinner's breach of his obligation, while both Selden and Hobbes took an expectation of their occurrence to constitute a rational man's obligation.[33] Selden was in fact rather cool about explicit talk of providence: 'we cannot tell what is a judgement of God; 'tis presumption to take upon us to know ... Commonly we say a judgement falls upon a man for something in him we cannot abide.'[34] Such judgements were unpredictable, and therefore no expectation of their occurrence could be formed; what mattered to both Selden and Hobbes was God's general, rule-governed providence, not his special or arbitrary judgements on sinners.

In Selden's arguments about the nature of obligation, we are at another of the roots of his Erastianism. The moral authority claimed by churches was merely a special case of the general claim that men can be bound by

---

[31] 'Quin ratio, quatenus talis solum est & simplex, suadet & demonstrat, non jubet, aut ad officium, nisi superioris eo qui jubetur accedat simul autoritas, obligat ... Nam undenam obligationis causae reperitur disparitas, ubi universi, ut diximus, habentur pariter sui juris & aequales, nec in civile aliquod corpus sociati?' Selden, *Opera*, I, cols. 139–40.

[32] Selden, *Opera*, III. cols. 2065–6.

[33] This is, I take it, the point of Cudworth's distinction between Hobbes's 'Divine Fatalism Natural' and the Calvinist 'Divine Fatalism Arbitrary'. For a discussion of the manuscript in which this point is made, see S. I. Mintz: *The Hunting of Leviathan* (Cambridge, 1962), pp. 126 ff.

[34] Selden, *Opera*, III, col. 2036.

institutions independently of the latters' capacity to administer physical punishments. By refuting this general proposition, Selden automatically ruled out the moral authority of churches. This was a theme which he was to develop in the years following the publication of the *De Iure Naturali*, both in his work in the Westminster Assembly and in his last major publication, the *De Synedriis Veterum Ebraeorum* (1650 and 1653). Clearly, this argument dominated Selden's last years, and a sign of the importance he attached to it is his description of Erastus as another Copernicus[35] (itself an interesting indication of the way in which he thought his own work fitted into the seventeenth-century scientific and mathematical revolution, at which the frequent use of geometrical examples in the *De Iure Naturali* also hints).

The position which Selden had adopted, however, had one major problem: it was difficult to give a substantive content to the law of nature, and to show that God had historically commanded the performance of its precepts on pain of terrestrial or celestial punishments. It was this which led to the otherwise highly idiosyncratic overall plan of the work – the attempt to flesh out the law of nature from the record of God's dealings with men immediately after the Flood, both in the Bible and in Talmudic traditions. The Decalogue, which might have been thought to represent God's commands to all men, Selden regarded as peculiar to the Hebrews: 'we read the commandments in the church-service, as we do *Davids* psalms, not that all there concerns us, but a great deal of them does'. The crucial stumbling-block was the status of the Sabbath: Selden always argued that the observance of the Sabbath was peculiarly Jewish, and that it was 'superstition' for non-Jews to observe it also.[36]

According to Talmudic tradition, there were seven matters dealt with in God's instructions to Noah and his children: idolatry, blasphemy, homicide, incest, theft, the eating of live animals and disobedience to the judgements of a civil power. Selden in fact modified this picture extensively, by insisting as he had done in the *Mare Clausum* on the primacy of contract in the cases of theft and civil disobedience: given the original community of property and freedom from commands enjoyed by men, what was wrong with theft or disobedience was the breaking of an implicit promise to accept the dispositions of society.[37] He also, like Grotius,

[35] Selden, *Opera*, I, col. 1076.
[36] Selden, *Opera*, I, cols. 313–430; III, cols. 2069, 2070. In Bodleian MS Selden Supra 108 there is a letter of November 1643 from Cudworth to Selden discussing this point, and agreeing that the Sabbath is 'never a jot the more Morall (as the Word of late in use, hath been) because it hath a Place in the Jewish Decalogue ...' (f. 268). Hobbes too was interested in this issue as early as 1635, and agreed with Selden's position. *English Works*, VII, p. 454.
[37] Compare his remarks in *Table Talk*: '*All power is of God*, means no more than, *fides est servanda*. When St. *Paul* said this, the people had made *Nero* emperor. They agree, he to command, they to obey. Then God comes in, and casts a hook upon them, *keep your faith,*

related the ban on homicide to the *ius zelotarum*: God had given men the right to execute murderers, and the *ius zelotarum* was a relic of this originally universal right.[38] In most other societies, the right had been wholly transferred to the sovereign. Any matters outside these seven were not dealt with by the preceptive law of nature, but came under the permissive *ius naturale*. So Selden argued that as long as incest was avoided, a wide variety of types of marriage was possible (polygamy, polyandry, etc.), as was divorce: the marriage contract could be a civil contract of the kind which can be broken unilaterally.

Indeed, an enormous variety of contracts was possible; the only definite rule was that whatever a contract specified had to be performed, on pain of divine punishment. It was in this way that Selden was able to arrive at a strong form of the Grotian position on the origin and nature of political authority. A contract of total servitude was possible, and could not be broken.

1. If our fathers had lost their liberty, why may not we labour to regain it?

Answer. We must look to the contract, if that be rightly made, we must stand to it. If we once grant we may recede from contracts, upon any inconveniency that may afterwards happen, we shall have no bargain kept. If I sell you a horse, and you do not like my bargain, I will have my horse again.

2. Keep your contracts. So far a divine goes, but how to make our contracts is left to ourselves; and as we agree upon the conveying of this horse, or that land, so it must be. If you offer me a hundred pounds for my glove, I tell you what my glove is, a plain glove, pretend no virtue in it, the glove is my own, I profess not to sell gloves, and we agree for a hundred pounds; I do not know what I may not with a safe conscience take it. The want of that common obvious distinction between *jus praeceptivum*, and *jus permissivum*, does much trouble men ... Every law is a contract between the king and the people, and therefore to be kept. An hundred men may owe me an hundred pounds, as well as any one man, and shall they not pay me because they are stronger than I?

Object. Oh but they lose all if they keep that law.

Answ. Let them look to the making of their bargain. If I sell my lands, and when I have done, one comes and tells me I have nothing else to keep me. I and my wife and children must starve, if I part with my land. Must I not therefore let them have my land that have bought it, and paid for it?[39]

Selden was able to say that men might promise anything, and be forced to keep their word even at the cost of great suffering, or even death, because of his general theory of obligation. The rational egotist will include in his calculations about prospective pleasure and pain information about how he will be treated by God after his death, as a consequence of breaking his promise or the rest of the natural law, and God's pronouncements to the Noachidae conveyed that information to mankind. Selden

[38] Selden, *Opera*, I, cols. 456–9. See Grotius, *De Iure Belli*, II, 20.9.
[39] Selden, *Opera*, III, cols. 2024, 2041.

then comes in, *all power is of God*. Never king dropped out of the clouds. God did not make a new emperor, as the king makes a justice of peace.' Selden, *Opera*, III, col. 2057.

assumed that somehow human societies had passed that information on to posterity; God had given it to man at a point in historical time, and it was the historical continuity of human societies that kept it alive. The attack on the theory that the natural law consisted of innate rational principles threw into prominence its historical dimension, and made Selden's life-work a consistent whole.

But Selden's theory of obligation had taken him much further along the road to absolutism than ever Grotius had gone. It allowed no right of resistance *in extremis*: a bad bargain or a foolish contract had to be kept to even at the cost of death. The difference between the two is clearest in their discussion of the question whether men may plead an original common right in extreme necessity to justify taking another's property. We have seen that Grotius allowed this, but Selden denied it. He pointed out (among other arguments) that Grotius's argument implied that if someone in necessity was offered charity and refused it, he would still have the right if he changed his mind of taking the charity by force. The implausibility of this suggested that no common right was revived; rather, there might be some kind of duty of charity laid on others (though he was pretty equivocal about this too).[40]

It would however be wrong to conclude from Selden's acceptance of the idea of a contract of total servitude that he thought that the contract underlying the English constitution was of such a kind. His position in English politics during the 1620s and 1630s is too well known to need rehearsing here: he consistently spoke in Parliament and law courts in favour of 'the liberty of the subject', and particularly of course the liberty of the subject's person. His famous motto 'περὶ παντὸς τὴν ἐλευθερίαν' presumably refers to this continuous concern, though there may also be a pun on his idea of a state of original liberty. But it is true that his notion of the 'ancient law of freedome' (as he was to call it when writing against the Commission of Array in 1642)[41] was distinctly more restricted than that, say, of the Levellers, since he always explicated the liberties of a free man by comparing them with the servitudes of a villein in English law. The technique was summed up in one of his speeches on the *habeas corpus* in 1628: 'in all our questions stirred amongst us, we cannot better determine them, than by comparing ourselves to *villeins*. A *villein regardant* must not be out of his Lord's manner, 22. Hen. VI. 31. but *liber homo est, qui potest ire quo vult*, saith the book of Domesday.'[42] As early as 1610, moreover, he had argued that villeinage and slavery had been fundamental features of English society: clearly, his picture of his society was that it was one in which only certain people had been free, but their freedom could be precisely specified. His acceptance of villeinage ties in with his general

---

[40] See Selden, *Opera*, I, col. 638.
[41] Bodleian MS Selden Supra 123, ff. 70v–71.
[42] Selden, *Opera*, I, p. xiii n. See also Selden, *Opera*, III, col. 1955.

theoretical position – a wide variety of constitutions was possible, including one in which a high degree of liberty for some was matched by a high degree of servitude for others. (It is interesting to compare his views on serfdom with his eloquent advocacy of political rights for women as early as 1610 – a fine example of his blending of (to our eyes) liberal and illiberal sentiments.)[43]

When the conflict between King and Parliament began in the 1640s, Selden's attitude appears to have been little different, in a number of ways, from that of his friend and protégé Hyde, though he believed that it would be foolish for anyone of his known opinions to join the King. (He remarked later that 'the king calling his friends from the parliament, because he had use of them at *Oxford*, is as if a man should have use of a little piece of wood, and he runs down into the cellar, and takes the spiggot, in the mean time all the beer runs about the house: When his friends are absent, the king will be lost.')[44] When the Commons debated episcopacy, he spoke in its defence, and it is notable that he and Hyde both believed (unusually, for the early 1640s) that the bishops were the third estate of the realm, and could not be abolished or excluded from Parliament without fundamental damage to the constitution.[45]

Hyde also said, famously, that in his opinion the constitution was 'so equally poised, that if the least branch of the prerogative was torn off, or parted with, the subject suffered by it, and that his right was impaired: and he was as much troubled when the crown exceeded its just limits, and thought its prerogative hurt by it'.[46] He was here employing one of the most deeply entrenched assumptions of seventeenth-century Englishmen, that their constitution represented a balance between sovereignty or prerogative and the liberty of the subject;[47] Selden shared this assumption, though he expounded it explicitly in terms of a contract, and so related it to his general political theory.

Question. Whether may subjects take up arms against their prince?

Answer. Conceive it thus; there lies a shilling betwixt you and me; ten pence of the shilling is yours, two pence is mine: By agreement, I am as much king of my two pence, as you of your ten pence: If you therefore go about to take away my two pence, I will defend it; for there you and I are equal, both princes.
Or thus; Two supream powers meet; one says to the other, give me your land; if you will not, I will take it from you: The other, because he thinks himself too weak to resist him, tells him, of nine parts I will give you three, so I may quietly enjoy the

---

[43] His refutation of Thomas Sprott's claim that 'the English, before the *Norman* Conquest, knew nothing of private servitude or bondage' is in *Jani Anglorum Facies Altera* (*Opera*, II, col. 1015; trans., p. 75). His defence of the equal status of women is *ibid.* (*Opera*, II, cols. 980–2; trans., p. 18–21).

[44] Selden, *Opera*, III, col. 2039.

[45] See B. H. G. Wormald, *Clarendon* (Cambridge, 1951), p. 12; Selden, *Opera*, III, col. 2038.

[46] Clarendon, *History*, pp. 940–1. See Wormald, *Clarendon*, p. 12, for a (rather strange) scepticism about Hyde's sincerity in using this as an explanation of his conduct in 1640–2.

[47] See above all M. A. Judson, *The Crisis of the Constitution* (New Brunswick, 1949), pp. 60–5.

rest, and I will become your tributary. Afterwards the prince comes to exact six parts, and leaves but three; the contract then is broken, and they are in a parity again.

To know what obedience is due to the prince, you must look into the contract between him and his people; as if you would know what rent is due from the tenant to the landlord, you must look into the lease ...[48]

Selden thus believed that it was possible to attribute precise rights to both the King and the people, and that either side could break the presumed contract by which those rights had been allocated. He acted on this belief in his opposition to both the Militia Ordinance (which he stigmatised as 'without any shadow of law or pretence of precedent')[49] and the Commissions of Array issued by the King (which he described as against 'the ancient law of freedome [from] compulsion to find arms or to be led out of the county' other than according to the precise forms of the various statutes).[50] Although he seems to have been increasingly happy to remain on the Westminster Parliament's side, believing presumably that the King had broken the contract by such moves, he never took either the Covenant or the Engagement. Despite this, he was always treated with great deference by the new regime after 1649, and in this he resembled some of his friends such as Bulstrode Whitelock or Matthew Hale, though he differed of course from others such as Hyde or Falkland.

His opposition to the ideology of the radicals in the Westminster Parliament is illustrated interestingly by his criticisms of the work of Henry Parker (as they almost certainly are) preserved in *Table Talk*. Central to Parker's *Observations*, published in 1642 and one of the most important apologias for Parliament in the early course of the war, were the two principles that *salus populi suprema lex esto*, and *quicquid efficit tale, est magis tale*. In most attacks on Parker, even from committed royalists, the way in which he understood these two maxims was not questioned; what was criticised was his application of them to the particular English circumstances. Selden however went deeper into the matter, and drew characteristic conclusions:

There is not any thing in the world more abused than this sentence, *Salus populi suprema lex esto*, for we apply it, as if we ought to forsake the known law, when it may be most for the advantage of the people, when it means no such thing. For first, 'tis not *salus populi suprema lex est*, but *esto*, it being one of the laws of the twelve tables, and after divers laws made, some for punishment, some for reward, then follows this, *salus populi suprema lex esto*; that is, in all the laws you make, have a special eye to the good of the people; And then what does this concern the way they now go?

---

[48] Selden, *Opera*, III, col. 2076.

[49] Clarendon, *History*, p. 267; see Bodleian MS Selden Supra 124 for a draft of the letter to Falkland which Hyde quotes from here.

[50] Bodleian MS Selden Supra 123, ff. 70v–71. See also MS Selden Supra 124, and Clarendon, *History*, p. 267.

Objection. He that makes one, is greater than he that is made; the people make the king, *ergo*, &c.

Answ. This does not hold. For if I have 1000*l*. *per annum*, and give it to you, and leave my self never a penny, I made you; but when you have my land, you are greater than I. The parish makes the constable, and when the constable is made, he governs the parish. The answer to all these doubts is, Have you agreed so? If you have, then it must remain until you have altered it.[51]

Though Selden was always unwilling to spell out exactly what would count as evidence for such an agreement, it seems that he could only interpret a settled constitution as the result of a presumed agreement; the law which Englishmen had accepted until recently represented the terms of the agreement, and Parker's avowed object of going beyond it was anathema.

We can now see clearly what kind of ideology Selden represented in England: it was in many ways close to Grotius's, but there were nevertheless important differences. They were both capable of sustaining the practices of mercantile capitalism such as slavery and usury (Selden was quite definite about the legitimacy of money-lending)[52] and prepared to accept a high degree of absolutism in theory while denying that the constitutions of their own countries were absolutist. But Selden pushed this theory much further than Grotius had done, and turned it into a completely brutal and illiberal doctrine. He did so, quite simply, because he was prepared to hypothesise an original state of total freedom, on which the laws of nature supervened, and because he made contracts play a much more important role at each stage of his theory. Both features are connected with his doctrine of obligation: for if the prospect of God's punishments provided an obligation or motivation for egotistical men to follow the law of nature, it followed both that the laws of nature could be independently specified and not simply reduced to the general principle of observing other people's rights, and also that before men received information about those punishments they were under no obligation. In formal character, this theory (as I have suggested) is close to Hobbes's. But the fact that Selden allowed God a more central role in his theory than Hobbes was to, meant that men could find themselves completely divested of any rights. In some ways, paradoxically enough, the timorous Hobbes was a more liberal theorist than the brave fighter for Parliamentary liberties.

[51] Selden, *Opera*, III, col. 2053.
[52] Selden, *Opera*, III, col. 2075.

5

Selden's Followers

If we are to understand the importance of the ideas which Selden put forward, we have to recognise the strength of their influence in England during the 1640s to the 1670s. Just as Grotius's theory did in Holland, Selden's provided a whole generation of politically active and intelligent Englishmen with a new ideology, which they were able to apply to the most important issue of the day, the war between the King and Parliament. The most interesting of these followers, and the most original in his adaptation of the ideology, was Thomas Hobbes; but before considering his work we ought to consider that of the more typical and faithful 'Seldenians', for it is they who represent the milieu out of which Hobbes's work grew.

The key group of these followers were the members of the so-called Tew Circle, the intellectuals (mainly from Oxford) who met at Falkland's house at Great Tew in the 1630s. We know in fact that Selden himself sometimes came there though he does not seem to have been one of the regular group immortalised in Clarendon's *Life*.[1] The Tew Circle writers modified the theory in various ways, of course, but in its basic outlines it remains recognisably the same sort of doctrine as that which Selden expounded, rather than those of Grotius or Hobbes (as has been suggested by, *inter alia*, Trevor-Roper and Sirluck).[2]

The Tew Circle ideas were put forward in various works, one of which (to complicate matters) was of joint authorship. The earliest was a pamphlet entitled *An answer to a printed book*, the 'printed book' being Parker's *Observations*, written by (according to Thomason's note on his copy) Falkland, William Chillingworth, Dudley Digges 'and the rest of the University' (i.e. Oxford), and published in November 1642. The following year Henry Hammond published *Of resisting the lawfull magistrate upon*

---

[1] The evidence for Selden's association with Tew is in Suckling's poem 'The Wits' (1637): 'There was *Selden*, and he sate hard by the chair; / *Wenman* not far off, which was very fair; / *Sands* with *Townsend*, for they kept no order; / *Digby* and *Chillingworth* a little further ...' J. Suckling, *Works*, I, ed. T. Clayton (Oxford, 1971), pp. 71–2. See *ibid.*, p. 268 for a note relating the poem to Tew. Hyde's account of the group, omitting Selden (whom he implies to have been a friend of his in a different London-based *milieu*), is in Clarendon, *The History of the Rebellion ... Also his Life* (Oxford, 1843), pp. 926–31.

[2] H. Trevor-Roper, 'Clarendon', *Times Literary Supplement* (January 10 1975), p. 31; J. Milton, *Prose Works*, II, ed. E. Sirluck (New Haven, 1959), p. 35.

colour of religion,[3] while in June 1644 there appeared a posthumous work exclusively by Dudley Digges, *The unlawfulnesse of subjects taking up armes* (Digges having died in October 1643). Finally in January 1649 Hammond composed a *Humble address to the right honourable the Lord Fairfax and his Council of War* appealing for the King's life to be spared. The work, in addition to being disregarded by its recipients, was attacked by John Goodwin the Independent divine, and a pseudonymous writer 'Eutactius Philodemius', and Hammond wrote a *Vindication* of it which appeared in July. In all these works we find different combinations of identical arguments, so that it is difficult and might be misleading to extract a general theory from them; but we can show what kind of ideological nexus they belong to.

Quite a lot of space in the earlier works was devoted to making incidental points against their opponents, and especially against Henry Parker. These points in themselves often show the kinship between their authors and Selden; thus *An answer* remarked of Parker that

he offers us a proofe; *for if the people bee the true efficient cause of power, it is a rule in nature, Quicquid efficit tale, est magis tale.* Strange that men upon such palpable Sophistry should endeavour to cast off Monarchy! Hee will be unwilling to follow the consequence of it. Hee hath an estate, which no question he would willingly improve, let him bestow it upon me, hee will make me rich, and himselfe richer. For, *Quicquid efficit tale, est magis tale* ...[4]

But the serious attack on Parker involved a refutation of his central claim that under the law of nature men have a duty to protect themselves from attack, and hence that military action against the King's forces was justified. This was to remain a staple feature of the Parliamentary case, and arguments against it were still relevant when Hammond composed his *Address* and *Vindication*.

In all the Tew Circle works, we find the same kind of argument against this claim. It turned initially on a distinction between a right of nature and a law of nature, which paved the way for a demonstration that any natural right could be renounced, including the natural right of self-defence. As Digges said,

If we looke backe to the law of Nature, we shall finde that the people would have had a clearer and most distinct notion of it, if common use of calling it *Law* had not helped to confound their understanding, when it ought to have been named the *Right* of nature; for *Right* and *Law* differ as much as Liberty and Bonds: *Jus*, or right

---

[3] The bibliography of this work is complicated. It was first published in 1643 in London as *Of resisting the lawfull magistrate upon colour of religion*, and in Oxford as *The scriptures plea for magistrates*. In the second edition at Oxford in 1644 a number of tracts, including the one on the zealots which I discuss below, were added to it, and they were included in its many subsequent reprints. For convenience, I quote from William Fulman's collected edition of Hammond's works, *Works*, I–IV (London, 1684).

[4] *An answer to a Printed Book, intituled, Observations upon Some of His Majesties late Answers and Expresses* (Oxford, 1642), sig. A4. See Selden's remark quoted above p. 100.

not laying any obligation, but signifying, we may equally choose to doe or not to
doe without fault, whereas *Lex* or law determines us either to a particular performance by way of command, or a particular abstinence by way of prohibition; and
therefore *jus naturae*, all the right of nature, which now we can innocently make use
of, is that freedome, not which any law gives us, but which no law takes away, and
lawes are the severall restraints and limitations of native liberty.[5]

His concept of 'native liberty' was of a state in which men were under no
constraint to recede from taking over anything:

If we looke upon the Priviledges of Nature, ... Freedome is the birth-right of
mankinde, and equally common to every one, as the Aire we breath in, or the Sun
which sheds his beames and lustre, as comfortably upon Beggars, as upon the
Kings of the Earth. This Freedome was an unlimited power to use our abilities,
according as will did prompt.[6]

The consequence was inevitably 'feares and jealousies, wherein every
single person look't upon the world as his enemy' or, as Hammond put it,
'a state of common hostility, ... a wilderness of Bears or Tygers, not a
society of men'.[7]

The way out of this situation was through a contract not to exercise this
right of self-defence: a contract obliges men to perform in a particular way,
and thus supervenes upon a natural right. Self-defence, again according to
Digges,

ceases to be lawfull, after we have made our selves sociable parts in one body,
because we voluntarily and upon agreement restrained our selves from making use
of this native right [;] and the renouncing this power by mutuall consent will
appeare very consonant to sound reason, whether we looke upon the benefits
issuing thereby, or the mischeifes avoyded. For it is a more probable meanes to the
attaining that very end, in relation to which they [e.g. Parker] plead for it, the
preservation of particular persons ... Reason induced men to enter into such a
Covenant, and to lay a mutuall obligation one upon another, not to resist authority
upon what ever grounds, whether of fancied, or reall injustice, but to submit their
actions and persons to the ordinary triall, though it might possibly happen, that
some particulars would be sentenced unjustly, because a farre more considerable
good could not be obtained, unlesse by agreement patiently to submit to this
possible evill, since the common peace and quiet, cannot be effectually provided
for, if it shall be indulged to any, to appeale from the lawes themselves, and to judge
their Judges ...[8]

What Digges was talking about here, it must be stressed, was the source
of the subject's obligation not to resist the magistrate, and not the source of
the magistrate's right to inflict penalties on the subject. This is an important distinction, as will become clear presently. Digges was arguing that
the source of the subject's obligation was a promise not to resist, even if the
magistrate were to take coercive action against the promissor, and that the

[5] *The Unlawfulnesse of Subjects, Taking up Armes against their Soveraigne* (n.p., 1644), sig. B3v.
[6] *ibid.*, sig. A1v.
[7] *ibid.*, sig. A2; Hammond, *Works*, 1, p. 311.
[8] Digges, *Unlawfulnesse*, sig. A3–A3v.

incentive for making such a promise was the improbability of the
individual covenanter actually suffering as a result. I think it is fair to take
seriously Digges's use of the terms 'probable' and 'possible', and their
similar use by the authors of *An answer*. Parker's claim that 'since all
naturall power is in those who obey, they which contract to obey to their
owne ruine, or having so contracted, they which esteeme such a contract
before their owne preservation, are felonious to themselves and rebellious
to nature', was answered by them as follows:

He cannot meane any people contracting to their owne certain ruine; there never
was Government guilty of this madnesse: therefore hee must understand a contract
to a possible ruine; as for example, an agreement patiently to submit themselves to
the ordinary tryall of Law, and to suffer, if it should so fall out, though under an
undeserved Sentence. In this case, he that doth not make resistance, and preferre his
preservation to his contract, is pronounced *Felo de se*; and a rebell to nature.
Unhappy thiefe who for felony is condemned to bee hanged, and will be guilty of
another felony in being hanged! . . . The Observer [i.e. Parker] takes no notice, that
it is in our power to part with this right of self-defence, yet doe nothing contrary to
nature, if reason tells us, wee shall thereby obtaine a more excellent good, the
benefit of Peace and Society . . . Because in probability, we shall be in lesse danger,
living amongst men who have agreed to be governed by certaine Lawes, then if
every one followed his owne inclination.[9]

The problem of decision-making in conditions of uncertainty was one
which exercised many of Falkland's friends in the Tew Circle, and they
were often drawn to a solution which depended upon the estimation of
probabilities (though without the sophisticated mathematics which was
shortly to be employed to do so by such men as Huygens). One of the best
examples is in fact provided by William Chillingworth, one of the authors
of *An answer*, in his earlier work *The Religion of Protestants*. Answering his
Jesuit opponent's objection, 'Shall I hazard my soul on probabilities, or
even wagers?' he remarked:

As if whatsoever is but probable, though in the highest degree of probability, were
as likely to be false or true! Or because it is but morally, not mathematically certain,
that there was such a woman as queen Elizabeth, such a man as Henry VIII, that is,
in the highest degree probable, therefore it were an even wager there were none
such! . . . you have confounded and made all one, probabilities and even wagers.
Whereas every ordinary gamester can inform you, that though it be a thousand to
one that such a thing will happen, yet it is not sure, but very probable.[10]

Chillingworth used such arguments to support his general contention that
although certainty was not to be looked for in religious matters, yet it
could be rational to believe religious propositions. It seems that his friends
believed that it could be similarly rational for men in a state of nature to

⁹ *An answer*, sig. C3–C3v.
¹⁰ W. Chillingworth, *The Religion of Protestants* (London, 1846), p. 277. See also R. R. Orr,
  Reason and Authority (Oxford, 1967), pp. 51–3.

contract away their right of self-defence, given the long odds against them suffering themselves.[11]

However, if the rationality of making such a promise not to resist is to be found in the probability of benefit as a result, the general obligation to keep promises when they result in harm is to be found elsewhere. We can deduce two different sources of this obligation from the writings of Digges and the others. The first, and most important one, is implied by the authors of *An answer to a printed book* in the following passage:

> though force bee not law, yet if after conquest a people resigne their right in part, or in whole, by a subsequent act of consent, they are obliged to stand to those conditions, which they made perchance out of a probable fear of harder usage. For the law of God generally, and the Civill law in this case makes the act binding. That covenants should not bee violated, will appeare by the revenge God tooke in behalfe of the *Gibeonites*. The Children of *Israel* suffered three yeares famine, and after this, seven of *Sauls* Sonnes were hanged to make an atonement for this breach of promise. Notwithstanding the *Gibeonites* had over-reached the Children of *Israel* by craft, yet they having sworne, were bound to perform their Oath unto the Lord. *Doli exceptio* could not take off this obligation. That they were deceived, gave no right to them to imitate what they condemned, and to deceive againe. Thus wee see what speciall care God takes to preserve the faith of Contracts, He will returne abondantly, what any mans honesty costs him; and therefore it is great reason, he that sweareth to his Neighbour, should not disappoint him, though it be to his owne hinderance.[12]

In this account, the obligation on men to keep their promises is the result of God's punishing them for not doing so, the punishment being either in this world or (presumably) in the next. It followed from this that contracts had to be kept even if doing so entailed the contractors' suffering or death, since God would make them suffer even more or condemn them to eternal punishment for breaking them. In the second account, however, God does not seem to have entered directly; after making the point about a condemned thief quoted above, the authors continued:

> though it should happen to me in particular, to be condemned by the Magistrate without cause, I am bound to suffer patiently, because having made such a bargaine, which might have beene profitable, I have no right to recall it, when it appeares disadvantagious. I ow, that I have beene safe thus long, to the benefit of this Covenant, and therefore am bound in justice to share the inconveniences.[13]

Here, the argument seems to be that there is a prior principle of justice which dictates that men must accept disadvantages consequent upon a formerly advantageous arrangement which they entered into freely, and that this principle generates an obligation to keep promises. The status of

---

[11] This clear use of the 'modern' concept of probability in fact antedates a number of Ian Hacking's examples in his *The Emergence of Probability* (Cambridge, 1975), and raises certain doubts about his account of the context in which the concept emerged. It is notable that Grotius, in the unpublished part of his *De Iure Praedae*, also uses such a modern concept. Trans. G. L. Williams (Oxford, 1950), p. 78.

[12] *An answer*, sig. A3v–A4.

[13] *ibid.*, sig. C3v.

such a principle is left unclear; and the authors in fact shortly afterwards brought God's punishments in again as a crucial feature. They replied to Parker's point that non-resistance is 'against Nature' by asserting that 'He must meane, nature guided by right reason; and doth that dictate, that rather then part with a temporall life, wee ought to forfeit an eternall [?]'[14]

Digges in *The unlawfulnesse* also seems to have been unsure about what might constitute an obligation to keep promises. His central belief, like that of the other authors of *An answer to a printed book*, was that the obligation must be capable of being spelt out in terms of *motivation*, and this belief is (as we have seen) an important pointer to the roots of this line of thought. But he (again) had two rather different accounts of what might provide such a motivation. One was an account simply in terms of physical coercion by the other members of the society:

the wills of men, though the fountaines of all voluntary actions, yet are not themselves the objects of choice; (for we cannot will to be willing, (this would be infinite) but to performe what is commanded) and so are not capable of being obliged by compacts; therefore this submission of all to the will of one; or this union of them agreed upon, is to be understood in a politique sense: and signifies the giving up of every mans particular power into his disposall, so that he may be inabled to force those who are unwilling upon some private ends, to be obedient to the common good; otherwise they would enjoy the benefits of others faith in observing lawes, and the advantages of their owne violations and breaches, which may probably be prevented, if penalties be appointed much greater then the profits which can come by their disobedience ...[15]

But Digges subsequently also brought in what we know about God's commands in order to explain our motivation for keeping contracts up to and *including* the point of death:

Naturally we love society below our selves, for the end of it was to convey to us such and such goods, and that which is loved in order to something else, is less amiable: But morally and in Christianity we are bound to preferre the publique good to whatever private Interest. And the obligation is very reasonable; For if we submit nature to religion, and be content to loose our lives for the present, we shall receive them hereafter with great advantage. So that charity to our neighbour, and love of our selves, doe sweetly kisse each other.[16]

One crucial point is that whatever the source of the obligation to keep promises, it is an obligation independent of the entry of men into civil society under a sovereign. Thus property rights, too, were independently acquired as a result of contracts which were not the same as the contract of government. Men in a state of nature are free to make contracts with each other about anything, but once made each contract is binding by virtue of the general obligation men are under, in or out of society, to keep their promises.

[14] *ibid.*, sig. C4.
[15] Digges, *Unlawfulnesse*, sig. A2v.
[16] *ibid.*, sig. Q2.

So far, it is clear that on the whole the Tew Circle writers are working very much within the ideological constraints set up by Selden. Like him, they believed in a state of complete freedom prior to the law of nature, and like him they thought that the obligatory force of the law of nature was given by man's knowledge of God's commands. Political authority was the result of a contract which could imply the death of the contractor, but it was rational for him to stick to his promise given what he knew of God's instructions. Unlike Selden, they went into some detail over the rationality of actually making such a promise in the first place, and elucidated it with very up-to-date considerations of probability. But I have to repeat what I said earlier, that we are dealing at the moment with the source of the obligation not to resist the magistrate, not with the source of the magistrate's rights over his subjects. This might seem a distinction without a difference, but it was in fact regarded as centrally important by the Tew Circle writers, and their exploitation of it constituted one of the major differences between them and Selden and (as we shall see) Hobbes. The issue was discussed primarily by Digges and Hammond, rather than by the authors of *An answer*, whose object was after all to meet Parker's points in detail and not to provide a general theory.

Selden had assumed, like Grotius, that the law of nature allowed private individuals to execute their fellows for appropriate crimes, and that the *ius zelotarum* of the Hebrews was an example of such a permission operating within and recognised by a civil law code. Hence there was no problem for him, any more than for Grotius, in explaining the right of execution possessed by a magistrate in a developed society. But this was a problem for both Digges and Hammond. As Digges said,

> The people could not agree together to dispence with Gods precept, *Thou shalt not kill*, nor distinguish sheeding bloud with the sword of vengeance from murther. It was not possible for any man to give away a greater right over his owne life than hee had, *Nemo plus juris ad alium transferre potest, quam ipse habet*; and hee had nothing to doe in the disposall of any others, and therefore except killing a mans selfe bee lawfull, the people cannot enable the Magistrate to take away their lives ... *Jus gladii*, (to beare the sword innocently, and to cut off offenders without deserving greater punishment than they inflict by transgressing against Gods knowne will, *Vindicta mea, ego retribuam*, Vengeance is mine, I will repay saith the Lord,) must referre to God as the author ...[17]

Precisely the same point was made with increasing fervour by Hammond in his three political pamphlets, and it is possible that Digges owed his apprehension of it to Hammond. In his first, *Of resisting the lawful magistrate under colour of religion*, he argued that 'though the Regal power were confest to be first given by the people, yet the power of the sword, wherewith regality is endowed, would be a superaddition of Gods ... for even in nature there is *Felonia de se*'.[18] Hammond was clearly worried by

[17] *ibid.*, sig. E1v.
[18] Hammond, *Works*, I, p. 313.

Selden's point about the *ius zelotarum*, and he devoted an appendix to marshalling Selden's evidence for it, but drawing the rival conclusion that 'the original and ground of it among [the Jews] is to be fetcht from hence; that among that people, God immediately presided, and reserved many things to be manag'd, and rul'd by his peculiar and extraordinary incitation and impulsion, and not by any rule of standing publick law'.[19]

In his later pamphlets, Hammond emphasised that, like Digges, he derived the obligation not to resist from the renunciation of a natural right founded on man's natural liberty:

That which is in the *Subject's power* the *Governour* may have by the Subject's *consent*, and by *virtue* of the *power which he received from him*: And therefore it is that the *power* of *violent resisting* invaders, the right of *repelling force by force*, which God and *Nature* hath give the *single* man in *community of Nature* is now, in case of submission to the *Governour*, parted with, and deposited by him, so far as it refers to the *Governour*; and though it be founded in *self-defence*, he that thus violently resists *the powers*, shall *receive to himself damnation*.[20]

Such a submission was involved when men changed 'absolute liberty for somewhat which seemed better, and more advantagious to them, to wit, for security, and *protection*, i.e. in changing a state of common *hostility*, (the unhappiest lot in nature), for ... a quiet setled peace'.[21] They were able to do so by virtue of the general power men have to renounce any rights which they possess, and Hammond instanced the fact that 'the *Jew* under God's own Government could give himself up wholly into the power of his *Master*'.[22] But 'still that which is not in the *Subject's power* is not, nay cannot be vested by the Subject in the Governour'.[23]

All that the *People* bestow, or part with by their act is their *own liberty*, or that part of it of which they voluntarily divest themselves, that they may by *obedience* empower him, whom they have set over them; and that they may reasonably part with for that greater benefit of *protection from him*, over them, which, while *he is obeyed by all*, he may by their united *obedience* to his commands be able to afford them, and could not probably without it; now this giving up their *liberties* to one, or more, makes that man, or men a *Ruler* over them; and being a *Ruler*, to him belongs (derived from God not from *them*) that *power of life, and death*, which God's forementioned decree hath enstated on the *Supreme power*, or *Ruler* . . .[24]

It is clear, then, that it was possible for the Tew Circle writers to argue in extremely Seldenian terms about a general state of liberty limited by contracts, the obligation to obey which was grounded on a law of God, and even to give a new and sophisticated twist to the argument by

[19] *ibid.*, I, p. 319.
[20] *ibid.*, I, p. 342 (*A Vindication*).
[21] *ibid.*, I, p. 339 (*ibid.*).
[22] *ibid.*, I, p. 336 (*ibid.*).
[23] *ibid.*, I, p. 342 (*ibid.*).
[24] *ibid.*, I, p. 333 (*The humble Address*).

introducing the element of probability calculations. But alongside this they denied a main assumption of Selden (as it had been of Grotius, their other great mentor), and derived the magistrate's right to use force against his subjects not from their contract of non-resistance, but from a direct grant by God. Because of this, they could appear much more like traditional divine-right theorists, and match their ideological with their political allegiance.

This should not surprise us: we misunderstand Great Tew if we expect too pure a Grotian or Seldenian account of politics from the men gathered there. It is useful here to compare the standpoint of Tew's great memorialist, Edward Hyde, both in his writings of the 1640s and in his later book against Hobbes's *Leviathan*. Even in 1648, Hyde was much more prepared to talk about the divine origin of all governmental rights than Digges or Hammond – he quoted Grotius as apparently in an unguarded moment endorsing the opinion of St Ambrose that the power of all kings came from God[25] – and in the 1670s he extended this into a fully fledged and highly un–Seldenian account of magistracy. According to his *A Brief View and Survey*, Adam had been given genuine political powers directly as a gift from God, and the current distribution of authority was to be explained in terms of a devolution from that state of affairs. Against Hobbes's claim that the right of punishment vested in the magistrate was the same as the natural right possessed by all men in a state of nature (which was in effect on the same kind of lines as Selden's or Grotius's theory), Hyde first pointed out quite validly that this meant that 'his Soveraign is vested in no other autority, than lawfully to fight so many Duels as the Law hath condemned men to suffer death', and then concluded:

How this right and autority of punishing came into the hands of the Soveraign, we shall now follow his example in repeting, having before confessed, that it neither is nor can be grounded on any concession or gift of the Subject, but is indubitably inherent in the office of being Soveraign, and inseparably annexed to it by God himself ...[26]

One of the most remarkable features of Hyde, and one which Trevor-Roper's account of him, for example, leaves unexplained, is precisely this difference between his general political theory and that of Selden or Digges or Hammond, however much his detailed political ideas might have agreed with theirs. But Hyde notoriously found Tew very agreeable, as Selden apparently did not, at least to the same extent, and what made it so congenial may well have been that aspect of it represented by Digges's divine right of punishment, rather than the more purely Seldenian elements of his theory. Moreover we should beware of assuming that because Hyde expressed his warm affection for someone, as he often did in his *Life*,

[25] [E. Hyde], *Full Answer to an Infamous and Trayterous Pamphlet* (1648), B2.
[26] E. Earl of Clarendon, *A Brief View and Survey of . . . Leviathan* (Oxford, 1676), pp. 139–40.

he either understood what they were saying or would have agreed with
them if he had understood it.

Another example of a much more traditional theory of politics than we
might expect to come from Tew, given many of the features of the line that
Digges and Hammond took, is provided by Chillingworth in his manuscript treatise *Of the Unlawfulness of Resisting the Lawful Prince*. It consists
simply of a rehearsal of the standard Biblical texts against resistance, and a
denial of the relevance of the law of nature – 'no law prevails against the *ius
divinum*'.[27] It is also interesting that though Thomason attributes coauthor-
ship of *An answer* to Chillingworth, the *Petition of the most substantiall
inhabitants of the Citie of London* (January 1643) which he attributed to
Chillingworth alone has none of the kinds of argument which we have
been considering.[28]

From all this, I think one can conclude that the Tew writers should be
seen as working within a rather more conservative or traditional atmos-
phere of political thought than has often been suggested. They deliberately
modified a theory of political association which came from Grotius via
Selden in such a way that it could link up in at least one important respect
with an older tradition – an older tradition which some of them (such as
Hyde) were not prepared to abandon at all. To say this, however, is not to
diminish the extent to which they did inherit many of their basic political
ideas from Grotius and Selden; undoubtedly they are the most important
figures after Selden in the early history of the adoption and development of
this natural rights theory in England, with the exception of course of
Thomas Hobbes.

It might be thought that one reason for Tew's modification of Selden's
position was their alarm at the consequences apparently drawn from it by
Hobbes in his early writings. As we shall see in the next chapter, Hobbes's
Elements of Law of April–May 1640 cannot have alarmed them, as it did not
differ from their own writings over the crucial question of non-resistance;
and while Hobbes had shifted his position by the time of *De Cive* in 1642, it
seems that that work was not known to his former friends in England until
much later (if Hyde's evidence is any guide).[29] The events of the war no
doubt took up most of their time by then. Moreover, on the fundamental
issue of the derivation of the natural law from God there was clearly such a
gap between them and Hobbes that it cannot have seemed a really substantial challenge.

In fact, Hobbes's use of some rather similar ideas seems to have been in

---

[27] Lambeth Palace Wharton MS 943, ff. 897–8. See also Orr, *Reason and Authority*, p. 194.
[28] Sirluck's remark that it 'displays many similarities with our *Answer* of November 20'
should be treated with some caution. (Milton, *Prose Works*, II, p. 35.)
[29] Hyde wrote from Jersey to a friend in Paris in January 1647, asking for a copy of *De Cive*
'which I have never seen since it was printed, and therefore know not how much it is the
same which I had the favour to read in English'. B. D. Greenslade, 'Clarendon's and
Hobbes's *Elements of Law*', *Notes and Queries*, CCII (1957), p. 150.

no way a deterrent to the continued deployment of Selden's theory throughout the 1650s and 1660s. Two men (both of them outside the circle at Tew) exhibit particularly pure versions of the theory in this period, the royalist theologian Jeremy Taylor and Selden's friend and executor John Vaughan. Taylor's ideas are put forward in his compilation of essays on difficult questions, the *Ductor Dubitantium*, which he printed in 1660, but which we know he was already working on in the early 1650s. He seems to have been unpopular with the Tew habitués – Chillingworth made a slighting reference to him in a letter of 1635; and Gilbert Sheldon had a quarrel with him which was not patched up until the 1650s as a result of his intrusion by Laud into an All Souls' fellowship.[30] Taylor was famous for his adherence to Grotius in theological matters, which led him into his well-known controversy about original sin and the freedom of the will (an echo of the kind of debate in the Low Countries which lay behind the emergence of a modern rights theory fifty years earlier). But it was Selden rather than Grotius who inspired his political theory. This comes out clearly from Book II, Chapter I of the *Ductor*, which is devoted to the law of nature, and is obviously based on Selden's *De Iure Naturali*. Thus he goes through the alternative theories of natural law just as Selden had done, rebutting them with the same arguments and coming himself to the same conclusions. At times, indeed, the discussion reads like a rough and ready translation of Selden's Latin.

He began with a distinction which we first saw made in these precise terms by Digges, though implied (of course) in all that Selden said. It was also a distinction made, famously, by Hobbes:

Jus naturae, and *Lex naturae* are usually confounded by Divines and Lawyers, but to very ill purposes, and to the confusion and indistinction of all the notices of them. *The right of nature*, or *Jus naturae* is no *Law*, and the *law of nature* is *no natural right*. *The right of nature* is a perfect and universal liberty to do whatsoever can secure me or please me. For the appetites that are prime, original, and natural, do design us towards their satisfaction, and were a continual torment, and in vain, if they were not in order to their rest, contentedness and perfection. Whatsoever we naturally desire, naturally we are permitted to. For natures are equal, and the capacities are the same, and the desires alike; and it were a contradiction to say that *naturally* we are restrained from any thing to which we *naturally* tend. Therefore to save my own life, I can kill another, or twenty, or a hundred, or take from his hands to please my self, if it happens in my circumstances and power; and so for *eating*, and *drinking*, and *pleasures*. If I can desire, I may possess or enjoy it: this is, *The right of nature*. *Jus naturae*, by *jus* or *right*, understanding not a *collated* or *legal right, positive* or *determined*, but a *negative right*, that is, such a right as every man hath without a Law, and such as that by which the stones in the streets are mine or yours; by a right that is negative, because they are *nullius in bonis*, they are appropriate to no man, and may be mine; that is, I may take them up and carry them to my bed of turf, where the *natural, wild*, or *untutored* man doth sit. But this is not *the Law of nature*, nor passes any obligation at all.[31]

[30] See J. Taylor, *Whole Works*, I, ed. R. Heber (London, 1854), pp. ccliii and xix.
[31] Taylor, *Ductor Dubitantium* (London, 1676), pp. 167–8.

Taylor argued that the law of nature was only natural in so far as it was a law relating to 'the natural necessities of mankind': laws are '*Civil* or *Religious,* or *Natural* according as they serve the end of the *Commonwealth,* or of the *Religion,* or of *Nature*'.[32] Its source, and the basis of its obligatory force, cannot be 'right reason' or the consent of mankind, or any of the other traditional possibilities. This is so precisely because 'nature is free to everything which it naturally desires', and that

where nature hath an appetite, and proper tendency, it cannot deny to it self satisfaction; whatsoever therefore is a law and a restraint to it, must needs be superinduc'd upon it: which nature her self cannot be supposed to be willing to do; and nothing had power to do but God only who is the Lord of Nature . . .[33]

Because 'in all laws there must be some penalty annexed, the fear of which may be able to restrain men from doing against the law: which cannot be unless the evil be greater than the benefit or pleasure of the praevarication can be',[34] God has annexed punishments to breaches of the law of nature, and the prospect of those punishments constitutes its obligatory force.

It can easily be seen that Taylor was straightforwardly following Selden in all this; where he differed was simply over the weakest point in Selden's case, the promulgation of the natural law by God. Whereas Selden believed that it had been promulgated once and for all to mankind through the *Noachidae,* Taylor thought that it had been promulgated in different ways at different times, and most recently through Christ:

Christianity is a perfect systeme of all the laws of nature, and of all the will of God, that is, of the obligatory will; of all the Commandments. In those things where Christianity hath not interpos'd, we are left to our natural liberty, or a *Jus permissivum,* a permission, except where we have restrain'd our selves by *contract* or *dedition.*[35]

It was via such a contract that the civil magistrate was set up, when everyone renounced the right of resistance which they had possessed in the state of nature. Taylor gives an account of this in just the same terms as the Tew Circle writers, except over the question of the origin of the magistrate's right to punish his subjects.[36] Instead of basing it on God's direct grant, he argued that it was founded at least in part simply on the necessity for securing the common good.

When the faults and disorders of Mankind have intangled their own and the publick affairs, they may make that necessary to them, which in the first order and intention of things was not to be endur'd. Thus we cut off a leg and an arm to save the whole body; and the publick Magistrate, who is appointed to defend every

[32] *ibid.,* p. 169.
[33] *ibid.,* p. 177.
[34] *ibid.,* p. 185.
[35] *ibid.,* p. 184.
[36] See *ibid.,* p. 541.

Mans rights, must pull an honest Mans house to the ground to save a town or a street: and peace is so dear, so good, that for the confirming and perpetuity of it, he may commence a war which were otherwise intolerable ...

His defence of punishment was thus wholly utilitarian – if highway robbers, etc. 'were to be free from afflictive punishments, the common-wealth would be no society of peace, but a direct state of war, a state most contrary to governments; but if there were any other less than death, the Gallies and the Mines, and the Prisons would be nothing but nurseries of villains'.[37]

If this is a relatively pure version of Selden's argument (which I think it clearly is), then equally clearly there is no sign of any concern that it is the sort of thing which in *Leviathan* backed up some very alarming conclu-sions. Taylor later applauded Bramhall for his refutation of Hobbes's ideas on determinism,[38] so he was presumably aware of what Hobbes said, but he did not see it as any sort of challenge. Indeed, there is not even any sign of an awareness that the generation of a magistrate's penal rights other than from God provided any problems for royalist orthodoxy.

Similar arguments were put forward by one of the most interesting and neglected of Selden's followers, John Vaughan. He was Chief Justice of Common Pleas from 1668 to 1674, and had been a close friend of the elderly Selden: Burnet in his life of Matthew Hale records that Hale 'was soon found out by that great and learned antiquary Mr. Selden, who though much superior to him in years, yet came to have such a liking of him, and of Mr. Vaughan, who was afterwards lord chief justice of the common-pleas, that as he continued in a close friendship with them while he lived, so he left them at his death, two of his four executors'.[39] Discus-sion of Hale's general theory properly belongs to a subsequent chapter, for he was more influenced by the need to rebut Hobbes than Vaughan was; Vaughan in fact represents a remarkably pure and untroubled application of Selden's ideas to actual legal problems. He left no works other than the records of his judgements, but they usually contain a long philosophical discussion of the general issues involved.

His ideas on the law of nature are set out in his judgement on a case in 1669, *Harrison* v. *Doctor Burwell*. At issue was the question of the legiti-macy of a marriage between a man and the widow of his great uncle, and although it was not strictly relevant, Vaughan argued the case from basic principles.

In the first place, he claimed, it did not make much sense to say that *any* marriage was unnatural:

[37] *ibid.*, pp. 466–7.
[38] See S. I. Mintz, *The Hunting of Leviathan* (Cambridge, 1962), p. 114.
[39] M. Hale, *Works, Moral and Religious*, I, ed. T. Thirlwall (London, 1805), p. 15. For a full account of Vaughan, see J. Gwyn Williams, 'Sir John Vaughan of Trawscoed, 1603–1674', *National Library of Wales Journal*, VIII (1953–4), pp. 33–48, 121–46, 225–43.

To speak strictly what is *unnatural,* it is evident that nothing which *actually* is, can be said to be *unnatural,* for Nature is but the production of effects from causes sufficient to produce them, and whatever is, had a sufficient cause to make it be, else it had never been; and whatsoever is effected by a cause sufficient to effect it, is as natural as any other thing effected by its sufficient cause. And in this sense nothing is unnatural but that which cannot be, and consequently nothing that is, is *unnatural,* and so no *Copulation* of any man with any woman, nor an effect of that *Copulation* by *Generation,* can be said *unnatural;* for if it were, it could not be, and if it be, it had a sufficient cause.[40]

Only if no desire to copulate was evidenced, as in the case of two creatures of different species, could the mating properly be described as unnatural.

This was of course just the same point that Taylor had made about what was natural for man: the state of nature, for Vaughan as for all the others in this tradition, was one of complete amorality. Vaughan then proceeded to explain *historically,* just like Selden, how moral feelings and laws had supervened upon this natural state:

A second way by which mens Acts are said to be unnatural (and are so in some measure) is, *When Laws Divine or Humane, do supervene upon mans original nature with great penalty for transgressing them. Mens education, a teneris Annis, to observe those Laws, the infamy attending their violation, and the religious customary observance of them, implant a horrour and averseness to break them; so that by long custome they are not observ'd, only to avoid the punishment, and as things which were otherwise indifferent, but are observed, from an averseness and loathing, begot by Custome, to transgress them. That though men were secure from the punishment, if they broke them, yet Nature denies all appetite and inclination to violate them* . . . In this secondary way, the *Copulation* with the Mother, Sister, and the like, do become odious and reluctant to Nature, and generally are so where *Humanity* is well planted, which in the original state of nature, and without those induc'd *Laws, Education,* and *Custome* of *Manners,* had been as indifferent as with other women . . .[41]

In this sense, laws which had a completely human origin could be construed as truly natural – custom was literally a second nature. Vaughan was clearly in the mainstream of the Grotian tradition, with its assimilation of natural and conventional laws, though neither Grotius nor Selden made this point with quite so much force. But Vaughan also suggested a totally Seldenian interpretation of the natural laws:

A third way of mens acting unnaturally is, when they violate Laws coeval with their *original being,* though the Laws be but *positive Divine,* or *positive Human Laws,* and not of nature, primarily, nor in any other sense, intelligible to be *Natural Laws.* But that they bind men as soon as men can be bound, and no Law can possibly precede them.
A *second* reason of their being natural Laws properly, is, because mans nature must necessarily assent to receive them as soon as it is capable of assenting, and hath no power to dissent from them; for a man hath no power to dissent from, or not to assent to his own preservation, or not to dissent from his own destruction: But not to assent to the will, that is, to the Laws, of an Infinite Power, to hurt and benefit, is,

[40] *Reports and Arguments,* ed. E. Vaughan (London, 1677), p. 221.
[41] *ibid.,* p. 224.

to assent to his own destruction and infinite hurt, and to dissent from his own preservation and infinite benefit; *for infinite power can hurt or benefit as it pleaseth.* Therefore to assent to the Laws of the *Deity* is natural to man ... Of the *Natural Laws,* in this sense given to all Mankind by the Deity, from the beginning of time, concerning *Marriage* and bodily knowledge, See excellent matter in that incomparable Work of Mr. *Selden, De Jure Naturali & Gentium juxta disciplinam Ebraeorum* ...[42]

Vaughan's judgement in *Harrison* v. *Doctor Burwell* shows convincingly that Selden's ideas were still alive and highly influential in the late 1660s; moreover it shows that there was no need for Vaughan to dissociate himself from Hobbes. Whether this was because contemporaries could easily distinguish his position from Hobbes's, or whether it was because Hobbes was in fact much closer to a main stream of seventeenth-century political thinking than has usually been admitted, is a question for the next chapter.

It is a striking fact that the political stance of all these followers of Selden, from Digges to Vaughan, was one of pretty unqualified royalism. The Tew writers were obviously committed to the King's side, as we have seen; Jeremy Taylor's loyalty was no less marked, while Vaughan retired into private life in 1649, remarking (apparently) 'that it was the Duty of an honest Man to decline, as far as in him lay, owning Jurisdictions that derived their Authority from any Power, but their lawful Prince'.[43] Selden's own position in the early 1640s had been equivocal, but he too never took the Engagement and lived privately for the five years left to him. The revolutionary break was one which none of them could easily accept, for it directly contradicted the fundamental principle of 'keep your contracts'. On no interpretation of the English constitution could the events of 1649 be seen as anything other than the breaking of a straightforward promise to stay loyal to a monarch of *some* kind.

But this did not necessarily mean that a Seldenian could not work under the new regime. The equivocal nature of the new ideology in some respects is brought out well by the self-doubts felt by Matthew Hale. Although his general theory as set out after the Restoration was in some ways a modification of Selden's ideas to cope with Hobbes, in the 1640s and 1650s he applied a more or less pure version of Selden's constitutional ideas to his current problems, and came up with an interesting answer.

In the 1640s he was clearly of the King's party – he was counsel to Strafford, to Laud and to Charles himself, as well as to the Duke of Hamilton, the Earl of Holland and Lord Capel. He took the Engagement in 1651 in order to plead at the trial of the royalist Christopher Love, and apparently (in the circumstances) without many scruples. But his real test came three years later, when Cromwell offered to raise him to the Bench.

[42] *ibid.,* pp. 226–7.
[43] *ibid.,* sig. A3v.

116 *Natural Rights Theories*

The arguments he rehearsed then were essentially the ones that others had gone through four years previously: according to Burnet,

Mr. Hale saw well enough the snare laid for him; . . . yet he did deliberate more on the lawfulness of taking a commission from usurpers; but having considered well of this, he came to be of opinion, 'That it being absolutely necessary to have justice and property kept up at all times, it was no sin to take a commission from usurpers, if he made no declaration of his acknowledging their authority', which he never did: he was much urged to accept of it by some eminent men of his own profession, who were of the king's party; as Sir Orlando Bridgeman, and Sir Geoffry Palmer; and was also satisfied concerning the lawfulness of it, by the resolution of famous divines, in particular Dr. Sheldon, and Dr. Henchman, who were afterwards promoted to the sees of Canterbury and London.

To these were added the importunities of all his friends, who thought that in a time of so much danger and oppression, it might be no small security to the nation, to have a man of his integrity and abilities on the bench . . .

But he had greater scruples concerning the proceeding against felons, and putting offenders to death by that commission, since he thought the sword of justice belonging only by right to the lawful prince, it seemed not warrantable to proceed to a capital sentence by an authority derived from usurpers; yet at first he made a distinction between common and ordinary felonies, and offences against the state; for the last he would never meddle in them; for he thought these might often be legal and warrantable actions, and that the putting men to death on that account was murder; but, for the ordinary felonies, he at first was of opinion, that it was as necessary, even in times of usurpation, to execute justice in those cases, as in matters of property . . . but, having considered farther of it, he came to think that it was at least better not to do it; and so, after the second or third circuit, he refused to sit any more on the crown-side, and told plainly the reason; for, in matters of blood, he was always to choose the safer side . . .[44]

In this story we can see very plainly the practical consequences of such an ideology. The issue which worried Hale most – whether a magistrate had the right to execute criminals – was precisely the point raised by Hammond and Digges, and he apparently decided eventually that it was safer to act on their principles. (It is worth mentioning that Gilbert Sheldon, to whom he turned for advice, was of course a frequent visitor to Tew and a close friend of Hammond.)

We are fortunate in possessing an independent elucidation of Burnet's story, in the form of a treatise on just this matter by Hale himself. It is structured as a discussion of the juridical problems raised by the Wars of the Roses (a device also employed by Anthony Ascham), but it obviously refers to the 1650s. In it, Hale shows that he was stretching the ideology to its very limits in order to accommodate his own actions, but he at no time clearly breaks it. From its tone, it is probable that it belongs to the period of the earlier circuits, before his change of mind.

Essentially, his argument was built upon Selden's observation that the King and people had sharply defined and separate bodies of rights, which neither could infringe and which could be transferred by their holders like

[44] Hale, *Works,* pp. 20–1.

any set of private rights. Hale drew the conclusion that if the rights of the King in possession were infringed by a usurper, that did not give the people any more rights against the usurper than they had had against his predecessor. Or any fewer rights: a conquest did not necessarily lead to servitude. As he said, in the case of England, 'the last Change was by the Normans; which was a Conquest *in Regem*, but not *in Populum*; so their Rights remained. But what these were, we are not unhappy in not knowing, and therefore we must resorte to our Customes . . .'[45]

The main problem was the rights of the subject against a usurper:

whether a Subject cannot make an Acquest, by Conquest, upon a Usurper, is not so clear; as in the Case of Henry VII. upon Richard III. The Reason is: because, That as against any subject He is truly King, and there is a Bond of Allegiance between an Usurper and the People, against all Persons but Him that is Rightfull King: which Bond, or contract, as it makes any Opposition after, to be Treason & Rebellion, so by consequence, it may take away that Right, that by the Law of Nations belongs to a Conquest.[46]

From this it followed that the usurper

in reference to the People, and all others but the Rightfull Heir, owner, or Inheritour, . . . is King to all intents. It is Treason to conspire his death, and shall be punished, notwithstanding the Reaccession. His Charters will binde his Heir & Successour, if not the Rightful heir, or Owner. The Reason is, because the People have tacitely submitted to him, and as far as in them lay, transmitted all their Right, which was in them, in the Person upon whom such Usurpation was made, whether of Power or Profit . . .[47]

Hale thus advocated a high degree of obedience to the usurper: only if the rightful king actually called on his subjects to follow him against the new regime could disobedience to it be justified. Otherwise, the usurper should be treated as the straightforward successor of the previous King, with no more and no fewer powers than he had possessed.

It is clear how Hale was able to justify his own behaviour in these terms, and also how important it was for the Protectorate to secure the obedience of such men by emphasising the similarity between its powers and those of the old monarchy. But it would be wrong to treat Hale as an apologist for the new regime along the same lines as, say, Ascham. Unlike many of the defenders of the Engagement, Hale was not prepared to say that the usurper's rights were the same in all respects as those of his predecessor. The crucial difference was that he had no rights against the exiled King, while the exiled King did have rights against him. It is certainly true that time might have weakened this distinction; but as it was, Hale and others like him were always able to treat the Protectorate as an interlude even while they worked for it.

[45] B. M. Lansdowne MS 632 ('Extracts from a MS of Sir Matt. Hale . . . by J. Anstis Esq'), f. 2v.
[46] *ibid.*, f. 9.
[47] *ibid.*, f. 9v.

Nevertheless, there remained something slightly suspicious about Selden's theories to more traditional and conservative royalists, and Hale's equivocation cannot have reassured them. The new ideology remained exotic and rather daring, even after its exponents received high positions in Church and State after the Restoration. As such, it shared in the suspicion directed against apparently the most outrageous of all Selden's followers, whose relationship to this tradition is the subject of my next chapter.

6

Thomas Hobbes

I

The nearest anyone has yet got to a proper assessment of the relationship of Hobbes to the line of thought which I dealt with in the previous chapter is Ernest Sirluck in his introduction to the Yale Milton, twenty years ago. He commented on *An answer to a printed book* that 'this anonymous pamphlet ... contains the essential elements of Hobbes's political thought (along with much that is foreign and even contradictory to it)', and pointed to the friendship between Hobbes and many of the Tew Circle, and the fact that Hobbes's manuscript *Elements of Law* had circulated among his friends after its composition in April and May of 1640.[1] The evidence for this friendship and the manuscript's circulation is good,[2] and it is clear that it is in just the *milieu* surveyed in the last chapter that Hobbes's theory was developed. His interest in and admiration for Selden is separately attested: not only is Selden's *Titles of Honour* one of the few books praised (or even mentioned by name) in *Leviathan,* but in 1635 when he was touring the Continent Hobbes wrote back to a friend asking for a copy of *Mare Clausum,* saying that he had 'already a great opinion of it'.[3] They did not actually meet until after the publication of *Leviathan,* when Hobbes sent Selden a complimentary copy – an act which in itself shows the esteem in which he held him. They apparently became quite close friends afterwards.[4]

However, the conventional interpretation of Hobbes would rule out too close a similarity between him and Selden or Digges. After all, central to their theory was the idea that men renounce their right of self-preservation in order to create civil society, and that they have no right to resist the magistrate subsequently. Hobbes in *De Cive* and *Leviathan* denied just this and was attacked by Hyde, among others, for doing so. Moreover if we accept the normal view of Hobbes's theory of natural law and its

---

[1] J. Milton, *Prose Works*, II, ed. E. Sirluck (New Haven, 1959), p. 35.
[2] See B. D. Greenslade, 'Clarendon's and Hobbes's *Elements of Law*', *Notes and Queries*, CCII (1957), p. 150; J. Aubrey, *Brief Lives*, I, ed. A. Clark (Oxford, 1898), pp. 333–4; and pp. 365–72 for a list of Hobbes's friends including most of the Tew Circle.
[3] Hobbes, *English Works*, VII, ed. W. Molesworth (London, 1839–95), p. 454.
[4] Aubrey, *Brief Lives*, I, p. 369.

obligatory force, nothing could be much further from Selden's picture, with God in a central place. In the first part of this chapter, I shall show that while the standard account of Hobbes's ideas on resistance is true for *De Cive* and *Leviathan*, and so true for Hobbes from 1642 onwards, it is not so obviously true for the *Elements of Law*. In the second part, I shall show the relationship between Hobbes's theory of natural law and Selden's.

One consequence of getting straight the relationship between Hobbes and Selden is that we can put the long argument between Professor Warrender and his critics in a new perspective. Warrender's case rests on the fact that in *Leviathan* Hobbes consistently refuses to treat self-preservation as a *duty* – it is the primary *right* of nature, and 'Law and Right, differ as much, as Obligation and Liberty; which in one and the same matter are inconsistent'. Duty, the law of nature, must therefore have some other basis than self-interest, and Warrender famously found its basis in God's will. But as his critics have always stressed, and as Hobbes's contemporaries also realised, the whole tenor of Hobbes's theory is that obligation is ultimately a matter of self-interest. As we shall see, Warrender isolated a real problem in the text of *Leviathan*; the solution to the problem, however, is not what he proposed but is to be found by looking at the development of Hobbes's thought during the 1640s.

The *Elements* is in fact ambiguous in just the area I want to consider first, the surrender of the right of self-preservation; but there are some passages which cannot really be interpreted in any way other than by accepting that he believed in such a surrender. In addition, contemporaries took him to be justifying the surrender, and that is evidence which cannot be disregarded. The general similarities between the *Elements* and the works of the Tew Circle or Taylor are clear: most obviously, Hobbes hung his argument on just the distinction between right and law which was central for Digges and others.

The names *lex,* and *jus,* that is to say, law and right, are often confounded; and yet scarce are there any two words of more contrary signification. For right is that liberty which law leaveth us; and laws those restraints by which we agree mutually to abridge one another's liberty. Law and right therefore are no less different than restraint and liberty, which are contrary ... (II.10.5)

The primary right of nature is self-defence: 'that which is not against reason, men call RIGHT, or *jus*, or blameless liberty of using our own natural power and ability. It is therefore a *right of nature*: that every man may preserve his own life and limbs, with all the power he hath' (1.14.6). But although it is the primary right of nature, it is not the only right. Hobbes was quite explicit in the *Elements* that the state of nature was the state of *total* freedom hypothesised by Selden and the others.

Every man by nature hath right to all things, that is to say, to do whatsoever he listeth to whom he listeth, to possess, use, and enjoy all things he will and can. For

seeing all things he willeth, must therefore be good unto him in his own judgement, because he willeth them; and may tend to his preservation some time or
other; or he may judge so . . .: it followeth that all things may rightly also be done
by him. (1.14.10)

As we shall see, this is significantly different from the theory put forward
in *De Cive*. Moreover, in the *Elements* Hobbes at various points went on to
argue that the right of self-defence has to be renounced by the contractors
if a sovereign with coercive power is to be set up. Thus he explained the
creation of a sovereign by remarking that 'the end for which man giveth
up, and relinquisheth to another, or others, the right of protecting and
defending himself by his own power, is the security which he expecteth
thereby, of protection and defence from those to whom he doth so
relinquish it' (11.1.5). And he said of the power of coercion that it

consisteth in the transferring of every man's right of resistance against him to
whom he hath transferred the power of coercion. It followeth therefore, that no
man in the commonwealth whatsoever hath right to resist him, or them, on whom
they have conferred this power coercive, or (as men use to call it) the sword of
justice; . . . (11.1.7)

After defining the power of domestic coercion in this way, he went on to
say that

forasmuch as they who are amongst themselves in security, by the means of this
sword of justice that keeps them all in awe, are nevertheless in danger of enemies
from without; if there be not some means found, to unite their strengths and
natural forces in the resistance of such enemies, their peace amongst themselves is
but in vain. And therefore it is to be understood as a covenant of every member to
contribute their several forces for the defence of the whole . . . (11.1.8)

His argument thus made a distinction between the case where the power
of coercion is based on men renouncing their right of resistance against
the sovereign, and the case where it is based on their agreement to help
the sovereign against a common enemy. This is a distinction which
makes little sense in the later Hobbesian theory, and of course disappears
totally in *Leviathan*, having survived in a very emasculated form in *De
Cive*.

Another example can come from his definition of a sovereign:

In all cities or bodies politic not subordinate, but independent, that one man or one
council, to whom the particular members have given that common power, is called
their SOVEREIGN, and his power the sovereign power; which consists in the power
and strength that every one of the members have transferred to him from themselves, by covenant. And because it is impossible for any man really to transfer his
own strength to another, or for the other to receive it; it is to be understood: that to
transfer a man's power and strength, is no more but to lay by or relinquish his own
right of resisting him to whom he so transferreth it. (1.9.10)

While the last example can come from his account of the marks of
sovereignty:

He that cannot of right be punished, cannot of right be resisted; and he that cannot of right be resisted, hath coercive power over all the rest, and thereby can frame and govern their actions at his pleasure; which is absolute sovereignty ... Secondly, that man or assembly, that by their own right not derived from the present right of any other, may make laws, or abrogate them, at his, or their pleasure, have the sovereignty absolute. For seeing the laws they make, are supposed to be made by right, the members of the commonwealth to whom they are made, are obliged to obey them; and consequently not to resist the execution of them; which non-resistance maketh the power absolute of him that ordaineth them. (II.I.I9)

Against these passages, there are some others which point the other way, and imply that no man can relinquish his right of 'protecting and defending himself by his own power'. First, II.I.7, quoted above as defining the power of coercion, continues '... sword of justice; supposing the not-resistance possible. For (Part I. chapter 15, sect. 18) covenants bind but to the utmost of our endeavour.' However, one interesting thing about this is that the section referred to, which justifies this modification of his stated position, was added to the circulated copies of the *Elements* later by Hobbes, and is found in only two of the manuscripts. The evolution of the *Elements* text, despite Toennies's work, is still unclear, but there is a strong implication that Hobbes's original draft did not include the provision about the possibility of non-resistance.

Second, when discussing the rights which men retain from the state of nature into the state of peace (which in the *Elements* include, as Goldsmith has pointed out, rights founded on contracts made in the state of nature *before* the contract of society),[5] Hobbes observed:

As it was necessary that a man should not retain his right to everything, so also was it, that he should retain his right to some things: to his own body (for example) the right of defending, whereof he could not transfer; to the use of fire, water, free air, and place to live in, and to all things necessary for life. Nor doth the law of nature command any divesting of other rights, than of those only which cannot be retained without the loss of peace ... (I.I7.2)

This is a passage which of course raises a number of problems for any account of Hobbes, as does the similar passage in *Leviathan* itself: men may, for example, have the right to the use of a place to live in, but do they have the right to take a place to live in without the sovereign's permission?

However, despite these pointers away from the idea that men must renounce their rights of self-defence in order to erect a sovereign, the *Elements* was undoubtedly read by its first readers as arguing for a renunciation. The relevant parts of the work were first published as a piracy in May 1650 under the title *De Corpore Politico*, from a copy supplied (prob-

[5] Hobbes, *The Elements of Law Natural and Politic*, ed. F. Toennies, second ed. M. M. Goldsmith (London, 1969), p. xii. (Goldsmith's Introduction). All quotations in the text of this chapter are from this edition.

ably) by Hobbes's former friend and later enemy, Seth Ward.[6] The first people to mention it were among the now well-known 'Engagers', but the Engagers who read the *Elements*, as distinct from *De Cive* or *Leviathan*, took him to be putting forward a royalist case for the complete renunciation of all rights.

The first reference to it came some ten days after its publication, in the answer of 'Eutactius Philodemius' to Hammond's attack on him; he remarked revealingly that Hobbes was 'one of this Doctors party', despite the difference between their treatments of the magistrate's penal powers.[7] But probably the best example is Marchamont Nedham, who in the second edition of his *Case of the Common-wealth stated*, published later in 1650, added an appendix rehearsing arguments for his position

out of *Salmasius* his *Defensio Regis*, and out of M. Hobbs his late book *de Corpore Politico*. Not that I esteem their Authorities any whit more Authentick than those which I have already alledged; but onely in regard of the great reputation allowed unto those Books by the two Parties, *Presbyterian* and *Royall*; And I suppose no man may triumph, or cry a victory, more honourably than my selfe, if I can foile our Adversaries with weapons of their own approbation …[8]

He proceeded to quote the passage from the *Elements* about the creation of the sovereign (II.1.5), and continued:

From whence may plainly be inferred, that since no security for *Life, Limbs* and *Liberty* (which is the end of all Governments) are now to be had here, by relinquishing our right of self-protection, and giving it up to any other Power beside the present; Therefore it is very unreasonable in any man to put himself out of the Protection of this Power, by opposing it, and reserving his obedience to the K. of *Scots* …[9]

Nedham thus believed that Hobbes had argued for the relinquishment of the right of self-protection. It is interesting that Ascham too thought that Hobbes had a very extreme theory about the abnegation of rights (indeed, a theory which was too extreme for Ascham himself). Ascham's book, *Of the Confusions and Revolutions of Government*, the second edition of his *A Discourse: Wherein is Examined, What is Particularly Lawfull during the Confusions and Revolutions of Government*, was published some months before the *De Corpore*, and he did not say what work of Hobbes he had read (which is itself interesting). What he says makes better sense of the *Elements* than *De Cive*, which seems to have been very scarce in England at this time, and it is possible that he had seen one of the manuscripts of it. What Ascham said was that

Mr. *Hobbes* and H. *Grotius* are pleased to argue severall wayes for obliging people to one perpetuall and standing Allegiance. *Grotius* supposes such a fixt Allegiance

[6] Hobbes, *Elements*, p. vii (Toennies's Preface).
[7] 'Eutactius Philodemius', *An answer to the vindication of Doctor Hamond* (London, 1650), B3.
[8] M. Nedham, *The case of the common-wealth of England stated* (London, 1650), O4.
[9] *ibid.*, P2v–P3.

in a people, because a particular man may give himself up to a private servitude for
ever, as among the Jewes and Romans. Mr. *Hobbes* supposes, that because a man
cannot be protected from all civill injuries, unlesse all his rights be totally and
irrevocably given up to another, therefore the people are irrevocably and perpetually the Governours ... Such a totall resignation of all right and reason, as Mr.
Hobbes supposes, is one of our morall impossibilities, and directly opposite to that
antient *Ius zelotarum* among the Jewes ... Our Generall and Originall rights are not
totally swallowed up either in the property of goods or in the possession of
persons, neither is all that which was naturall now made Civill ...[10]

Given that Ascham himself, as his opponent Sanderson pointed out,
believed in effect that self-preservation was 'the first and chiefest obligation in the world', it is hardly surprising that he felt it necessary to rebut
Hobbes at this point. Later Engagers, however, such as Warren or
Osborne, who had the *Philosophical Rudiments* (i.e. the English translation
of *De Cive*) and *Leviathan* itself, were able to quote Hobbes as an authority
for their position with a clear conscience, and not treat him (as Nedham
had done) as an opponent to be subverted by the unforeseen consequences
of his own theory.[11]

If later readers of the *Elements* were aware that it countenanced the idea
that all men's rights could be renounced, so apparently was Hobbes
himself, for in *De Cive* he systematically removed the ambiguities and
altered his argument away from the Digges or Tew Circle line. This
process seems to have begun while he was tinkering with the *Elements*
itself, if the addition of the point about promises only binding to best
endeavours is any guide; and perhaps one reason why he abandoned the
manuscript and started on a basically new work is that the task of revising
the *Elements* piecemeal proved too cumbersome.

Thus in *De Cive* Hobbes added to his general discussion of contracts a
long defence of the proposition that 'no man is obliged by any contracts
whatsoever not to resist him who shall offer to kill, wound, or any other
way hurt his body', and of the consequent invalidation of compacts of
self-accusation.[12] The insertion of this passage into what is otherwise a
more or less straight copy of the *Elements* is very striking, given the way of
reading the *Elements* which we have just been considering. Equally striking
is the insertion of a new and rather forced explication of what non-
resistance is, into his account of the union of contracting individuals
(represented in the *Elements* by 1.19.10).

Submission of the wills of all those men to the will of one man or one council, is
then made, when each one of them obligeth himself by contract to every one of the
rest, not to resist the will of that one man or council, to which he hath submitted
himself; that is, that he refuse him not the use of his wealth and strength against any

[10] A. Ascham, *Of the Confusions and Revolutions of Governments* (London, 1649), pp. 15–16.
[11] For these Engagers' reading of Hobbes, see Q. R. D. Skinner, 'Conquest and Consent:
Thomas Hobbes and the Engagement Controversy', in G. E. Aylmer ed., *The Interregnum*
(London, 1972), pp. 92, 95.
[12] Hobbes, *English Works*, II, p. 25.

others whatsoever; for he is supposed still to retain a right of defending himself against violence.[13]

In general, however, any talk of a right of resistance being renounced is avoided in *De Cive*, and even qualified passages of this kind are excised in *Leviathan*.

But perhaps the best example of the change is provided by his analysis of coercive power. In place of the passage on the power of coercion in the *Elements* (II.1.7), *De Cive* interpreted the power as the result of the citizens renouncing, not their rights of resistance, but their rights of assistance: 'the right of punishing is ... understood to be given any one, when every man contracts not to assist him who is to be punished. But I will call this right, *the sword of justice*.' He thus made the right of domestic punishment the same kind of thing as the right to wage foreign war, and in *Leviathan* he was to move even further in this direction.[14]

Not only did Hobbes argue after 1642 for the impossibility of renouncing the right of self-defence, he also revised his account of the state of nature. It is ironical that Hobbes's picture of an anarchic natural state should have haunted contemporaries who were indifferent to the Seldenians; for in *De Cive* Hobbes in fact outlined a much *less* frightening and anarchic picture than Digges, Taylor or Vaughan, or he himself in 1640, had put forward. We have seen that according to the *Elements*, natural man had the right 'to do whatsoever he listeth to whom he listeth', just as he did (for example) in Taylor: 'whatsoever we naturally desire, naturally we are permitted to'.[15] But in the later theory, he had the right merely to do what tended to his self-preservation, or what he judged to do so. That this was by no means the same was made clear by Hobbes in a note he appended to the second edition of *De Cive* in 1647. In the state of nature, a man 'hath a right to make use of, and to do all whatsoever he shall judge requisite to his preservation ... But if any man pretend somewhat to tend necessarily to his preservation, which yet he himself doth not confidently believe so, he may offend against the laws of nature ...'[16] Similar remarks have been marshalled by Wernham to show that Hobbes consistently in his later works limited man's natural rights to those actions which tended to preservation, and not to anything he wished to do.[17] In this, he was undoubtedly moving away from his own earlier position and that of his friends.

If what I have been suggesting is correct, and Hobbes in the *Elements* was much more like Digges and the others than he later became, and was taken by contemporaries to be saying the same kind of thing, then we have to

[13] *ibid.*, II, p. 68.
[14] *ibid.*, II, p. 75.
[15] See above p. 111.
[16] Hobbes, *English Works*, II, p. 10.
[17] B. de Spinoza, *The Political Works*, ed. A. G. Wernham (Oxford, 1958), pp. 12–14. See also L. Strauss, *The Political Philosophy of Hobbes* (Oxford, 1936), pp. 8 ff.

explain his move away from their position. To understand this, we have to
bear in mind the distinction which I made when discussing the Tew Circle
writers, between the general obligation to keep promises, and the ration-
'ality of making a particular promise. In Hobbes, both these issues were
treated differently from the beginning.

The first point to be stressed is that in Selden, the obligation to obey the
natural law, and hence to keep one's promises, is (as we saw) equivalent to
a *motivation* – to the fear, that is, of suffering at the hands of God either in
this life or in the next. It was because we can fear punishment in the
after-life that it makes sense to talk of being obliged to keep a contract of
non-resistance; if belief in the after-life or in the possibility of talking about
it is dropped out, such a contract must go as well. It is fairly clear that
Hobbes never in fact believed that the after-life was relevant to the prudential calculations of all men, even in 1640, although he did accept that it
could be rational to accept death if one happened to believe that by doing
so one would avoid a worse penalty in the life to come. His position was
always (roughly speaking) Selden's without the premiss of God's eternal
punishments, though it was not stated as clearly as it could be until the
mature period of *Leviathan*. The famous passage on 'natural punishments'
there shows what he believed:

Having thus briefly spoken of the natural kingdom of God, and his natural laws, I
will add only to this chapter a short declaration of his natural punishments. There is
no action of man in this life, that is not the beginning of so long a chain of
consequences, as no human providence is high enough, to give a man a prospect to
the end. And in this chain, there are linked together both pleasing and unpleasing
events; in such manner, as he that will do any thing for his pleasure, must engage
himself to suffer all the pains annexed to it; and these pains, are the natural
punishments of those actions, which are the beginning of more harm than good.
And hereby it comes to pass, that intemperance is naturally punished with diseases,
... negligent government of princes, with rebellion; and rebellion with slaughter.
For seeing punishments are consequent to the breach of laws; natural punishments
must be naturally consequent to the breach of the laws of nature; and therefore
follow them as their natural, not arbitrary effects.[18]

It was because of this view that Hobbes seems to have equivocated so
often about the status of the laws of nature: 'they are but conclusions, or
theorems concerning what conduceth to the conservation and defence of
[men]; whereas law, properly, is the word of him that by right hath
command over others. But yet if we consider the same theorems, as
delivered in the word of God, that by right commandeth all things; then
are they properly called laws.'[19] On Selden's account, the laws of nature are
equally such 'conclusions, or theorems' – they prescribe what must be
done if we are to avoid suffering, and they have no obligatory force except
in so far as we are frightened of suffering by their neglect. But equally they

[18] Hobbes, *Leviathan*, ed. C. B. Macpherson (Harmondsworth, 1968), pp. 406–7.
[19] *ibid.*, p. 217.

can be seen as 'proper' laws, since there has been a definite decision by a law-maker that we shall suffer if we break them. Our suffering is the consequence of that decision, which could have been different. If God's construction of nature is taken to be a series of similar decisions, then the Hobbesian laws of nature are also 'proper' laws.

Hobbes's theory of obligation, despite its very different consequences, is thus not very different in its overall structure from Selden's: one empirical premiss has disappeared, that we know what we will be punished for after our death. Instead, we simply look at what we are punished for in this life, and act accordingly. Selden's attack on the deontology of the scholastics opened up a space for Hobbes's theory to slip into. Moreover, Hobbes's laws, like Selden's, are necessarily not coeval with mankind: they depend for their recognition, and hence for their force, not on intuition but on historically acquired experience of the natural punishments. This is the significance of another note which Hobbes added to the second edition of *De Cive* explaining what he meant by the 'right reason' by which the laws of nature are found out – 'by right reason in the natural state of men, I understand not, as many do, an infallible faculty, but the act of reasoning, that is, the peculiar and true ratiocination of every man concerning those actions of his, which may either redound to the damage or benefit of his neighbours'.[20] By a comparison of this kind between Selden and Hobbes, we can cut through much of the confusion that has surrounded Hobbes's 'theory of obligation', though we have still not sufficiently met Warrender's main argument, which will be dealt with presently.

But it remains true that in the *Elements* men are supposed to be bound to keep their covenants not to resist the sovereign. How could Hobbes justify this, given the absence of eternal punishment as a relevant feature of the situation? He did so simply by making the claim that if it is rational to *make* a promise, then it is rational to *keep* it: no separate source of obligation is needed.

The law of nature mentioned in the former chapter, sect. 2, namely *That every man should divest himself of the right* [to all things, in order to bring about peace] were utterly vain, and of none effect, if this also were not a law of the same Nature, *That every man is obliged to stand to, and perform, those covenants which he maketh*. For what benefit is it to a man, that any thing be promised, or given unto him, if he that giveth, or promiseth, performeth not, or retaineth still the right of taking back what he hath given? (1.16.1)

This led him into the curious doctrine, perpetuated in *De Cive*, that to break a promise is equivalent to a contradiction: 'he that covenanteth, willeth to do, or omit, in the time to come; and he that doth any action, willeth it at that present, which is part of the future time, contained in the covenant: and therefore he that violateth a covenant, willeth the doing and

[20] Hobbes, *English Works*, II, p. 16.

the not doing of the same thing, at the same time; which is a plain contradiction'. (1.16.2)[21]

The problem about this argument is that it seems to be the wrong way round: a condition of its being rational to make a contract must be the independent expectation that it will be kept. It is true that there is no point in making a promise unless it is kept, but it could be that there is in fact no reason to keep a promise, and hence no point in making it. But by using this argument, Hobbes was able to conclude that it could be rational not to resist: it was rational to promise not to do so since such a promise was a necessary condition of leaving the state of nature, and any promise which it is rational to make, it is rational to keep.

This was clearly an unsatisfactory position to adopt, and Hobbes was hampered even more in his argument by his views on probability. We have seen that the Tew Circle writers explicated the rationality of making a promise of non-resistance in terms of probability calculations: we are less likely to suffer as a consequence of being held to our promise than we are by not making it in the first place. Hobbes was just as idiosyncratic in his relationship to this aspect of the Tew theory as to its other manifestations. Hacking has recently pointed out that Hobbes in the *Elements* clearly had a modern notion of probability[22] – his famous remark that 'experience concludeth nothing universally' was part of an argument that 'though a man have always seen the day and night to follow one another hitherto, yet can he not hence conclude that they should do so . . . If the signs hit twenty times for one missing, a man may lay a wager of twenty to one of the event; but may not conclude it for a truth'. (1.4.10) But the striking feature of Hobbes's argument is not so much that he shared this modern notion of probability with people like Chillingworth, but that he refused to apply it to his political theory. The men in his state of nature are not supposed to make probability calculations; they are supposed to be certain that they are going to be (at the very least) no worse off by making the covenant than they would be by staying in their original position. If certainty of this kind is required, then clearly it is going to be difficult to argue that it can ever be rational to promise not to resist someone else. Hobbes's reluctance to talk about men gambling in the state of nature, despite his firm grasp of the idea of probability calculation, stems from his general epistemology: he wanted to argue both that the laws of nature were learned through experience, and also that they could be presented as deductive conclusions comparable to those of Euclidean geometry, precisely because of his eccentric view of the logical status of geometry.[23]

If this is right, then we must conclude that Hobbes's argument in the

---

[21] Hobbes, *English Works*, II, p. 31.

[22] I. Hacking, *The Emergence of Probability* (Cambridge, 1975), p. 48.

[23] The best recent discussion of this relatively neglected feature of Hobbes's thought is in F. S. McNeilly, *The Anatomy of Leviathan* (London, 1968), especially p. 63.

Elements was simply inconsistent. While he agreed with Selden and the Tew writers about the means whereby a civil society is established, he disagreed fundamentally with them over a number of issues. That being so, we can now see why he moved away from his earlier position and why he took the particular direction that he did. First of all, the Seldenians were happy to talk about a state of total natural freedom: they did not have to link all men's natural rights up to the principle of self-preservation in this world. After all, one of the rights which men enjoyed in the state of nature was precisely the right to renounce their own self-defence. But Hobbes did not believe this, and in any consistent theory would have had to limit man's natural freedom: men could only have the right to do those things that conduced to their own preservation. This explains the move to the more limited account of the state of nature outlined particularly in the notes to *De Cive*, in which Hobbes explicitly denied that men can have a natural right to do anything other than what leads to their own protection.

Secondly, he had to propose a mechanism whereby a sovereign could be erected without his subjects losing their right of self-defence. In *De Cive* he suggested that all that was needed was for the natural men to promise not to assist the enemies of the sovereign – 'the right of punishing is then understood to be given to any one, when every man contract not to assist him who is to be punished'.[24] A great deal of fun was made of this by his opponents; as one of them, Roger Coke, said, 'what power of life or death is here any more, then if a company of Men contract one with another, that they will afford Mr. *Hobbs* no relief, if another man will kill, maim, or punish Mr. *Hobbs*, that then this Man hath power over Mr. *Hobbs* his life and person? and this Right forsooth he will call *gladium justitiae*'.[25] But in fact it would have been no poorer a theory than that of Selden or Digges, had Hobbes not altered his account of the state of nature.

As it was, while such a sovereign in the old theory would have had the unlimited right to do anything to anyone (for all men possessed that right in the state of nature which the ruler had never left), in the new theory all he could possess was the right to defend *himself* – for that was now the only right anyone possessed. And clearly, that was no use if he was to act in the way that sovereigns are normally supposed to. It was almost certainly a consideration of this kind that led Hobbes to drop this proposal, and replace it in *Leviathan* with the famous theory of *authorisation*. According to this, the only way for natural men to erect a sovereign is for them 'to appoint one man, or Assembly of men, to beare their Person; and every one to owne, and acknowledge himselfe to be Author of whatsoever he that so beareth their Person, shall Act, or cause to be Acted, in those things

[24] Hobbes, *English Works*, II, p. 75.
[25] R. Coke: *A Survey of the Politicks of Mr. Thomas White, Mr. Thomas Hobbs, and Mr. Hugo Grotius* (London, 1662), p. 29.

which concerne the Common Peace and Safetie'.[26] As a result, the
sovereign did not simply defend himself: he acted as agent for the defence
of each member of the community, and was thus capable of performing all
the interventionary actions associated with sovereigns.

But although in this area by 1651 Hobbes had developed a consistent
theory, there still remained one major difficulty in his account. This
has caused great confusion among modern scholars, as a result of the
interpretation of *Leviathan* put forward by Professor Warrender. At
the beginning of the discussion of natural law in *Leviathan* occurs
the famous passage distinguishing the right of nature from the law of
nature:

Though they that speak of this subject, use to confound *jus*, and *lex*, *right* and *law*:
yet they ought to be distinguished; because RIGHT, consisteth in liberty to do, or
to forbear: whereas LAW, determineth, and bindeth to one of them: so that law,
and right, differ as much, as obligation, and liberty; which in one and the same
matter are inconsistent.

The right of nature is 'the liberty each man hath, to use his own power, as
he will himself, for the preservation of his own nature'.[27] Now, in the
Elements, just as in the Tew Circle pamphlets or Jeremy Taylor or Selden
himself, this distinction does some real work. Self-preservation is a right
and not a law precisely because a right does not have to be exercised – one is
at 'liberty to do, or to forbear' in the matter. So it makes sense to promise
not to exercise any right. But in *De Cive* or *Leviathan* this is no longer the
case: men are not free *not* to exercise their right of nature, and its status as a
right is therefore questionable.

One of Hobbes's first critics, Sir Robert Filmer, spotted this:

If the right of nature be a liberty for a man to do anything he thinks fit to preserve
his life, then in the first place nature must teach him that life is to be preserved, and
so consequently forbids to do that which may destroy or take away the means of
life, or to omit that by which it may be preserved: and thus the right of nature and
the law of nature will be all one: for I think Mr. Hobbes will not say the right of
nature is a liberty for man to destroy his own life. The law of nature might better
have been said to consist in a command to preserve or not to omit the means of
preserving life, than in a prohibition to destroy, or to omit it.[28]

But it is this discrepancy between the notion of a right as formally defined
by Hobbes and the fact that men are apparently *not* at liberty to forbear to
preserve themselves, which is at the heart of the case argued by Professor
Warrender:

Hobbes describes the fundamental *law* of nature as 'seek peace' and the *right* of
nature as 'defend ourselves'; likewise his precept or general rule of reason is that

[26] Hobbes, *Leviathan*, p. 227.
[27] *ibid.*, p. 189.
[28] R. Filmer, *Patriarcha and other Political Works*, ed. P. Laslett (Oxford, 1949), p. 242.

men *ought to* endeavour peace when it is possible; and when that is impossible that they may use the advantages of war. If self-preservation were meant to be taken as the principal duty of each individual, one would expect Hobbes to have regarded the precept that we should defend ourselves as a law and not a right, and that we *ought to* use the advantages of war where peace is unobtainable. As his words stand, however, the fundamental law of nature is not 'preserve thyself', but 'seek peace', and the further laws of nature are derived from the latter precept ... 'Preserve thyself' plays the part of the supreme motive for the individual but 'seek peace' is his supreme duty.[29]

This distinction between *motive* and *duty* in Hobbes is the gap through which Warrender is able to introduce his theory that the obligation to seek peace must be founded on something other than prudential calculations of self-preservation. I think it would be fair to say that were it not for this distinction, Warrender's case would have very little plausibility. As it is, many of his critics have failed to see the strength of his case, though there are one or two notable exceptions.[30]

But we are now in a position to provide a different account of the discrepancy from Warrender's, without simply ignoring it, as most of his more recent critics in particular have done. In the work in which the distinction between right and law first appeared, there was an important point in regarding self-preservation as a right, since it could be renounced: what we have to explain is thus not why the distinction was developed, but why it was retained into the later works. And here a number of factors become relevant. One of them is of course the fact that Hobbes had already publicly committed himself to treat self-preservation as a right and not a duty; explicitly to change his stand on this issue would have pointed up the oddity of his new position, and might also have laid him open to the sort of attack which the Tew Circle writers launched on Parker. But most importantly, it would also have rendered impossible his account of the state of nature in terms solely of *rights*, upon which the law of nature supervened. Instead, he would have had to postulate a primary law, from which both rights and further laws could be derived – in other words, a more traditional account of the natural state of men. The alterations in fundamental

[29] H. Warrender, *The Political Philosophy of Hobbes* (Oxford, 1957), p. 216.
[30] Thomas Nagel in particular focussed on this aspect of Warrender's case. He rehearsed Hobbes's position on rights and duties, and concluded that it 'appears in fact to be self-contradictory ... I confess that I do not know what is intended, but I do not think that it is possible on this basis to show that Hobbes felt we do not have an obligation to preserve ourselves.' T. Nagel, 'Hobbes's Concept of Obligation', *Philosophical Review*, LXVIII (1959), p. 71. But virtually none of Warrender's other critics (for the most up-to-date list of whom see McNeilly, *Anatomy of Leviathan*, pp. 257–61) have gone into the matter in any detail. Warrender himself replied to Professor Plamenatz's criticism of him by making just this point, which Plamenatz had not dealt with: 'personal self-preservation in Hobbes is not what makes actions obligatory, but what suspends the obligation from actions that would otherwise be obligatory ... personal self-preservation in Hobbes is a right, and not a duty, and so to be distinguished as a principle from the laws of nature'. H. Warrender, 'A Reply to Mr. Plamenatz', in K. C. Brown ed., *Hobbes Studies* (Oxford, 1965), p. 97.

features of his theory that would have been required were so many and so great that it is hardly surprising that he chose to continue treating self-preservation as a right.

If the interpretation of Hobbes which I have been suggesting is correct, then it follows that Sirluck got the relationship between Hobbes and the Tew Circle the wrong way round. The Tew writers developed a consistent theory out of Selden's ideas; Hobbes began along lines similar to theirs, and as a result was left with some awkward features in his theory when he diverged from them. But in some ways, what he did was to draw the logical conclusion from some of Selden's suggestions; his powerful vision proved a constant threat to the 'Seldenian' tradition when it revived in 1660, until what seemed to many to be the death-blow was delivered to it by Pufendorf in 1672.

II

Confirmation of this interpretation of Hobbes comes from the reaction to his later writings, particularly his post-Restoration *Dialogue between a Philosopher and a Student of the Common Laws*. Here too we can see that his ideas never fundamentally diverged from those of Selden's other followers, with embarrassing consequences for the more orthodox of them. To understand this, we must go back to Selden's original account, in his notes on Fortescue, of English legal history in terms of constant change and constant continuity. At the heart of his argument was the image of a ship altered plank by plank at sea – natural laws were originally

> limited for the conveniency of civil society here, and these limitations have been from thence, increased, altered, interpreted, and brought to what now they are; although perhaps, saving the meerly immutable part of nature, now, in regard of their first being, they are not otherwise than the ship, that by often mending had no piece of the first materials, or as the house that's so often repaired, *ut nihil ex pristina materia supersit* . . .[31]

As we saw earlier, in its acceptance of change in English legal history, this view developed from the standard attitude of late sixteenth- and early seventeenth-century common lawyers, but in the systematic account it gave of such change, and the full awareness that it was no argument against the laws of England, Selden's note was highly original.

Two people in particular, Matthew Hale and John Vaughan, developed Selden's ideas on the law in the years after 1660. It was Selden's picture of English legal history which Hale enlarged upon in his justly famous *History of the Common Law*, published posthumously in 1713 (Hale died in 1676). His relationship to Selden is much clearer than his relationship to Coke, though both his major recent commentators, Pocock and Gray,

---

[31] See above p. 84.

have wanted to associate him primarily with Coke.[32] Hale even borrowed Selden's imagery:

Use and Custom, and Judicial Decisions and Resolutions, and Acts of Parliament, tho' not now extant, might introduce some *New* Laws, and alter some *Old*, which we now take to be the very Common Law itself, tho' the Times and precise Periods of such Alterations are not explicitly or clearly known: But tho' those particular Variations and Accessions have happened in the Laws, yet they being only partial and successive, we may with just Reason say, They are the same English Laws now, that they were 600 Years since in the general. As the Argonauts Ship was the same when it returned home, as it was when it went out, tho' in that Long Voyage it had successive Amendments, and scarce came back with any of its former Materials; and as Titius is the same Man he was 40 Years since, tho' Physicians tell us, That in a Tract of seven Years, the Body has scarce any of the same Material Substance it had before.[33]

He was clear that the reason for these changes was the constant attempt by law-makers to adjust to new circumstances, and that as a consequence it was a fruitless task to sort out the history of the English law; different parts had been introduced at different times, and the knowledge of the actual occasions could well now be lost.

Pocock has taken this picture of a constant change to have arisen from the idea of the English law as custom,

or rather from that aspect of the idea of custom which emphasizes its universality and anonymity, the myriad minds who, not knowing the importance of what they do, have, each by responding to the circumstances in which he finds himself, contributed to build up a law which is the sum total of society's response to the vicissitudes of its history and will be insensibly modified tomorrow by fresh responses to fresh circumstances.[34]

But we need to make a distinction here in order to understand what both Hale and Vaughan thought. Pocock slides from talking (in the context of Hale) about the constant change and adaptation of law to new circumstances, to talking about *custom*, that is, the creation of law without the deliberate decision of a law-making authority. (It is for this reason above all that he wants to associate Hale with Coke, who undoubtedly did want to protect the common law from such an authority.) But this is not a necessary transition – after all, modern law is constantly being changed and adapted, but it is not at all a customary law. And it is precisely that transition which Hale and Vaughan were in fact rather unwilling to make.

Hale's remarks on this subject in his *History* need to be read in the light of the closely parallel remarks of Vaughan in some of his judgements. The

---

[32] See J. G. A. Pocock, *The Ancient Constitution and the Feudal Law* (Cambridge, 1957), p. 173; M. Hale, *The History of the Common Law of England*, ed. C. M. Gray (Chicago, 1971), pp. xxi ff.

[33] Hale, *History*, p. 40.

[34] Pocock, *Ancient Constitution*, p. 173.

important passages in Hale's *History* are in chapter IV, where he distinguishes between three 'formal Constituents' of the Common Law: common usage or custom, the authority of Parliament, and judicial decisions. But one cannot take it for granted that these three formal constituents are all alternative ways of making the common law. Hale specifically ruled this out in the case of the third:

It is true, the Decisions of Courts of Justice, tho' by Virtue of the Laws of this Realm they do bind, as a Law between the Parties thereto, as to the particular Case in Question, 'till revers'd by Error or Attaint, yet they do not make a Law properly so called, (for that only the King and Parliament can do); yet they have a great Weight and Authority in Expounding, Declaring, and Publishing what the Law of this Kingdom is.[35]

This suggests that the formal constituents could simply be the various ways in which the common law could be *known*, rather than *made* – precisely the distinction which seems to have exercised Hale. On the other two constituents, he remarked first that 'Usage and Custom generally receiv'd, do *Obtinere vim Legis* . . . And if it be enquired, What is the Evidence of this Custom, or wherein it consists, or is to be found? I answer, It is not simply an unwritten Custom, not barely *Orally* deriv'd down from one Age to another; but it is a Custom that is deriv'd down in Writing . . .'[36] But it is his remarks on the role of Parliament which are most interesting:

We are to know, that although the Original or Authentick Transcripts of Acts of Parliament are not before the Time of Hen. 3. and many that were in his Time are perish'd and lost; yet certainly such there were, and many of those Things that we now take for Common Law, were undoubtedly Acts of Parliament, tho' now not to be found of Record. And if in the next Age, the Statutes made in the Time of Hen. 3. and Edw. 1. were lost, yet even those would pass for Parts of the Common Law, and indeed, by long Usage and the many Resolutions grounded upon them, and by their great Antiquity, they seem even already to be incorporated with the very Common Law . . . Those Constitutions and Laws being made before Time of Memory, do now obtain, and are taken as Part of the Common Law and immemorial Customs of the Kingdom; and so they ought now to be esteem'd tho' in their first Original they were Acts of Parliament.[37]

Here, Hale seems to have assimilated the first and second constituents: an unspecified proportion of the customs were in fact Acts of Parliament, that is, decisions by a clear and precise authority, which had simply continued in force for so long that lawyers ceased to refer to them as specific enactments. Hale was not entirely clear about the status of the customs which did not have this origin; Vaughan, characteristically, was much harder headed. In the case of *Edward Thomas* v. *Thomas Sorrell*, in 1667, he observed,

many things are said to be *prohibited* by the *Common Law*, and indeed most things *so prohibited* were primarily *prohibited* by *Parliament*, or by a Power equivalent to it in

[35] Hale, *History*, p. 45.
[36] *ibid.*, p. 44.
[37] *ibid.*, p. 44–5.

making Laws, which is the same, but are said to be *prohibited* by the *Common Law*, because the Original of the *Constitution* or *prohibiting Law* is not to be found of *Record*, but is beyond memory, and the.Law known onely from practical proceeding and usage in *Courts of Justice*, as may appear by *Laws* made in the time of the *Saxon* Kings, of *William the First*, and *Henry the First*, yet extant in *History*, which are now received as *Common Law*. So if by accident the *Records* of all *Acts of Parliament* now extant, none of which is older than 9 H. 3. (but new Laws were as frequent before as since) should be destroyed by fire, or other casualty, the memorials of proceeding upon them found by the *Records* in Judicial proceeding, would upon like reason be accounted *Common Law* by *Posterity*.[38]

And in the case of *Edmund Sheppard* v. *George Gosnold*, in 1672, which turned on the status of the ancient customs chargeable upon imports and exports, Vaughan argued that they were originally due by an Act of Parliament (now lost) of Edward I. But he remarked:

Nor is it a true Inference, That if the *Antiquae Custumae* were at *Common Law* (as every thing in one sense is taken for *Common Law*, if it be Law, when it appears not to be by *Act of Parliament*) therefore it was by *Arbitrary Imposition* of the King, for it might be by *Act of Parliament* not extant, as this of 3 E. 1. and in truth, most of the *Common Law* cannot be conceived to be Law otherwise than by *Acts of Parliament*, or *Power equivalent* to them, whereof the *Rolls* are lost; for alwaies there was a power and practise of making new Laws.[39]

Both Hale and Vaughan thus viewed the common law as possibly the creation of past Parliaments, or their equivalent (whatever Vaughan may have intended by that expression). If it was such a creation, then it was clearly not custom in Coke's (or Pocock's) sense; it was quite compatible even with a Hobbesian view of sovereignty, provided that the Hobbesian sovereign was taken to be Parliament. Neither Hale nor Vaughan were particularly worried about the uncertainty over the history of Parliament: the debates over the origin of the Commons which Pocock has traced were of course not debates over the antiquity of Parliament itself. Many people throughout the late sixteenth and seventeenth centuries (including Dodderidge, Selden and Spelman) could believe both that some kind of Parliament had been a continuous feature of the English constitution, and that the Commons had not always been part of it.[40]

It is worth remembering at this point Aubrey's reminiscences of how he got Hobbes to write his *Dialogue between a Philosopher and a Student of the Common Laws*, and how it was received. Some time after 1664 Hobbes yielded to Aubrey's persuasion, and wrote the *Dialogue* after studying Bacon's *Elements of Law*. 'He drives on, in this, the King's Prerogative high. Judge Hales, who is no great Courtier, has read it and much mislikes it, and is his enemy. Judge Vaughan has perused it and very much

[38] *Reports and Arguments*, ed. E. Vaughan (London, 1677), p. 358.
[39] *ibid.*, p. 163.
[40] For Dodderidge, see *A Collection of Curious Discourses*, i, ed. T. Hearne (London, 1771), p. 283; for Selden see his *Opera Omnia*, ii, ed. D. Wilkins (London, 1726), cols. 1026-7; for Spelman, see *Reliquiae Spelmannianae* (London, 1723), pp. 57-66.

commends it, but is afraid to license it for feare of giving displeasure.'[41]
Aubrey's remarks about people's reactions to each other are often the most
misleading parts of his reminiscences, but it is clear that Hale felt much
more strongly about the *Dialogue* than Vaughan. But it is also clear that in
their ideas on the status of the common law, Hale and Vaughan did not
diverge a great deal from each other – it was rather that Hale was prepared
to accept a greater degree of unclarity. This should prompt us to read
Hale's well-known attack on the *Dialogue* with some caution: what did
Hale actually criticise in Hobbes's argument? Was there a fundamental
difference between them?

To answer this, we have first to consider the arguments of the *Dialogue*,
which have often been misunderstood (though less so by its most recent
commentator, Joseph Cropsey). The Philosopher in the *Dialogue* accepted
the Lawyer's distinction between the common law and statute law, and
also the description proferred by the Lawyer (explicitly following Coke)
of the common law as the law of reason. He gave a general Hobbesian
account of law – 'I grant you that the knowledge of the Law is an Art, but
not that any Art of one Man, or of many how wise soever they be, or the
work of one or more Artificers, how perfect soever it be, is Law. It is not
Wisdom, but Authority that makes a Law . . .'[42] – but this was intended to
apply to both common and statute law, and not to undermine the distinction. Hobbes had after all argued just this about the law of nature itself, so
the Philosopher could accept the Lawyer's point about the common law
being the law of reason in a way that statute law was not. He continued (in
the passage which was the occasion for the first half of Hale's critique),

'Tis very true; and upon this ground, if I pretend within a Month or two to make
my self to perform the Office of a Judge, you are not to think it Arrogance; for you
are to allow to me, as well as to other Men, my pretence to Reason, which is the
Common Law (remember this that I may not need again to put you in mind, that
Reason is the Common Law) and for Statute Law, seeing it is Printed, and that
there be Indexes to point me to every matter contained in them, I think a Man may
profit in them very much in two Months.[43]

Hale's response to this was by no means to come to Coke's defence in a
straightforward way. His repudiation of Hobbes in fact rested more on a
rejection of the distinction between common and statute law – a rejection
that we should expect, given what we have seen of his theory of the
common law's origins. He had to establish against Hobbes the conven-
tionality and arbitrariness of the common law, such that it was not accessible to an untrained, natural reason, and he did so by arguing in the
following kind of way:

[41] Aubrey, *Brief Lives*, I, p. 394; see also pp. 341–2.
[42] Hobbes, *A Dialogue between a Philosopher and a Student of the Common Laws of England*, ed. J. Cropsey (Chicago, 1971), p. 55.
[43] *ibid.*, p. 56.

It is a part of the Law of England that all the Lands descend to the eldest Sonne without a particular Custome altering it. That a Freehold passeth not without Livery and Seisin, or Attornement by an Act in Paijs. But where Statutes have altered, then an Estate made by Deed to a Man for ever passeth only for life without the word Heires and Infinite more of this kind. Now if any the most refined Braine under heaven would goe about to Enquire by Speculation, or by reading of Plato and Aristotle, or by Considering the Laws of the Jewes, or other Nations, to find out how Lands descend in England, or how Estates are there transferred, or transmitted among us, he would lose his Labour, and Spend his Notions in vaine, till he acquainted himselfe with the Lawes of England, and the reason is because they are Institutions introduced by the will and Consent of others implicitely by Custome and usage, or Explicitely by written Laws or Acts of Parliament.[44]

Hale's case was that whether one took the laws to be introduced by custom or statute (and he did not here enlarge on the difference between the two modes), they would appear arbitrary to a contemporary student, as the various occasions for their introduction had now been forgotten – the same point which he made in his *History*. It did not follow, he was at pains to emphasise, that such laws were now out of date or unjustifiable: the rational procedure was to assume that their original purpose still held good, even if no adequate historical account of it could now be given. It is this element in his argument which looks extremely Burkean, and which has led Pocock to think that Hale was putting forward a theory of the gradual and insensible modification of the common law through the decisions of innumerable private individuals;[45] but as we have already seen, that is an unfounded extension of Hale's more limited point. Hale's case is in fact perfectly compatible with a complete denial of the genuinely customary status of the common law, which Pocock takes to be the characteristic position of Hobbes. The reason why in Hale's theory we should not only obey but take as prudentially justified five hundred year old *statutes* was exactly the same as the reason why we should treat six hundred year old *customs* in the same way.

Hale's objection to the second part of the *Dialogue* was similarly compatible with at least some of Hobbes's premises. Hobbes argued in the second and subsequent sections that the king of England was a genuinely Hobbesian sovereign, with the right and duty if he thought the common interest demanded it of taking his subject's goods without their consent. The justification for this was of course general considerations of what it was rational for a sovereign to do, and those same considerations (he believed) would generally lead a sovereign to consult with his subjects in something like a Parliament before issuing laws or demanding taxation. But that was a prudential constraint, and therefore to be disregarded in cases of need, such as a military emergency.

[44] *Reflections ... on Mr. Hobbes His Dialogue of the Law*, printed as Appendix III to W. Holdworth, *History of English Law*, V (London, 1924), p. 505.
[45] Pocock, *Ancient Constitution*, p. 173.

Hale's reply to this consisted firstly of a discussion of what the law of England actually was, which he intended as a demonstration that the king was not allocated such powers. But secondly he tried to justify the limitations on the king, and he used two arguments to do so. The first was that a long succession of kings had promised to be so bound, and 'tho' it is true that the Kinges Person is Sacred, and not under any Externall Coertion, nor to be arraigned by his Subjects for the violation of that Sacred Oath yett no man can make a Question whether he be not in the Sight of God and by the bond of Naturall Justice oblidged to keepe itt'.[46] In other words, he was employing the characteristic Seldenian argument against Hobbes, about the obligation to keep any promises; but with a surprising degree of diffidence and qualification. More important to his case was a set of prudential arguments, based on the clearly Hobbesian (though also, of course, Seldenian – as shown in Hammond's works) principle of the relationship between protection and obedience.

The greate happiness of any Government rests Principally in this, namely the Mutuall Confidence that the Governours have in the people as to point of Duty and obedience and that the Governed have in their Governours as to point of Protection, and to Secure this mutuall Confidence was that Ancient and Solemne Institution of Oath of Fidelity of the People to the Prince and of Preotection and upholding their first Liberties & Laws by the Prince to the People. And the first breach that happens in this Golden Knott as by miserable Experience we have learned, [is when it comes to be believed that] the Prince is bound to keepe none of the Lawes that he or his Ancestours have by the advice of his great Councill Established that he may repeale them when he sees cause. That all his Subjects Properties depend upon his Pleasure [etc.].[47]

Against the claim that it might be necessary for a sovereign to act in this way, he made simple empirical points – 'this is but an imaginary feare as appeares by Experience. For this Kingdome hath been now these 500 yeares govern'd by Laws made by Parliamentary advise and noe time yett affords us an Instance wherein a Parliament might not be timely Enough called for such a Supply ...'[48]

It is clear from this that Hale was not in fact putting forward a radically different theory as an alternative to Hobbes's: many of his premises were similar to Hobbes's, and what was at stake was the kind of conclusions to be drawn from them. Hobbes himself, as Cropsey has pointed out, provided one of his least outrageous accounts of government in the *Dialogue*.[49] It is not therefore particularly surprising that someone like Vaughan, who did not have very different views from Hale's in this area, should have admired the work. This is not to say, of course, that Hale did not genuinely

[46] Hale, *Reflections*, p. 511.
[47] *ibid.*
[48] *ibid.*, p. 512.
[49] Hobbes, *Dialogue*, pp. 9–10, 48.

feel strongly about it: the difference between his ideas on the actual
constitution and Hobbes's was sufficient to make the attack very necessary. But this difference should not be seen as based on the kind of fundamental divergence which Pocock (for example) has suggested.

III

So far, the particular theory put forward by Hobbes has appeared rather
isolated: in England, men who were attracted to this new way of looking at
politics seem to have gone (as we have seen) for Selden's version of it.
There was no one like Taylor or Vaughan to put forward a genuinely
Hobbesian point of view, as I have diagnosed it, in the 1650s or 1660s. The
one country where Hobbes's arguments as set out in *De Cive* or *Leviathan*
rather than the *Elements* attracted support as well as abuse was Holland.
There a whole series of writers, mostly associated with the liberal republican and anti-clericalist regime of the De Witts, produced works
endorsing and utilising at least some of Hobbes's ideas, and in the process
revealing some of the differences between Hobbes and the Seldenians.

The first person to do so was Lambert Velthuysen, who in 1651 published an *Epistolica Dissertatio de Principiis Justi et Decori* in which he
defended his version of Hobbes's theory against an anonymous critic with
whom he had recently been in correspondence. Velthuysen later became
one of the political commissaries appointed by the Utrecht city council to
attend the meetings of the church consistory, and achieved fame as an
enthusiastic opponent of ecclesiastical power.[50] His ideas are perhaps best
summed up in a work belonging to this period, *Tractatus de Poena Divina et
Humana* of 1664. In this he argued that the right to punish derived from the
right of self-defence, along orthodox Hobbesian lines; but he departed
from them when he interpreted that right as derived from our knowledge
of God's purposes. It is clear (he argued) from a consideration of our
biological make-up and our passions, that self-preservation is the prime
function of the organism, and such a biological fact carries moral over-
tones when we recognise God's design in it.[51]

This kind of interpretation of the right of self-defence was in fact
common to all the Dutch Hobbesians that we shall be looking at, and was
associated with another of their common features, their Cartesianism.[52]
Although Hobbes and Descartes had been very critical of each other, there
was in Descartes's *Passions de l'Ame* (published in 1649) material for a

[50] For Velthuysen, see E. H. Kossmann, *Politieke Theorie in het Zeventiende-eeuwse Nederland*,
Verh. der K. Ned. Akad. v. Wet., Afd. Lett. N.R., LXVII, No. 2 (Amsterdam, 1960), pp.
34–6; see also P. Geyl, *The Netherlands in the Seventeenth Century*, II (London, 1964), p. 115.
[51] See his *Opera Omnia*, I (Rotterdam, 1680), pp. 54–75.
[52] See C. L. Thijssen-Schoute, *Nederlands Cartesianisme*, Verh. der K. Ned. Akad. v. Wet.,
Afd. Lett. N.R., LX (Amsterdam, 1954).

psychological theory which could easily be adapted to Hobbes's developed political ideas. In particular, there was the claim that 'the customary mode of action of all the passions is simply this, that they dispose the soul to desire those things which nature tells us are of use, and to persist in this desire, and also bring about that same agitation of spirits which customarily causes them to dispose the body to the movement which serves for the carrying into effect of those things.'[53] In Descartes, of course, this view of man's psychology was associated with a strong and very un-Hobbesian emphasis on his free will – man could control his passions and distinguish between their effective working and their harmful excess. But this in some ways made the task of linking Cartesian psychology to Hobbesian politics rather easier, for it allowed these Dutch Hobbesians to exploit Hobbes's point that the law of nature did not permit *everything possible*, but rather whatever was thought to be necessary to self-preservation (and in the process to reveal that this distinction was fully apparent to contemporary readers).

Thus Velthuysen argued that in a state of nature all men are judges of their own interests; in civil society the right to decide on such matters is transferred to the sovereign, and resistance to him is forbidden not because 'from subjection to a magistrate arises more right to inflict harm than individuals possess in a state of nature', but because 'the defendant is convicted in his conscience, and recognises that he has perpetrated a crime because of which his neighbour, or rather his *judge*, rightly expects vengeance in the public interest. And indeed even in the state of *nature* no one can resist their neighbour without sin, if their conscience tells them that he has been treated by them in an unworthy way, with cruelty, avarice or other vices ...'[54] This is of course far more extreme than anything Hobbes ever said, though it is implied by his note to 1.10 of *De Cive*. It is also, it must be said, a more extreme argument than these Dutch writers usually put forward: in general, they insisted that one was always justified in preserving oneself, but one was not always justified in doing more than that, even in a state of nature. And they were able to combine this with their Cartesianism precisely because Descartes provided the psychological explanation of how men could refrain from doing whatever they had an impulse towards, and how they should restrict their activities to those things that were genuinely beneficial.

In addition to Velthuysen, we find the same kind of points being made by

[53] Descartes, *Philosophical Works*, I, ed. E. S. Haldane and G. R. T. Ross (Cambridge, 1931), p. 358.
[54] 'ex subjectione Magistratui jus magis [non] nascitur ad infligendum malum, quam singuli habent in statu *naturali* ... reus in conscientia convictus, agnoscit se ea perpetrasse, propter quae proximus, vel dicam potius *iudex*, merito ad salutem reipublicae tuendam expetit vindictam. Et certe in statu *naturali* etiam nulli licet sine peccato resistere proximo, si conscientia ipsum arguet se concedentem crudelitati, avaritiae aut aliis vitiis, proximum indignis accepisse modis.' Velthuysen, *Opera*, I, p. 72.

the pseudonymous 'Lucius Antistes Constans' in his *De Jure Ecclesiasticorum* (1665) – a work which drew more explicitly than any other the anti-clerical implications of the theory, and which enjoyed a European reputation (the Earl of Shaftesbury is known to have possessed a copy)[55] – and most interestingly in the *Consideratien van Staat ofte Polityke Weeg-Schaal* (1661) of Johann de la Court (or, in Dutch, van Hove). The interest of de la Court's work is that while he argued in general very like Velthuysen, stressing that it was possible in a state of nature to break the law of nature,[56] and being if anything even more explicit in his use of a Cartesian psychology, he combined this with a Machiavellian political science.

It is notorious that Descartes and the early French Cartesians had no proper political theory – their ethics were entirely a nosology of an individual's emotions and a set of recommendations for coping with them. The one political theory they were interested in was Machiavelli's (though even then it was not a very deep interest), for Machiavelli portrayed politics as the public arena of the passions, and political techniques as based on a correct understanding of how those passions could be manipulated.[57] De la Court was the first person to marry this aspect of Cartesianism to Hobbesianism: the men in his state of nature were deemed to be capable of making Machiavellian calculations about what constitutions and social arrangements were likely to utilise and control their passions in such a way that the community benefited, and the conclusions they came to were taken to be those of the *Discorsi* – the republican regime of active citizens.[58]

It is with this group of writers that the most famous Dutch political theorist of the period, Benedict de Spinoza, is usually associated. He corresponded with Velthuysen (though on the basis of mutual opposition) and is known to have been deeply influenced by the 'political scientific' sections of the *Polityke Weeg-Schaal*. The book by 'Constans' was attributed to him by contemporaries, though he denied its authorship. He himself displayed the same kind of interest in Machiavelli as de la Court, and his relationship with Descartes, though complex and certainly not one of straightforward influence, is vital to any understanding of his work. And yet there is a striking and neglected fact about Spinoza, which is that a substantial part of his theory looks more like that of the *early* Hobbes or the Seldenians than like that of *De Cive*.

It is well known that he differed from the later Hobbes over the question of whether the law of nature permits *anything*: as he said, 'the right and law

[55] K. H. D. Haley, *The First Earl of Shaftesbury* (Oxford, 1968), p. 219.
[56] See W. Roed, 'Van den Hoves "Politische Waage" und die Modifikation der Hobbesschen Staatsphilosophie bei Spinoza', *Journal of the History of Philosophy*, VIII (1970), p. 37. See also Kossmann, *Politieke Theorie*, pp. 36–50.
[57] See G. Rodis-Lewis, *La Morale de Descartes* (Paris, 1957), pp. 100–5.
[58] This Dutch Machiavellianism and its links with later economic theory (as suggested by de la Court's brother Pieter's *Interest van Holland*) badly needs a good treatment; it is unfortunate that Pocock chose not to discuss it in his *The Machiavellian Moment* (Princeton, 1975), for it might have thrown a different light on some of his conclusions.

of nature, under which all are born and for the most part live, forbids nothing save what nobody desires and nobody can do: it forbids neither strife, nor hatred, nor anger, nor deceit; in short, it is opposed to nothing that appetite can suggest'.[59] The only contemporaries who said anything like this were men such as Jeremy Taylor:

Whatever we naturally desire, naturally we are permitted to. For natures are equal, and the capacities are the same, and the desires alike; and it were a contradiction to say that *naturally* we are restrained from any thing to which we *naturally* tend. Therefore to save my own life, I can kill another, or twenty, or a hundred, or take from his hands to please my self, if it happens in my circumstances and power; and so for *eating*, and *drinking*, and *pleasures*

or John Vaughan:

it is evident that nothing which *actually* is, can be said to be *unnatural*, for Nature is but the production of effects from causes sufficient to produce them ... so no *Copulation* of any man with any woman, nor an effect of that *Copulation* by *Generation*, can be said *unnatural*; for if it were, it could not be, and if it be, it had a sufficient cause.[60]

Clearly, no one could suppose that Spinoza had read either Taylor or Vaughan. But their basic theory was available to him in two places. One was Hobbes's *Elements of Law*, published in French (which he could read) in 1652, but the other was Selden's *De Jure Naturali et Gentium juxta disciplinam Ebraeorum* itself – a work which was likely to be particularly attractive to a Jew. This can be no more than conjecture, and it is equally probable that Spinoza simply converged on the same kind of theory as the Seldenians from his very different and idiosyncratic metaphysics; given the absence of references to any influences or analogous arguments which is so notorious a feature of Spinoza's work, we can say little more.[61] But it is certainly plausible to see Spinoza not against a background solely of Hobbes and Descartes, as has been customary, but against the more complicated background I have depicted, in which Hobbes had his rivals; and not all the positions which seem superficially to derive from *Leviathan* or *De Cive* did indeed do so.

[59] 'jus et institutum naturae, sub quo omnes nascuntur et maxima ex parte vivunt, nihil nisi quod nemo cupit et quod nemo potest prohibere; non contentiones, non odia, non iram, non dolos, nec absolute aliquid quod appetitus suadet aversari.' Spinoza, *Works*, pp. 126–7; see also pp. 15–16.

[60] See above pp. 111, 114.

[61] He did not possess a copy of either work at his death – see the probate inventory in J. Freudenthal, *Die Lebensgeschichte Spinoza's* (Leipzig, 1899), pp. 160–4. See also pp. 203–4.

7
The Radical Theory

The years 1640–3 saw not only the publication of the major works in the conservative natural rights tradition, but also the appearance of a rival way of talking about natural rights. As we saw in Chapter Three, Grotius provided the basic language for both traditions: the conservatives drew on the central idea of free men being capable of renouncing their freedom, while the radicals drew on the (in Grotius, more peripheral) idea of interpretative charity applied to fundamental political agreements. Radicalism of this kind seems in the present state of our knowledge to have been at this time an exclusively English phenomenon: some Dutch lawyers took up Grotius's remarks in the *Inleidinghe* about inalienable liberty and used them to attack slavery,[1] but no Dutchmen before the 1650s seem to have used the rather different and much more general arguments of the *De Iure Belli*.

It must be stressed that while the principle of interpretative charity led directly to the notion of 'inalienable rights', the radicals never abandoned the basic rights theory common to both traditions. *Logically*, according to both, it is possible for free men to renounce all their natural rights; but charity, according to the radicals, requires that we assume that they have not done so. We must presume that our predecessors were rational, and hence that they could not have intended to leave us totally bereft of our rights. This is the argument that Grotius had used to defend the pos-sibilities of resistance and common ownership *in extremis*, and it is the argument that was to occur year after year in the pamphlets of the English radicals, sometimes with direct references to Grotius. There is no reason to suppose that anyone using this argument had to have read Grotius: inter-pretative charity is an obvious principle to use in order to modify a strong rights theory, and once the language of natural rights became sufficiently common it was likely to be developed independently of Grotius. On the

---

[1] See in particular Simon van Groenewegen van der Made, *Tractatus de Ligibus Abrogatis* (Leiden, 1649), on *Institutes* 1.1.8 (2nd edn Nijmegen, 1664, p. 5). For a discussion of the influence of both the *Inleidinghe* and *De Iure Belli* on Arnold Vinnius, greatest of the mid-century Dutch lawyers, see R. Feenstra and C. J. D. Waal, *Seventeenth-Century Leyden Law Professors and their Influence on the Development of the Civil Law*, Verh. der K. Ned. Akad. v. Wet., Afd. Lett. N.R. xc (Amsterdam, 1975), p. 30.

other hand, there is good evidence that many of the more important radical theorists had indeed read the *De Iure Belli*.

At the beginning of the English civil war, the work of ideological opposition to the King was still done (largely) by the radical Calvinism of the sixteenth century and its derivatives. Throughout the revolutionary period, Calvinist Presbyterians continued to provide an ideology of opposition which must be distinguished from that of the radical natural rights theorists if we are to understand the latters' ideas.

The sixteenth-century Calvinists (as I argued in Chapter 2) had fused the insights of juridical humanism with their own strong sense of the divine, non-natural character of political association, and their seventeenth-century successors kept to this. We can see in all the great works produced by Presbyterians in the 1640s and 1650s – such as Samuel Rutherford's *Lex, Rex* (1644), Philip Hunton's *A Treatise of Monarchy* (1643), Edward Gee's *The Divine Right and Originall of the Civill Magistrate* (1658) and George Lawson's *Politica Sacra et Civilis* (1660) – that they wished to combine a stress on the need for consent with a reluctance to construe magisterial power as *constituted* by individuals promising not to exercise their natural rights.

This second point is the more important, and is embodied in the constant distinction the Presbyterian consent theorists drew between the origin of government and its determination into a particular person or institution. Gee put the distinction as well as anyone:

Gods derivation of authority to men must needs import two things.
1. His institution of authority in the general, with the several species of it, as conjugal, parental, herile, magistraticall.
2. His communicating, conferring or conveying that power, which he hath so instituted to be, to particular persons. There must be this latter as well as the former to the real & actual constituting of an authority, or putting it into existence. Gods ordaining at the first the conjugal, parental, herile, and political power, that is, his appointing that the husband, parent, master, or prince shall have authority over their respective correlatives (suppose by those words of the commandment, *Honour thy Father*, &c.) doth not of it self put any of those authorities in being, or in one person more than another; or it makes no man a husband, father, master, or Prince.[2]

This, as the royalists were fond of pointing out, may seem a distinction without a difference, but it was at the heart of the Presbyterian cause. While the natural rights theorists from Grotius onwards believed that any form of *dominium* was constituted by a transfer by humans of their own natural rights of *dominium* over themselves and alien objects, the Presbyterians believed that the developed social forms of *dominium* were constituted by God as correlatives of his commandments, and in particular the commandments to punish evildoers and to honour parents. As Lawson

[2] E. Gee, *The Divine Right and Originall of the Civill Magistrate from God* (London, 1658), pp. 33–4.

said, '*The fundamentall Charter of all civil Majestie, is the fifth Commandment*, taken in a large sense, and understood by other Scriptures, which speak more expressly and distinctly of civil Government.'[3] Or as Hunton said, 'It is Gods expresse Ordinance, that in the societies of Mankind, there should be a Magistracie or Government. At first when there were but two, God ordeyned it, Gen. 3. 16.'[4] Even Rutherford, who came as close as any of this group to the natural rights theorists, accepted that the power of government was a separate kind of thing, given by God to mankind and not created by them through transfers of right – 'God and nature intendeth the policie and peace of mankinde, then must God and nature have given to mankinde, a power to compasse this end; and this must be a power of *Government*.'[5]

But – and here was the crucial point of difference between the Presbyterians and their royalist opponents – men had to be seen as free either not to have some of these kinds of power among them, or to decide on who should exercise them. To that extent, civil society could be seen as the artificial construct of consenting individuals: as Lawson said, from the union of individuals 'ariseth a communion and participation in some things which agree and belong unto the whole body as a body. This union doth not arise merely from some accident or cohabitation, or natural instinct, but from a rational and just consent, *ex juris consensu*, saith *Cicero*.'[6] A good analogy might be with the polluting effect of power stations. Men can decide whether to have such power stations, and where to put them, given what they know about their effects; but the nature of their effect on the environment is beyond the scope of human decision. Rutherford put it very neatly:

The question is, Whether the Kingly Office it self come from God; I conceive it is, and floweth from the people, not by formall institution; as if the people had by an act of reason, devised and excogitated such a power: God ordained the power; it is from the people onely by a virtuall emanation, in respect that a community having no Government at all, may ordain a King, or appoint an Aristocracie.[7]

There was sufficient room for debate over this question to allow for the production of vast quantities of pamphlets by Presbyterians and royalists; but because the Presbyterians in the 1640s and 1650s never abandoned the idea of the special, divine origin of governmental *dominium*, they lie outside the area of natural rights theories proper.

At the same time as the Presbyterians were expounding these kinds of ideas, the men who actually made the revolution of 1649 had enlisted in their support a very different group of theorists. As early as 1642 we can find a radical natural rights theory being put forward, and the beginning of

[3] G. Lawson, *Politica Sacra & Civilis* (London, 1660), p. 45.
[4] [P. Hunton], *A Treatise of Monarchie* (London, 1643), sig. B1v.
[5] [S. Rutherford], *Lex, Rex* (London, 1644), sig. B1v.
[6] Lawson, *Politica*, p. 10.
[7] Rutherford, *Lex. Rex*, sig. C1.

an open debate between the two kinds of rights theorists. The important work here is Henry Parker's justly famous *Observations* of July 1642 – perhaps the most influential pamphlet of the entire civil war. Parker was a lawyer who was undoubtedly acquainted with the *De Iure Belli*,[8] and who may have been aware of the Seldenian arguments: the *Observations* immediately became one of the prime targets of the Tew Circle. In order to refute any claims to absolute power, Parker used a combination of the principle of interpretative charity and the traditional idea of the natural *duty* of self-defence in order to argue that a people must always have reserved rights to itself in any bargain with its sovereign.

> Though all Monarchies are not subiect to the same conditions, yet there scarse is any Monarchy but is subiect to some conditions, and I thinke to the most absolute Empire in the world this condition is most naturall and necessary, That the safetie of the people is to bee valued above any right of his, as much as the end is to bee preferred before the meanes; it is not just nor possible for any nation so to enslave it selfe, and to resigne its owne interest to the will of one Lord, as that that Lord may destroy it without injury, and yet to have no right to preserve it selfe: For since all naturall power is in those which obay, they which contract to obey to their own ruine, or having so contracted, they which esteeme such a contract before their owne preservation are felonious to themselves, and rebellious to nature.[9]

To explicate the relationship between sovereign and people, he used the notion of a *trust*:

> I conceive it is now sufficiently cleared, that all rule is but fiduciarie, and that this and that Prince is more or lesse absolute, as he is more or lesse trusted, and that all trusts differ not in nature or intent, but in degree only and extent: and therefore since it is unnaturall for any Nation to give away its owne proprietie in it selfe absolutely, and to subject it selfe to a condition of servilitie below men, because this is contrarie to the supreme of all Lawes, wee must not think that it can stand with the intent of any trust, that necessarie defence should be barred, and naturall preservation denied to any people.[10]

The idea that the King was entrusted with his power had first been employed in a pamphlet of the preceding April,[11] and had been bitterly attacked by those members of the Tew Circle who counselled Charles. In a royal declaration penned by Hyde in June, he tried to give a Seldenian interpretation of the trust between king and people: Power was 'irrecoverably committed to his majesty, and his heirs for ever': 'might any thing be taken from a man, because he is trusted with it? Nay, may the person

---

[8] Though he does not quote him directly until 1644; see below, p. 147. A good study of Parker is still needed. Until one appears, see W. K. Jordan, *Men of Substance* (Chicago, 1942), and M. A. Judson, 'Henry Parker and the Theory of Parliamentary Sovereignty', *Essays in Honor of C. H. McIlwain* (Cambridge Mass., 1936). See also my 'Power and Authority in Seventeenth-Century England', *Historical Journal*, xvii (1974).

[9] [H. Parker], *Observations upon Some of His Majesties Late Answers and Expresses* (London, 1642), 2nd edn, sig. A4v.

[10] *ibid.*, sig. C2v.

[11] *A Question Answered: How Laws are to be Understood, and Obedience Yeelded*, reprinted in J. Rushworth, *Historical Collections*, iv (London, 1721), pp. 542–3.

himself take away the thing he trusts, when he will, and in what manner he will?'[12] But the advantage of the notion of a trust for the radicals was precisely that it was difficult to interpret in this way: it was not the case that anything entrusted was irrecoverably lost, for that was exactly the distinction between trust and alienation. Henceforward the idea of a trust was a regular feature of this kind of radical argument.

In the *Observations,* Parker used the notion of an inalienable right exclusively in the context of his defence of the rights of a community *as a whole* against its ruler. But when his royalist opponents pushed him on this issue, and countered with the point (made by the Tew writers in *An answer to a printed book*) that pre-social individuals had to renounce *all* their rights, Parker was forced to consider the possibility of inalienable individual rights. In his defence of the *Observations* against his critics, published in October 1644 under the title *Jus populi,* he both explicitly repudiated Grotius's theory of voluntary autocracy – 'by the favour of *Grotius,* I think there is stronger reason, that no Nation yet ever did voluntarily or compulsorily embrace servitude, or intend submission to it'[13] – and denied the possibility of rational individuals becoming slaves.

That Dominicall power which we oppose, is unnaturall; it is such, as has no eye at all upon the good or conservation of the slave, or at least, none but secundary; the very definition of it leaves the slave utterly disinherited of himself, and subject to his masters sole ends: Now that which tends not to the preservation, is not naturall, but violent, and consequently, to be abhorred . . .[14]

Nevertheless, that was as far as Parker went in the direction of accepting individual inalienable rights, and even in *Jus populi* he was determined to explain the evils of slavery as due in part to its infringement of a *social* right.

Servile Government does not onely shew it self injurious and violent in devesting the propriety of those which are subjected to it, but also the more publicke and sublime propriety; which the Common-wealth, the Society of Mankinde, nay God himself has in the parties enslaved. If the Lord may destroy his slave at pleasure, then he may destroy that, which in part is belonging to another . . .[15]

This unwillingness is important and interesting, for it shows us what was happening among the radicals. Parker was theoretically and professionally committed to support the Army leaders (which at this stage still meant supporting Parliament): their authority had to be safeguarded at the same time as the king's authority had to be weakened, and the obvious way to do this was to stress the rights of the commonwealth *as a whole.*

But among the radicals, there were some who wished to use the doctrine of inalienable rights *against* Parliament and the Independent grandees. One of the earliest examples of this was in 1644, when an old opponent of

[12] See Clarendon's *The History of the Rebellion . . . Also his Life* (Oxford, 1843), p. 248; and see B. H. G. Wormald, *Clarendon* (Cambridge, 1951), pp. 111–12.
[13] [H. Parker], *Jus Populi* (London, 1644), sig. K1v.
[14] *ibid.,* sig. F3.
[15] *ibid.*

Parker's (formerly from a more royalist standpoint),[16] William Ball, delivered a paper to Major-General Skippon at Reading. His argument as it was later published in an expanded form was that the basic rights of the people of England were such that they could be pleaded against any government. If asked what should happen if Parliament began to seize men's property, then

I answer that for my part, I suppose it almost impossible that the King and Parliament should doe such a thing; but admitting of a kinde of *impossible possibility*, I answer further, that in such case, the Counties, Cities, and Townes corporate might and ought first to petition against so great an injury, and if not remedied then they might *declare* and *protest* against such an act; if violated then they might defend themselves by Armes; for if the *Representative* Body of the Kingdome, may in the behalfe of the Kingdome, raise Arms for the defence of themselves and the Kingdome, may not the *essentiall*? ... by reposing or granting such Trust, they doe not disinvest themselves of their *right naturall* (no more than one that passeth an estate to feofees in Trust for some causes and considerations, disinvesteth himself of the use intended or reserved) so that they may defend their liberties and proprieties even by law of *Nature*, which no speciall or Nationall Lawes can *nullifie*, unlesse men will become, or be made slaves, and lose the *right of Nature*.[17]

Ball meant this; he was not simply making a royalist debating-point of the kind which had been made earlier (i.e. using this argument as a *reductio ad absurdum* of the Parliamentary case – there was nothing absurd about it in Ball's eyes). He quickly became involved in a heated controversy about it with John Cook, later the Independent Attorney-General, for Cook (like Parker) wished to assert that Parliament must have supreme power over the people of England taken as individuals or as members of the smaller local societies envisaged by Ball.[18]

Thus already by 1644 the lines were drawn between the radicals which were to become more familiar in the Leveller agitation of the succeeding years (which incidentally disposes of Brailsford's contention that the Levellers were the intellectual vanguard of the radicals).[19] Ball was no member of the Leveller 'party', and yet his ideas were very close to theirs. What the Levellers did was to seize on the notion of individual inalienable rights and insist that Parliament was indeed trampling on them; the reply from their radical opponents was that individual rights were subordinate to collective social rights. To this extent, the arguments even at Putney

---

[16] See his *A Caveat for Subjects, Moderating the Observator* (London, 1642). It is interesting that this pamphlet was issued anonymously at about the same time at Oxford under the title, *An Appendix to the late Answer* (i.e. the *Answer to a Printed Book*), thus associating Ball with the Tew group's polemic. (The identity of the two pamphlets has not hitherto been recognised; *An Appendix* is only to be found in the Bodleian.)

[17] *Tractatus de Jure Regnandi, & Regni* (n.p., 1645), sig. C1–C1v.

[18] See J. Cook, *The Vindication of the Professors & Profession of the Law* (London, 1646), answered by Ball's *Constitutio Liberi Populi. Or, the Rule of a Free-Born People* (n.p., 1646).

[19] H. N. Brailsford, *The Levellers and the English Revolution*, ed. C. Hill (Stanford, 1961), p. xii.

were arguments within a single ideological group, and it can be said that the Levellers were often embarrassed by their opponents' case precisely because they too still believed in the strength of collective rights. Lilburne indeed revealed that he had learned his basic political theory from the *Observations*.[20]

The truth of this is shown by Lilburne's *Englands birth-right justified* of 1645. Asserting that Parliament must abide by the law, he remarked,

take away the declared, unrepealed Law, and then where is *Meum & Tuum*, and Libertie, and Propertie? But you will say, the Law declared, binds the People, but is no rule for a Parliament sitting, who are not to walke by a knowne Law. It is answered: *It cannot be imagined that ever the People would be so sottish, as to give such a Power to those whom they choose for their Servants*; for this were to give them a Power to provide for their woe, but not for their weal ...[21]

The principle of interpretative charity, of course, is only applicable in the absence of any clear historical evidence: it remains true that *logically*, all rights are renounceable. Thus the Levellers' use of history, which Pocock (for example) takes as incompatible with their rationalistic politics,[22] was in fact vital to it: they had to be confident that natural freedom had not been validly renounced at any point in the past, and only empirical facts, not logic, could give them that confidence.

Undoubtedly the best statements of the Leveller case are in Richard Overton's pamphlets of 1646 and 1647. It is summarised most neatly in *An appeale from the degenerate representative body* (1647): authority

alwayes is either in the hands of the *Betrusted* or of the *Betrustees*, while the *Betrusted* and *dischargers* of their *trust*, it remaineth in their hands, but no sooner the *Betrusted* betray and forfeit their *Trust*, but (as all things else in dissolution) it returneth from whence it came, even to the hands of the *Trustees*: For all iust *humaine powers* are but betrusted, confer'd and conveyed by ioynt and common consent, *for to every individual in nature, is given individuall propriety by nature, not to be invaded or usurped by any . . . for every one as he is himselfe hath a selfe propriety, else could not be himselfe*, and on this no second may presume without consent; and by naturall birth, all men *are equall and alike borne to like propriety and freedome, every man by naturall instinct aiming at his owne safety and weale* . . . Now as no man by nature may abuse, beat, torment or afflict himself, so by nature no man may give that power to another, seeing he may not doe it himselfe . . .[23]

The particular inalienable right which Overton put at the centre of his theory was the right of self-preservation, but he derived from that a fairly extensive set of other rights which no rational man could be deemed to alienate. The kind of thing which he had in mind is implied later in the *Appeale*, when he encouraged an armed struggle 'for the recovery of our

[20] See his *Innocency and Truth Justified* (London, 1646), sig. H1–H2v.
[21] *Englands Birth-Right Justified* (London, 1645), sig. A2–A2v.
[22] J. G. A. Pocock, *The Ancient Constitution and the Feudal Law* (Cambridge, 1957), pp. 126–7.
[23] *Leveller Manifestoes of the Puritan Revolution*, ed. D. M. Wolfe (New York, 1944), p. 162.

naturall humane rights and freedomes, that all orders, sorts, and societies of the *Natives* of this Land, may freely and fully enjoy a joynt and mutuall neighbourhood, cohabitation and humane subsistence'.[24] In other words, anything which it was reasonable to want, could now be construed as an inalienable right, the recovery of which was entirely justifiable: it was unlikely that any rational man would renounce his rights to such reason-able gratifications. The principle of interpretative charity had been stretched very wide, and we have here clearly the eighteenth-century notion of the inalienable rights of mankind.

Awkwardly for their polemics, the Levellers still accepted that societies might be the subjects of rights also – they (or many of them) simply wanted to allow individuals the same kind of rights. Much of their lan-guage in this area is just like that of the less radical Independents: thus at one crisis of the Revolution Cornet Joyce justified his seizure of the King by appealing to the principle that 'every member in the Nation ought to preserve the Nation as much as in him lyes; it is a universall principle, *non nobis solum nati sumus, &c.* We are not borne for our selves alone, but the *Country* in which we live chalenges an interest in us, this principle made many rejoyce in dying, esteeming it, *dulce & decorum pro patria mori.*'[25] On the other hand, their main inclination could often be towards spelling out the rights of societies in terms of individual rights. Again, Overton is the best example: in the *Appeale* he wrote that

all degrees and titles Magisteriall, whether emperiall, regall, Parliamentarie, or otherwise are all subservient to *popular safety,* all founded and grounded thereon, all instituted and ordained only for it, for without it can be no humane society, cohabitation or being, which above all earthly things must be maintained, as the earthly soveraigne good of mankind, let what or who will perish, or be con-founded, for mankind must be preserved upon the earth, and to this preservation, all the Children of men have an equal title by Birth, none to be deprived thereof, but such as are enemies thereto . . .[26]

In addition to the natural and inalienable right men possess to protect themselves as individuals, they also have an inalienable claim on other people that the communities to which they belong should be protected and preserved. Admittedly, Overton is unusual in making the point in just this way, but he does represent a definite aspect of Leveller thinking.

But critics of the Levellers such as Parker were able to home in on this sort of point and exploit the contradictions in the Leveller position. Parker produced the most formidable arguments against the Levellers in an Engagement tract, *An answer to a paper, entituled, some considerations,* annexed to *Scotlands Holy War* in 1651 (and published, unusually, under his name).

[24] *ibid.,* p. 182.
[25] G. Joyce, *A Vindication of His Majesty and the Army* (London, 1647), sig. B2.
[26] Wolfe, ed., *Leveller Manifestoes,* p. 178.

Liberty is the due birth-right, of every Englishman: but Liberty has its bounds, and rules; and the liberty of every member must be subordinate to the liberty of the whole body. By the Laws of Liberty every man is to injoy, that which is his own: but since one man has far greater, and better things to injoy, than another, the liberties of one may extend further, than the Liberties of another. Likewise, when our Liberties are equall[y] extensive, one man may voluntarily renounce, or maliciously forfeit, that which another does not. Therefore we must not suppose, that any man in *England* by the Protestation, or Covenant, or any Law else, has such an estate, or inheritance in his Liberty, as is altogether indefeasible, and unreleasible, whatsoever He does, or saies. But in the last place, there is a Liberty of the whole State, as well as of any particular subject: and that Liberty of the whole State must supersede the Liberty of every particular subject, whensoever both accord not: the lesser, to avoid repugnance, must alwaies give place to the greater.[27]

If this kind of argument was taken seriously, then it could lead to an attitude towards individual rights which resembled that of the Seldenians. This is strikingly true of Parker's employer, Henry Ireton, at Putney. He is to be found at one point attacking the Levellers' plea for liberty by (apparently) denying that the principle of interpretative charity works for individuals: 'liberty cannot be provided for in a general sense, if property be preserved. For if property be preserved, that I am not to meddle with such a man's estate, his meat, his drink, his apparel, or other goods, then the right of nature destroys liberty. By the right of nature I am to have sustenance rather than perish; yet property destroys it for a man to have [sustenance], by the right of nature.'[28] Elsewhere, he even argued (again, very like Selden) that

The government of Kings, or of Lords, is as just as any in the world, is the justest government in the world. *Volenti non fit injuria.* Men cannot wrong themselves willingly, and if they will agree to make a King, and his heirs, there's no injustice. They may either make it hereditary or elective. They may give him an absolute power or a limited power. Here hath been agreements of the people that have agreed with this. There hath been such an agreement when the people have fought for their liberty, and have established the King again ... Any man that makes a bargain, and does find afterwards 'tis for the worse, yet is bound to stand to it.[29]

The one thing that kept Ireton from becoming a completely conservative rights theorist was his insistence on the principle of interpretative charity as applied to a *society*. 'That's one maxim, that all government must be for the safety of the people,' he said at Putney,[30] and in his *Army Remonstrance* the following year he argued forcibly for the social right of self-defence under necessity, though stressing that care must always be taken that the plea of necessity was well-founded.[31]

But the Levellers could also be opposed by men who were much more

[27] *Scotlands Holy War* (London, 1651), sig. 14.
[28] A. S. P. Woodhouse, *Puritanism and Liberty* (London, 1951), p. 73. (I have omitted Woodhouse's conjectural additions to Clarke's text.)
[29] ibid., p. 122.
[30] ibid.
[31] ibid., pp. 456–7.

open to the idea of individual inalienable rights than either Parker or Ireton. The best example of this is Anthony Ascham, whose work is in some ways the purest expression of a radical rights theory, and who shows graphically the debt the radicals as much as the conservatives owed to Grotius. We have already seen that Ascham was concerned to differentiate his own ideas from those of conservatives such as Hobbes and Hammond, but he was also concerned to show how they differed from those of the Levellers. His developed argument, as it was put forward in his *Of the confusions and revolutions of governments* (1649), is now well known, largely as a result of the work of Perez Zagorin, Irene Coltman, John Wallace and Quentin Skinner.[32] He began with (as Wallace has pointed out) a highly Grotian account of the growth of property in a state of nature, according to which the possession of necessary commodities gave rise to property rights. These rights were formalised and regularised subsequently by agreement, given the difficulty of sustaining a non-conventional distribution, 'it being but naturall, and no injury, that in a state where there is no mutuall obligation, the inferiour in force should give way to him that is so much superiour. This necessarily breeding feare in many, could not but breed generall compact or conditions for secure neighbour-hood, and for holding what was first laid hand on, though in unequall parts.'[33]

But that was not the whole story, as it would have been (if fleshed out) for a conservative theorist. Ascham also endorsed Grotius's claim that *in extremis* the original common right is revived:

Our generall rights surely are not yet all lost, though all the world be now trampled over, & impropriated in particular possessions & rights: there yet remaines some common right, or naturall community among all men, even in impropriation; so that that which is necessary for any naturall subsistence and necessary to another belongs justly to mee, unless I have merited to lose the life which I seeke to preserve.[34]

The same argument could be applied to politics, for among the rights which we have lost are certain kinds of right against rulers. Again, the beginning of governmental *dominium* was possession, the subjection of the weaker by the stronger. That proved to be a shaky foundation, 'wherefore Compact was judg'd a securer way than meer power for the coalition of societies'.[35] But this compact did not entail the renunciation of all rights, any more than the compact of property had done, and here Ascham's

---

[32] See P. Zagorin, *The Political Thought of the English Revolution* (London, 1954), pp. 64–7; J. Wallace, 'The Cause too Good', *Journal of the History of Ideas*, XXIV (1963), pp. 150–4; I. Coltman, *Private Men and Public Causes* (London, 1962); Q. R. D. Skinner, 'History and Ideology in the English Revolution', *Historical Journal*, VIII (1965), pp. 151–78, and 'The Ideological Context of Hobbes's Political Thought', *Historical Journal*, IX (1966), pp. 286–317; J. Wallace, *Destiny His Choice* (Cambridge, 1968).

[33] *Of the Confusions and Revolutions of Governments* (London, 1649), sig. C3.

[34] *ibid.*, sig. B6v.

[35] *ibid.*, sig. H6v.

argument began against the conservative theorists (including, at this point, Grotius himself).

Mr. *Hobbes* and H. *Grotius* are pleased to argue severall wayes for obliging people to one perpetuall and standing Allegiance. *Grotius* supposes such a fixt Allegiance in a people, because a particular man may give himselfe up to a private servitude for ever, as among the Jewes and Romans. Mr. *Hobbes* supposes, that because a man cannot be protected from all civill injuries, unlesse all his rights be totally and irrevocably given up to another, therefore the people are irrevocably and perpetually the Governours.[36]

Against Grotius and Hobbes (whom Ascham took, as we have seen, to be arguing like an unmodified Seldenian) he argued first that there were no good historical cases of voluntary servitude – the year of Jubilee among the Jews involved automatic manumission, and that would be known to anyone who voluntarily enslaved himself. Second he claimed that

such a totall resignation of all right and reason, as Mr. *Hobbes* supposes, is one of our morall impossibilities, and directly opposite to that antient *Ius zelotarum* among the Jewes, who though they reverenc't their Magistracy, and their *Sanhedrim* very much, yet they conceiv'd they had a right of judging and punishing acts notoriously contrary to the light of nature and reason, without consulting the forms of either.[37]

Ascham was aware that Grotius had denied that this right generally survived into civil society, regarding the Jewish case as a freak, but he pointed out that if Grotius was right, it would follow that no father could exercise domestic justice on his children and servants, or a husband kill his wife taken in adultery. 'Out of which, and many other arguments, it is evident, That our Generall and Original rights are not totally swallowed up either in the property of goods or in the possession of persons, neither is all that which was naturall now made Civill.'[38]

From this, we can deduce that among the rights which Ascham believed could not reasonably be renounced were those of self-defence, of taking the necessities of life, and of punishing malefactors. The last is an important instance, as it shows how his argument (and that of the other radical theorists) worked: inalienable rights were not simply rights which it would be irrational not to exercise, as clearly it could be rational (and indeed merciful) not to exercise the right to punish criminals. Rather, they were rights which rational individuals would be aware that they might want to exercise and which they would therefore not be likely to renounce. The distinction is vital, as otherwise Ascham and the others would have landed themselves in the same difficulties as Hobbes, dealing with a right which looks more like a duty.

The importance for Ascham's overall case of making this kind of point

[36] *ibid.*, sig. I4v–5.
[37] *ibid.*, sig. I5.
[38] *ibid.*, sig. I6.

was that he was then able to argue precisely that men could not be bound to a 'perpetuall and standing Allegiance', and that when government broke down, men were free to act on the basis of their retained rights. If a new party seized the institutions of government, it did not affect the conduct of just relationships between the members of the society. One problem was that his way of talking about retained rights made him sound like a more radical theorist – and it is striking that one of the new chapters he added in *Of the Confusions* was explicitly intended to set out the points of difference between him and more radical writers who claimed to have detected a 'Tyranny in Property', and who urged a return to basic natural rights.[39]

His reply was essentially that according to a Grotian theory, one's natural property was extremely sparse. Civil society was necessary to meet all the exigencies of real life and to ensure fairness; to seek merely one's natural property was to seek a primitive existence. Despite a passing reference to Selden, he does not appear to have considered that the state of nature was one of total freedom, a Hobbesian condition of *bellum omnium contra omnes*; rather, it was (in line with his general account) the Grotian picture of men owning solely what they require for their continued existence. Such a way of life was insecure – 'there is no such thing as *Salus populi*, or protection there'[40] – but Ascham never said clearly that it was an *amoral* condition. In this respect too he resembled the other radicals: none of them was prepared to follow Selden and Hobbes into abandoning Grotius's account of the state of nature. Ireton, as one might expect, came nearest to it of any of them, but the notes Clarke took at Putney (admittedly, fragmentary and difficult evidence) never reveal him unequivocally abandoning Grotius's theory of original property.

This reply of Ascham's in no way cut him off from the radicals: his sentiments could have been endorsed by any of the Levellers. Obviously the overall thrust of his argument was towards a more conservative regime than they wanted, but their basic convictions were not so far removed from his. The ideology of the Independent radicals in the 1640s was a more pervasive and main-stream phenomenon than has often been realised.

The fact that there was not a great gulf between the Levellers and other apparently more conservative radicals such as Ascham or Parker is important not only for assessing their role in the 1640s, but also for deciding who their ideological heirs were. The more radical Whigs of the post-Restoration period talked the same language as the Independents and Levellers of the 1640s, and it is a mistake both to overestimate the peculiarity of the Levellers and to underestimate the radicalness of the Whigs. A fine example of this is provided by perhaps the most interesting work of political theory published in England between 1660 and 1689, James Tyrrell's *Patriarcha non Monarcha* of 1681. It is of course an important work

[39] *ibid.*, Chapter v. See C4 for the expression 'Tyranny in Property'.
[40] *ibid.*, sig. C5.

in the historiography of John Locke, for there is now conclusive evidence that Locke and Tyrrell were aware of each other's work at this time and that Tyrrell incorporated some of Locke's ideas into his own book.[41] But characteristically Lockean insights occur in only one section, added while the book was in the press, and in the rest Tyrrell used a rather different theory. Those sections of the work in fact represent an admirable statement of the kind of theory which Locke is notable for *not* putting forward, as I will show in the next chapter; instead, they contain arguments identical to the ones we have been considering.

Tyrrell's use of the principle of interpretative charity is shown by his discussion of the residual rights of slaves:

no man can be supposed so void of common sense (unless an absolute Fool, and then he is not capable of making any Bargain) to yield himself so absolutely up to anothers disposal, or to renounce all hopes of safety or satisfaction in this life, or of future happiness in that to come. So that I conceive that even a Slave (Much more a Servant hired upon certain Conditions) in the state of Nature, where he hath no civil power to whom to appeal for Justice, hath as much right as a Son or Child of the Family, to defend his life, or what belongs to him, against the unjust violence or Rage of his Master ... Since we have no notions of happiness but in life, nor is that farther than it is accompanied with some contentment of mind, no rational man can be supposed to consent to renounce all the pleasures and ends thereof, (and which onely make life desireable) much less the Right of living and preserving himself ...[42]

Here, on the eve of the appearance of a new radical natural rights theory from the pen of his friend, Tyrrell made one of the clearest statements of the older theory. As in Grotius (whom Tyrrell quoted frequently), the argument turns on what a rational man can be presumed to have consented to: in principle, as in all these writers, any rights are renounceable, but some are unlikely ever to have been renounced. Because of this, both the conservatives and the radicals remained in the confines of the natural rights theory as set out in the writings of men like Molina and Grotius: men are totally free, and may logically do anything with that freedom. The differences between the two groups were given by their differing estimates of what men would *actually* do with it. Not until Locke was there to be a radical theory which was fundamentally divorced from this tradition.

[41] See below, p. 169.
[42] J. Tyrrell, *Patriarcha non Monarcha* (London, 1681), sig. H4–H5. The 'Lockean' section begins sig. L1.

8

The Recovery and
Repudiation of Grotius

Neither of the two traditions of thought which we have seen developing out of Grotius's ideas proved generally attractive in the years after 1660, though Grotius's basic theory continued to exercise an enormous attraction. Some people, such as Vaughan, continued to talk like Selden; others, such as Velthuysen or de la Court, like Hobbes. And yet both Selden and Hobbes had used what was to many other contemporaries the extremely disquieting idea of a state of total natural freedom. Others again, like the English Whigs, continued to use the principle of interpretative charity, and to put forward a theory that was in some ways the most genuine extension of Grotius available; and yet this tradition had been compromised by its support for the English revolution. In the twenty years after 1660 we find many people trying to recapture something of the authentic character of the original natural rights theory, without finding themselves committed to either of its mid-century adaptations. This was a difficult enterprise, and most of the attempts failed; only one, that of John Locke, came anywhere near success.

The most radical attempt was by the most famous political philosopher of his day, Samuel Pufendorf. A German Protestant working largely in the courts of northern Europe (first Sweden and finally Prussia), he devoted the first part of his working life to a reconstruction of the new natural law ideology.[1]

After the publication of his first work, the *Elementa Jurisprudentiae Universalis* of 1660 (written in 1658 at the age of twenty-six), he was hailed as the man who had 'bravely followed in the footsteps' of Grotius,[2] and was appointed by the Elector Palatine to a chair at Heidelberg to lecture on the *De Iure Belli*. This understanding of the work was on the whole correct: in it Pufendorf did not depart radically from the Grotian tradition. But interestingly, he did not feel under any threat from Hobbes either. The book was written in a Danish prison during a brief war between Sweden

[1] For Pufendorf, see L. Krieger, *The Politics of Discretion; Pufendorf and the Acceptance of Natural Law* (Chicago, 1965), and H. Denzer, *Moral-philosophie und Naturrecht bei S. Pufendorf*, Munch. Stud. z. Pol., XXII (Munich, 1972).
[2] S. Pufendorf, *The Law of Nature and Nations*, ed. J. Barbeyrac, trans. B. Kennet, 5th edn (London, 1749) p. 68. (Barbeyrac's 'Historical and Critical Account of the Science of Morality'.)

and Denmark, and was based largely on Pufendorf's memories of *De Iure Belli* and *De Cive*. In the preface he praised Grotius, and remarked of Hobbes that his 'basic conception in his book, *De Cive*, although it savours somewhat of the profane, is nevertheless for the most part extremely acute and sound'.[3] It was between 1660 and 1672, when he published his major work *De Iure Naturae et Gentium*, that Pufendorf changed his ideas.

Thus the account of the origin of property which he gave in the *Elementa* was well within the Grotian tradition. By right of occupation as well as concession from God,

> the first man received his authority over all things, and he needed no further title, because there existed no one whose right could stand in his way ... Yes, and the same right would have been sufficient, even if a number of men had been created by God at the same time. For the pact which under these circumstances they would have regarded as necessary to make about the division of things for the sake of preserving concord would not have given them a new title or a new right, but would merely have circumscribed within definite limits a right which was common, and would have assigned to each his proportional share; since, of course, such a pact about things does altogether presuppose a certain right to the same.[4]

He combined this with ideas taken directly from Selden or Hobbes. Thus he remarked that in areas where there was no relevant law of nature, men had a natural right to do what they liked – 'a man has the authority or right to do all those things which can proceed from his natural powers, except such as are prohibited by law'.[5] Moreover and perhaps most strikingly, he adopted the same theory of obligation which Selden and Hobbes had developed. This comes out clearly from a passage in Definition XIII of Book I:

> the nature of law consists principally in this, namely, that it is a notional norm for actions, showing how far they should be conformed to the will of some superior. I use the expression 'a notional norm', because it touches actions only through the intellect, in envisaging to the intellect the will of a superior relative to doing or avoiding something. For, when this is made known, immediately there arises in the subject the obligation to act in accordance with that law, and this because he understands that he who enjoins that law upon him has the authority to compel him by the imposition of some evil, if he refuses to obey, and that he will exercise

---

[3] 'hypothesis in libro de Cive etsi quid profani sapiat; pleraque tamen caetera satis arguta ac sana.' Pufendorf, *Elementorum Jurisprudentiae Universalis Libri Duo* (Cambridge, 1672), photographically reproduced and edited for the Carnegie Endowment by W. Wehberg (Oxford, 1931), sig. *6. Translation Vol. II of the Carnegie edition by W. O. Oldfather (Oxford, 1931), p. xxx.

[4] 'potestatem in res omnes accepit primus homo, nec ullo praeterea opus fuit, quippe nemo extaret, cujus jus ipsi impedimento esse posset ... Atque idem jus suffecisset, etiamsi plures simul homines a DEO fuissent creati. Pactum enim, quod tunc circa divisionem rerum ob servandum concordiam inire necessum habuissent, novum titulum aut jus ipsis non dedisset, sed commune duntaxat jus certis limitibus circumscripsisset, ac ratam cuique partem adsignasset. Quippe cum tale pactum circa res jus aliquod in easdem omnino praesupponat.' *ibid.*, p. 41; trans., p. 36.

[5] 'homo omnia ea agendi potestatem seu jus habeat, quae a viribus suis naturalibus proficisci possunt, nisi quae per legem prohibentur.' *ibid.*, p. 170; trans., p. 148.

this authority [potestas] is well established from the fact that no one is presumed to wish his action to have no effect.[6]

Clearly, the notion of *authority* or *potestas* is important here, for it seems to make all the difference between Pufendorf and Hobbes: but in the following definition he observed that 'a man is judged to have authority to do all that which can be done by him through the exercise of his natural power, whatever, namely, is not forbidden by the laws, or is also enjoined by the same, or left indifferent'.[7] Thus in a situation where one being has the power to compel another and is not itself under any kind of compulsion from another source, that being (according to Pufendorf) will be a law-giver for the other. God was of course such a being, and therefore was the source of ultimate law, the natural law; but as in Selden, he was its source primarily because of his known capacity to *punish*.

All this was subtly changed by 1672. Pufendorf now devoted a large part of his massive work to attacking Hobbes and other rights theorists whom he saw as a danger, such as Velthuysen; in a later edition he added Spinoza to the list. Barbeyrac records that it was his daily lecturing on Grotius at Heidelberg that led him to be dissatisfied with *De Iure Belli*,[8] and his worries about Hobbes were probably part of that general dissatisfaction. The change (in the areas in which we are interested) took two forms: one was a loosening of his theory of obligation, and the other was an open attack on the notion of primary natural rights.

The theory of obligation put forward in *De Iure Naturae et Gentium* and in its shorter version, *De Officio Hominis et Civis* (published in the following year), has been a source of debate ever since its first appearance. Leibniz thought that he detected in it the same kind of theory as Hobbes's, and gave a critical account of it that would have been wholly true of the *Elementa*; Barbeyrac replied with a spirited defence of the difference between Pufendorf and Hobbes.[9] The truth seems to be that Pufendorf produced a genuinely muddled theory precisely because he modified his formerly prudential account in such a way that he now stressed the need

---

[6] 'Consistit autem natura legis potissimum in hoc, ut sit norma notionalis actionum, quatenus ad voluntatem superioris alicujus debent formari. Dico *norma notionalis*, quia ad actiones duntaxat concurrit notionaliter, dum intellectui repraesentat voluntatem superioris circa aliquid agendum aut omittendum. Haec enim ubi innotuit, statim in subdito exoritur obligatio juxta legem illam faciendi. Idque quia intellegit, eum qui istam injungit, potestatem habere detrectantem malo imposito adigendi; quam potestatem actu eum exseriturum inde constat, quod nemo actionis suae nullum esse effectum velle praesumatur.' *ibid.*, p. 176; trans., p. 153.

[7] 'Judicatur autem homo habere potestatem ad agendum omne id, quod per potentiam naturalem ab eo agi potest, quidquid legibus non est interdictum, sive iisdem quoque praecipiatur, sive indifferens relinquatur.' *ibid.*, p. 194; trans., p. 168.

[8] Pufendorf, *Law of Nature and Nations*, p. 69. This change in Pufendorf has often been ignored, e.g. by Krieger in *Politics of Discretion*.

[9] For Leibniz's critique of Pufendorf, see his *Political Writings*, ed. and trans. P. Riley (Cambridge, 1972), pp. 64–75. Barbeyrac's reply was appended to his French translation of the *De Officio*, first published at Amsterdam, 1718.

for a *legitimate* superior as the source of law, with the capacity to lay an obligation on men's *conscience*. As he said, in a passage that Leibniz leaped on as evidence for Pufendorf's confusion,

Obligation is properly introduced into the mind of a man by a superior, that is, a person who has not only the power to bring some harm at once upon those who resist, but also just grounds for his claim that the freedom of our will should be limited at his discretion. For when these conditions are found in anyone, he has only to intimate his wish, and there must arise in men's minds a fear that is tempered with respect, the former in view of his power, the latter in consideration of the reasons, which, were there no fear, must still induce one to embrace his will. For whoever is unable to assign any other reason why he wishes to impose an obligation upon me against my will, except mere power, can indeed frighten me into thinking it better for a time to obey him, to avoid a greater evil; but, once that fear is removed, nothing further remains to prevent my acting according to my will rather than his.[10]

Barbeyrac interpreted Pufendorf as saying at this point that obligation strictly speaking requires the awareness of another's right over us, and that in the case of the natural law the very idea of God implies that he possesses such rights, and not simply sufficient power to direct us.[11] Such an interpretation is probably fair enough, but it emphasises how far from a prudential theory of morality Pufendorf had come.

The second aspect of Pufendorf's retreat, his attack on primary natural rights, relied essentially on a new and important argument – nothing less than the 'correlativity thesis' which has been so much discussed by modern philosophers. What he said in the context of an attack on Hobbes's ideas about the state of nature, was:

it is necessary to observe, That not every natural Licence, or Power of doing a Thing, is properly a *Right*; but such only as includes some moral Effect, with regard to others, who are Partners with me in the same Nature. Thus, for Instance, in the old Fable, the Horse and the Stag had both of them a natural Power or Privilege of feeding in the Meadow; but neither of them had a *Right*, which might restrain or take off the natural Power in the other. So Man, when he employs, in his Designs and Services, insensible or irrational Beings, barely exercises his natural Power, if,

---

[10] '*Introducitur obligatio* in animum hominis *proprie a superiore*, i.e. tali, cui non solum *vires* sunt malum aliquod repraesentandi contranientibus; sed & cui *justae* sunt *causae*, quare postulare queat, ex suo arbitrio voluntatis nostrae libertatem circumscribi. Talia enim ubi in aliquo fuerint, postquam quid velit significavit, necessum est in animo hominis oriri metum reverentia temperatum: illum quidem ex potentia, hanc autem ex consideratione causarum, quae etiam remoto metu allicere aliquem debebant ad istius voluntatem amplectandum. Qui enim nullam rationem allegare novit, quare mihi invito obligationem velit impingere, praeter solas vires, is terrere quidem me potest, ut effugiendo majori malo ipsi tantisper parere satius ducam. Sed eo metu remoto nihil amplius obstat, quo minus meo potius, quam illius arbitrio agam.' *De Officio Hominis & Civis* (Cambridge, 1682), photographically reproduced and edited for the Carnegie Endowment by W. Schuecking (New York, 1927), pp. 13–14. Translation, Vol. II of the Carnegie edition by F. G. Moore (New York, 1927), p. 13. For Leibniz's use of this passage see Leibniz, *Political Writings*, p. 73.

[11] See S. Pufendorf, *Les Devoirs de l'Homme & du Citoien*, I, ed. and trans. J. Barbeyrac (Amsterdam, 1735), pp. 415–19.

without regard to other Men, we here precisely consider it in reference to the
Things, or Animals, which he uses. But then, at length, it turns into a proper Right,
when it creates this moral Effect in other Persons, that they shall not hinder him in
the free Use of these Conveniences, and shall themselves forbear to use them
without his Consent. For 'tis ridiculous Trifling to call that Power a *Right*, which,
should we attempt to exercise, all other Men have an *equal Right* to obstruct or
prevent us. Thus much then we allow, that every Man has naturally a Power or
Licence of applying to his Use any Thing that is destitute of Sense, or of Reason.
But we deny that this Power can be call'd a *Right*, both because there is not inherent
in those Creatures, any *Obligation* to yield themselves unto Man's Service; and,
likewise, because all Men being *naturally* equal, one cannot fairly exclude the rest
from possessing any such Advantage, unless by their Consent, either express or
presumptive, he has obtain'd the peculiar and sole Disposal or Enjoyment of it.
And when this is once done, he may then truly say he has a *Right* to such a Thing.[12]

   This is of course a vitally important passage. In it Pufendorf provided a
fundamental theoretical criticism of Hobbes, at a level far removed (as we
shall see) from that of his English colleagues. According to him, a Hobbesian 'right' simply was *not* a right, since any right requires a definite
obligation on someone else. This is the claim .which Bentham and the
Utilitarians were to make a hundred years later and which has remained
one of the central issues of the philosophy of rights.[13] But it was of course
tantamount to the repudiation of the whole history of rights as *dominia*, as
active rights expressing their possessor's sovereignty over his world. The
implication of the criticism was that individuals could only be said to have

---

[12] 'sciendum est; non quamlibet facultatem naturalem aliquid agendi proprie jus esse, sed
   illam demum, quae effectum aliquem moralem involvit aliud alios, qui ejusdem mecum
   sunt naturae. Sic, uti est in fabulis, facultatem naturalem habebat equus pascendi in prato,
   habebat eandem & cervus; neuter tamen jus habuit, quod illa utriusque facultas alterum non
   afficeret. Sic homo, quando res sensu destitutas, aut bruta in usum suum adhibet, meram
   duntaxat facultatem naturalem exercet; siquidem illa praecise consideretur in ordine ad res,
   & animantes, quibus utitur, citra respectum ad alios homines. Sed quae tunc demum in juris
   proprie dicti naturam evalescit, quando in caeteris hominibus hic effectus moralis pro-
   ducitur, ne alii eum impedire debeant, aut ipso invito ad easdem res usurpandas concurrere.
   Ineptum quippe est, eam facultatem juris nomine insignire velle, quam exercere volentem
   alii omnes pari jure impedire queant. Igitur hoc quidem admittimus, naturaliter competere
   homini facultatem ad usus suos adhibendi res quasvis sensu carentes, ut & bruta. Verum ea
   facultas, ita praecise considerata, jus proprie vocari nequit, tum quia in istis nulla est
   obligatio ipsius sese usibus praebendi; tum quia propter aequalitatem naturalem hominum
   inter se non potest unus caeteros ab iisdem rebus recte excludere, nisi ex eorum consensu
   expresso aut praesumto id sibi peculiariter comparaverit. Quod ubi factum est, tunc
   demum recte jus se ad eam rem habere dicere potest.' Pufendorf, *De Iure Naturae et Gentium*
   (Lund, 1672), p. 321 (III.v.3). Trans. B. Kennet, p. 267. The position about editions and
   translations of Pufendorf's main work is remarkably similar to that about Grotius's *De Iure
   Belli* (above, p. 73). The Carnegie Endowment reprinted and translated the 1688 Amsterdam edition, which contains extensive revisions and additions by Pufendorf (notably, all
   the references to the arguments of Cumberland and Spinoza) first added in the Frankfurt
   edition of 1684. I have judged it better to go to the original edition. As for the translation,
   Basil Kennet's translation of Barbeyrac's edition is as impressive and important a work as
   its sister volume, the translation of Barbeyrac's Grotius, and much to be preferred to any
   subsequent version.
[13] See above, p. 6.

rights when they had claims on one another, and that any idea of their having rights or property *in themselves*, outside the network of social obligations, was fundamentally misleading. Pufendorf made this point explicit in his discussion of property later in the work. There were certainly not private property rights of a Grotian kind in the state of nature; there could not even be said to be the unrestricted common rights of Selden.

> The Right of *Adam* over Things was of a different Kind from that Dominion, which is now settled amongst Men; We may call it an indefinite Dominion, not formally posses'd, but absolutely allow'd; not actual, but potential. It has, indeed, the same Effect which Dominion now obtains; that is, the using Things at Pleasure; yet was it not Dominion, strictly speaking, by reason that there was no other Person against whom this Effect might pravail [sic]; but 'twas capable of passing into Dominion, when the Number of Mankind should afterwards Increase. And thus, on the Whole, whilst *Adam* was the only Man, Things, in respect of him, were neither *proper*, nor *common*. For Community supposeth a Partner in the Possession; and Propriety denotes an Exclusion of the Right of others to the Thing enjoy'd: So that neither of them can be understood, 'till the World was furnish'd with more than one Inhabitant... Therefore the *Property* of Things flow'd immediately from the Compact of Men, whether *tacit,* or *express.* For altho', after the Donation of GOD, nothing was wanting but for Men to take Possession; yet that one Man's seizing on a Thing should be understood to exclude the Right of all others to the same Thing, could not proceed but from mutual Agreement.[14]

It is clear that with this argument Pufendorf renounced the attempt to live up to his youthful reputation as the preserver of Grotius. Any theory of a natural right of *dominium* or *quasi-dominium,* and of social relationships as built up through the transfers of such natural rights, had to be abandoned. Grotius could not be preserved if Hobbes was to be refuted: that was the melancholy conclusion to which Pufendorf had clearly been led by 1672. And of the two options, it now seemed more important for Hobbes to be refuted than for Grotius to be preserved. Out with Grotius and Hobbes went radical natural rights theories: Pufendorf made short work of the principle of interpretative charity as applied to both property and resistance. Instead, he retreated to a theory which laid stress on the fact that general agreements for social utility confer rights, and hence that rights

---

[14] 'jus Adami in res diversum fuit ab illo dominio, quale jam est inter homines constitutum; quod quis vocare possit dominium idefinitum non formaliter, sed concessive, non actu sed potentia. Idque eundem obtinebat effectum, quem jam dominium, rebus nempe pro libitu utendi; dominium tamen proprie loquendo non erat, quod nullus praeterea homo tunc existeret, adversus quem effectum id exsereret: hominibus autem postea subnatis in dominium transire poterat. Adeoque Adamo, quamdiu is solus extit, neque propriae neque communes res fuerunt. Nam communitas involvit socium possessionis; proprietas autem connotat exclusionem juris alterius ad eandem rem; sic ut utraque non possit intelligi, nisi postquam plures uno homines coeperunt existere... Ergo proprietas rerum immediate ex conventione hominum, tacita aut expressa, profluxit. Etiamsi enim, posita concessione Dei, nihil reliquum erat, quam ut homo res occuparet: tamen ut per occupationem seu adprehensionem caeterorum jus ad eam rem exclusum intelligeretur, conventione utique opus fuit.' Pufendorf, *De Iure Naturae,* pp. 456–8 (IV.IV.3–4); trans., pp. 365–7.

may not be pleaded against them – a theory which could easily be manipulated in support of authoritarian regimes (as indeed it was).

While Pufendorf was trying to rework the Grotian tradition in this manner, in England the same sort of enterprise was under way. But as one might expect, it proved much more difficult for the English to come to the same kind of conclusion as Pufendorf: the influence of Selden and Hobbes remained too strong. It is in the context of this enterprise that we must view the work of Matthew Hale (linked by strong personal ties to Selden) and Richard Cumberland; but we ought also, less familiarly, to read Locke in the same light.

The feature that all these writers had in common was their desire to rehabilitate what we might characterise as the early Grotian theory of property. The ideas of Selden and Hobbes, as we have seen, represented a complete break with the theory set out by Grotius in his *Mare Liberum* and only partially modified in *De Iure Belli*, for they argued that the state of nature was a state of *total* freedom and that property rights as commonly understood had to be created by a contract. The attack on their view of the state of nature involved the claim that property antedated such a contract, and all these post-Restoration writers were deeply concerned to establish that proposition. But they were not prepared to repudiate totally the rest of Selden or Hobbes, and the result was a delicate and often unsuccessful balancing-act.

The least known of the three is Matthew Hale. We have seen that he was a friend of the elderly Selden, and of Vaughan; he was also of course acquainted with Hobbes. But in an undated manuscript, probably composed during the 1660s, entitled a *Treatise of the Nature of Lawes in Generall*, he tried to produce a synthesis of Selden's theory of obligation with Grotius's original theory of property.

He began by defining a law in clearly Seldenian terms as 'a rule of moral actions, given to a being endued with understanding and will, by him that hath power or authority to give the same and exact obedience thereunto *per modum imperii*, commanding or forbidding such actions under some penalty expressed or implicitly contained in such law'. He thus committed himself to explicating the obligatory force of the laws of nature in terms of punishment, and that is precisely what he proceeded to do. But he wished to make a distinction between laws and prudential precepts like doctor's orders:

the physician hath no authority to exact his [patient's] observance under any penalty to be inflicted by him or by his authority, but only to withdraw himself and leave his unruly patient to taste and undergo the fruit and inconvenience of his own wilfulness.

And upon this account, if Atheistical persons could, as they would, exterminate the good God of heaven from having to do in this world, that, which they call reason and the law of reason, would be indeed a rule, but not truly and formally a law. For let us suppose any one man to be of the most exquisite reason that human nature is capable of; and hath reason chalked out to him, the just end and exquisite measure and order of all his moral actions in order thereunto. Yet this rule of reason would not be a law to him, unless there were some superior that gave this rule to him *per modum imperii et sub ratione legis*; for he could be under no obligation to observe this rule of reason but only to himself, and therefore may absolve himself by the liberty of his will from observing of that rule and from all obligation to it... for though he remain a reasonable nature, and is well acquainted with the rule of his reason, yet he remains still a free and voluntary agent, and as to the exercise of his actions is lord still of himself and them.[15]

Hale thus refused to accept that 'natural' punishments, of the sort which can follow a refusal to act on doctor's orders, are properly *punishments* unless God's role in arranging them is taken seriously – more seriously (it is implied) than Hobbes was prepared to. The difference between a doctor and God is presumably that the doctor has not determined what the punishment shall be, he merely predicts it, though conceivably with absolute certainty. But Hobbes too, of course, did say that the natural laws could only properly be seen as *laws*, and the punishments as *punishments*, if God was brought into the picture: so far, Hale had not really disentangled his own position from Hobbes's.

He proceeded to outline the source of the natural laws in very Seldenian terms: they were not naturally intuited, but had been made known historically to mankind, first through the seven *praecepta Noachidarum* and then through the Decalogue. Although only the Jews preserved in any detail the tradition of the *praecepta*, they had been issued to all the men living on earth at that time, and were therefore not the preserve of a particular people. The Decalogue was, on the other hand; but although God gave it

to one particular nation, the jewish chirch; yet he made that nation signal and eminent and conspicuous to all the world by signs, wonders and observable providence, that they might be like a beacon upon a hill, like a mighty and stately pillar set up in the middle of the world to hang up upon it those tables of natural righteousness, which might be conspicuous and legible to the greatest part even of the gentile world of many ages ...[16]

This was one of the most eloquent expressions of the centrality of Hebrew studies which marks this whole English theory of natural law, and which had a considerable influence even on their ideas about Parliament, through works such as Selden's *De Synedriis* and Bulstrode Whitelocke's manuscript historical treatises.[17]

However, alongside this Seldenian account of the natural law, Hale wished to put a more Grotian account of the state of nature. In particular he

[15] B. M. Hargrave MS 485, ff. 3v–4.
[16] *ibid.*, ff. 23–v.
[17] See particularly Whitelocke's treatises in B.M. Add. MSS 4993 and 37341, and Stowe MS 333. There is some discussion of these in R. Spalding, *The Improbable Puritan* (London, 1975), pp. 245 and 262–3. Whitelocke was a close friend of Selden; see *ibid.*, p. 202.

sought to deny the possibility, central to the Seldenian position, of a state of untrammelled freedom prior to the law.

Altho' there were no instituted human government or lawes, but men were in that natural state wherein they were propagated into the world, yet even in that state there would be some things *justa honesta et decora,* and somethings *injusta inhonesta et indecora.* Every thing would not be lawfull to every man; and that imaginary state of war; wherein every man might lawfully do what he thinks best without any law or controll, is but a phantasy; or if it be admitted, it must not, cannot be supposed the just state of nature, but as a disease disorder and corruption in it . . . [18]

In such a state of nature, men would have *private* property rights independent of and prior to any contract, just as Grotius had argued in his early work and Selden had denied. While Selden thought that all that men had prior to a contract of property was a general right to use whatever they chose and not a right to exclude others from its use, Hale argued that

there be some things in the world, that antecedently to any contract or pact a man hath an undoubted property in, that may not without natural injustice and violation of the law of nature be causelessly invaded by another. So every man hath an unquestionable property in his own life and in his own self. And therefore if for the purpose A. gives himself up to the propriety of B. as in matrimonial contracts and contracts of servitude, as A. may not contravene his own contract without violation of the law of nature; so neither can C. between whom and B. there intervenes no contract, devest B. of such his profession or property, because it is given up to B. by him that had the full dominion or propriety of what he so gave up . . . Much may be said to maintain a secondary law of nature for the acquest of property by the first possession or occupation; because that in as much, as before the institution of the lawes of property it is admitted, that all have an equal right to all things, the man that hath acquired the first possession hath somewhat superadded to that primitive right in common, that puts him in a better condition than any other, and to his interest in common there is superadded somewhat by his industry that another hath not, namely a prior possession. And the same may be said in reason of such acquisitions, that are made by art or industry, whereby the things so acquired are in some kind become his effects; as by planting, semination, culture, artificial manufacture, and the like. [19]

And he characterised the original state in terms very like those of Locke. The primitive condition of mankind was neither *bellum omnium contra omnes* nor civil society:

There is a third state, either between man and man or nation and nation, which hath neither the superinduction of a capitulation or contract to make it perfect peace, nor any hostility between them either denounced or begun; which at its best or highest advance is a mutual commerce or intercourse, as there is between the English and the Persian or Indian at this day. [20]

The most impressive part of Hale's theory is this discussion of property and his reconstruction of the early Grotian account of the origins of private

[18] B. M. Hargrave MS 485, ff. 35–v.
[19] *ibid.,* ff. 36–7.
[20] *ibid.,* f. 40.

dominium in individual action. His use of Selden's theory of obligation is less happy, however, for the obvious reasons. Selden had rejected Grotius's theory of property precisely because he had a different theory of obligation, according to which men were obliged at a specific point in historical time to the performance of specific actions, notably the keeping of contracts. Such a theory cannot be squared with the idea that the rights and duties attached to private property arise gradually in the course of nature without any contracts being necessary, and it is perhaps for that reason that Hale left his manuscript unpublished. It was an inadequate response to the problem posed most extremely (in his eyes) by Hobbes, just as in a rather different way had been his reply to Hobbes's *Dialogue of the Common Laws*. Anyone who wished to preserve Selden's theory of obligation was going to find it hard to refute Hobbes and to abandon the Seldenian or Hobbesian state of nature.

Richard Cumberland tried a different approach, though with the same overall objective. He came from the same kind of *milieu* as Hale, though he was a clergyman and not a lawyer: his early career was under the patronage of Orlando Bridgeman, another of the breed of realistic Restoration lawyers who had lived and worked under Cromwell. In his *De Legibus Naturae Disquisitio Philosophica* of 1672 he made public another version of the same attempt. What he did was to put forward not only a Grotian interpretation of property, though one rather closer to *De Iure Belli* than to *Mare Liberum,* but also a Grotian account of the content of the law of nature. That is to say, he took it to require the acts necessary to sustain a social being (which in Cumberland's eyes turned out to be the acts necessary to maximise general utility). But in addition he tried to provide a Seldenian account of the obligatory force of such a law.

He made his dependence on Selden at this point quite explicit:

> Mr. *Selden* denies, 'That the Conclusions of Reason, consider'd barely in themselves, have the Authority of Laws', upon no other account, than in order to *shew* 'the Necessity of having recourse to the Legislative Power of God, and of proving that God has commanded our Obedience to them, and by making them known to us, has proclaim'd them his Laws'. And indeed he has *judiciously*, as far as I can judge, *given this Hint* to the moral Philosophers, who are wont to consider the *Conclusions of their own Reason* as *Laws*, without due Proof, that they have the necessary *Form* of a Law, or that they are establish'd by God.[21]

---

[21] 'Seldenus autem ideo tantum causatur defectum Authoritatis in dictatis Rationis Humanae per se consideratis, ut ostendat opus esse, ut inde recurramus ad Potestatem Legislativam Dei; doceatque ejusmodi dictamina inde tantum propriam Legum virtutem acquirere quod hominibus a Deo eorum omnis cognitio derivetur, qui dum haec iis nota facit suas Leges reipsa promulgat. Atque hoc sane (si quid ego judicio) non imprudenter suggessit Philosophis Moralibus, qui Rationis suae dictata velut Leges considerare solent absque idonea probatione quod aut formam habeant Legum necessariam, aut quod a Deo stabiliantur.' *De Legibus Naturae Disquisitio Philosophica* (London, 1672), sig. a2v. The translation is *A Treatise of the Laws of Nature*, trans. J. Maxwell (London, 1727), p. 12.

Where he principally differed from Selden was over the question of how God had promulgated the natural laws: they had not been issued by him at a specific point in history, but were learned by men in the course of their experience of the world. As a result of this experience, it would become obvious to anyone who was aware of the 'nature of things' that the promotion of the general good involved promoting his own good – hence there was a definite egotistical motivation for benevolence. The good and bad consequences for individuals were arranged by God as the sanctions of the laws of nature: 'such consequences (thus *naturally known* from the *Nature* of Things) of such human Actions, because they are *foreshewn* by *God*, to *Men deliberating* concerning their Actions, in order to *incline* them to, or deter them from, Action, are intirely in the Nature of *Rewards* and *Punishments*, by which a Law receives its Sanction'.[22]

The problems about this approach are obvious. First, it did not disengage Cumberland from Hobbes any more than his approach had disengaged Hale, and Cumberland admitted that in this area there was in fact no divergence between him and his adversary.[23] He was extremely unwilling to introduce divine punishment in an after-life into his theory in order to refute Hobbes. Although he did talk in various places about the reasonable expectation that God will punish transgressions of the natural law not only in this life, but in the next life also, when he came to answer the objection that the connexion between wickedness and natural punishment was extremely uncertain, his only answer was that

altho' *some wicked Actions* may escape *some kind of Punishment*, that is, such as is inflicted by *Man*, yet even these Crimes do not wholly go *unpunished*; and therefore, there is not wanting an *Obligation* arising from the consideration of this Punishment, which *cannot be avoided*. For it is impossible to separate from the Crime all degrees of *Anxiety of Mind*, arising from the struggle between the sounder Dictates of Reason, which enforce our Duty, and those rash Follies which hurry Men on to Wickedness: There likewise ensue *Fears* (which cause present Grief) of *Vengeance*, both *Divine* and *Human*, and an *Inclination* to the same *Crimes*, or even *worse*; which, because it hurts the Faculties of the Mind, seems to me that it ought to be also reckon'd among Punishments.[24]

---

[22] 'Praecognita autem e Natura consequentia hujusmodi actuum humanorum bona & mala, quoniam a Deo hominibus de actionibus suis deliberantibus praemonstrantur ut ad agendum impellantur, aut inde deterreantur, integram habent rationem praemiorum poenarumque quibus Lex sancitur.' *ibid.*, sig. c4; trans., p. 27.

[23] See *ibid.*, pp. 45 and 250; trans., pp. 73 and 241.

[24] 'Quanquam aliquod poenarum genus, ultio scilicet humana, ab actibus aliquot flagitiosis deparari posse contingat, non tamen prorsus poenam ejusmodi crimina effugiunt; adeoque nec deficit obligatio a consideratione poenae certo secuturae. Non possunt enim a scelere divelli gradus aliqui aegritudinis animi, e conflictu inter saniora rationis dictata, quae officium suadent, & temerarios illos impetus qui in scelera homines rapiunt, enascentes: accedunt etiam metus (qui praesentem afferunt dolorem) ultionis tam Divinae quam humanae, & propensio ad eadem crimina, aut etiam deteriora; quae quia mentis facultates laedit, mihi inter poenas quoque enumeranda videtur.' *ibid.*, pp. 261–2; trans., p. 249.

The advance that Cumberland made on Hale was that he was able to integrate his theory of obligation with his theory of property. While Hale believed in the law of nature as the *praecepta Noachidarum*, and hence could not easily deal with obligation in a state of nature, Cumberland by using a much looser and worse-defined theory was able to explain why property should be natural. All men are under an obligation to maximise general utility, and it is simply the case that the means to such an end are provided most plausibly by property. It is evident

'That the Nature of Things discovers, that it is necessary to the Happiness, Life, and Health, of every particular Person, upon which all other Advantages depend, that the Uses of Things should be limited, at least for a time, to particular Persons exclusive of other.' It is hence further evident, 'That the same is likewise necessary to the Common Happiness of All, because the Whole is not distinguish'd from all its Parts taken together.'[25]

So although Cumberland talked briefly about men consenting to this, as in *De Iure Belli* this reference to consent carries very little real weight: the thrust of Cumberland's argument was against any strong theory of property based on consent. (It is curious that Pufendorf in the second edition of his *De Iure Naturae et Gentium* should have hailed Cumberland as an ideological ally – presumably it was on the principle that my enemy's enemy is my friend.)

Although both Hale and Cumberland thus tried to rehabilitate Grotius, it must be stressed that neither did so from a politically radical standpoint. Hale explicitly attacked the principle of interpretative charity, as one might expect given his still close relationship to the Seldenian tradition. Using a number of Selden's arguments in *De Iure Naturali,* Hale concluded in another manuscript work that

I do therefore take it, that, where persons live under the same civil government, as here in *England*, that rule [of common ownership in necessity], at least by the laws of *England*, is false; and therefore, if a person, being under necessity for want of victuals, or clothes, shall upon that account clandestinely and animo ferendi steal another man's goods, it is a felony ... For 1. Men's properties would be under a strange insecurity, being laid open to other men's necessities, whereof no man can possibly judge, but the party himself. 2. Because by the laws of this kingdom sufficient provision is made for the supply of such necessities by collections for the poor, and by the power of the civil magistrate.[26]

Cumberland was characteristically more circumspect, but he did suggest that Grotius should have extended his remarks about accepting existing

[25] 'Manifestum est itaque rerum Naturam indicare necesse esse ad singulorum foelicitatem, vitam, ac valetudinem a quibus alia omnia pendent commoda, ut limitentur, saltem ad tempus, rerum usus singulis, exclusis aliis. Manifestum inde est porro idem ad communem omnium foelicitatem pariter necessarium esse: quia Totum a partibus simul sumptis non distinguitur.' ibid., pp. 337–8; trans., p. 314.
[26] *History of the Pleas of the Crown*, I, ed. G. Wilson (London, 1778), p. 54. (This work was probably written in the 1670s judging by various internal references.)

forms of government to cover the acceptance of existing property distributions.[27] Both men clearly saw their objective as a conservative rendering of the tradition.

This was true also of some of the lesser figures who made the same kind
of point. For example, Richard Baxter, a known (though qualified)
enthusiast for Grotius and a close friend (after 1667) of Hale, occasionally
revealed that he shared much the same ideas. In the late 1660s he put
forward a basically Seldenian theory of natural law in his *Reasons of the
Christian Religion*,[28] while in a work of 1680 he remarked that 'Propriety is
naturally antecedent to *Government*, which doth not *Give it*, but *regulates* it to
the *Common good*: Every man is born with a propriety in his *own members*,
and nature giveth him a propriety in *his Children*, and his *food* and other just
acquisitions of his industry.'[29] But he elsewhere ruled out any right to take
another's goods in necessity,[30] and was always extremely equivocal about
whether or not men could renounce all their rights and commit themselves
to slavery.[31]

However, ideas not very far removed from those of Hale, Cumberland
or Baxter could be used to make a much more radical point, and the great
example of this is of course John Locke's *Two Treatises of Government*.
Locke began as a fairly orthodox, conservative Protestant political theorist, outlining in his lectures at Oxford in the 1660s a straightforwardly
voluntarist theory of the law of nature which explicitly ruled out anything
like Selden's account of it: 'all obligation binds conscience and lays
a bond on the mind itself, so that not fear of punishment, but a rational
apprehension of what is right, puts us under an obligation'.[32] This is
in striking contrast to what Pufendorf had already argued in the *Elementa*,
but it is also in contrast to what Locke himself was to suggest in the
1670s.

In his manuscript *Of Ethics in General*, one of the first full statements of
what was to be his developed theory, we can find remarks very like those
of Hale in his manuscript treatise (which of course Locke had no access to).

The difference between moral and natural good and evil is only this; that we call
that naturally good and evil, which, by the natural efficiency of the thing, produces
pleasure or pain in us; and that is morally good or evil which, by the intervention of
the will of an intelligent free agent, draws pleasure or pain after it, not by any
natural consequence, but by the intervention of that power. Thus, drinking to
excess, when it produces the head-ache or sickness, is a natural evil; but as it is a

[27] See Cumberland, *Disquisitio Philosophica*, pp. 349–50; trans., p. 323.
[28] Baxter, *Practical Works*, II (London, 1707), pp. 18–19.
[29] Baxter, *The Second Part of the Nonconformists Plea for Peace* (London, 1680), p. 54.
[30] Baxter, *Practical Works*, I, p. 490.
[31] See Baxter, *The Second Part*, p. 38; R. Schlatter, *Richard Baxter and Puritan Politics* (New
Brunswick, 1957), p. 154. (Baxter's paper on the Oxford Decree, 1683.)
[32] 'omnis enim obligatio conscientiam alligat et animo ipsi vinculum injicit, adeo ut non
poenae metus sed recti ratio nos obligat.' *Essays on the Law of Nature*, ed. W. von Leyden
(Oxford, 1958), pp. 184–5.

transgression of law, by which a punishment is annexed to it, it is a moral evil. For rewards and punishments are the good and evil whereby superiors enforce the observance of their laws; it being impossible to set any other motive or restraint to the actions of a free understanding agent, but the consideration of good or evil; that is, pleasure or pain that will follow from it.[33]

Locke's theory of obligation remained notoriously loose, as his famous correspondence on the subject with Tyrrell much later shows; but as in the case of Cumberland, this looseness was important for his general theory. Any prudential or hedonistic theorist of obligation who wishes to combine such a theory with a non-anarchic interpretation of the state of nature will be wise to avoid specifying too clearly how and when men come to perceive what obligations they are under.

Similarly, we find Locke by the end of the 1670s putting forward a theory of property very like that of the other English post-Restoration Grotians, though with one important difference.[34] The theory found public expression first in James Tyrrell's *Patriarcha non Monarcha* of 1681. This fact has been rather neglected because it seemed that Locke, though Tyrrell's friend at the time, did not know that he was the author and therefore could not have been consulted about it. It is now clear that this was not so, and as it is also clear that the peculiarly Lockean material is all to be found in a section of the work which was added while it was at the press, it is probable that the final book was indeed the result of a collaboration at a late stage between Locke and Tyrrell.[35] Among other things, this confirms

[33] Lord King, *The Life and Letters of John Locke* (London, 1864), p. 311.
[34] The brief note entitled 'Morality', edited by T. Sargentich, *Locke Newsletter*, v (1974), pp. 26–8, represents a transitional position; it includes a hedonistic account of obligation, but implies that an *explicit* contract is necessary to avoid the potential evils of a world left in common.
[35] Despite the obvious parallels between the two works, and despite Locke's known friendship with Tyrrell at this time, Laslett was led to conclude that Locke did not know of Tyrrell's authorship by a note in Locke's journal for 2 June 1681 that he bought a copy 'for Mr Tyrrell'; as Laslett said, 'no man buys a book to give to its anonymous author, if he knows who wrote it'. (J. Locke, *Two Treatises of Government*, ed. P. Laslett (Cambridge, 1963), p. 74 n. 39.) But this entry in his journal is explained by a letter from Tyrrell to Locke, c. 24 June 1681, printed in the new edition of Locke's correspondence. In it, he asked after their mutual friend Nathaniel Hodges, and remarked 'I have a book for him: but if he be gone (as I feare he is) I doe not think it worth while to send it so far: and therefore had not put you to the trouble of sending Adrians [Dr David Thomas's], (as I suppose you did) but that I know he is one that troubles himself more with the Politicks then our Master.' (J. Locke, *Correspondence*, ii, ed. E. S. De Beer (Oxford, 1976), p. 418.) It is clear from this that Locke sent Thomas a copy of *Patriarcha non Monarcha* on Tyrrell's behalf, and that the entry in his journal refers to the purchase of this copy; 'for Mr Tyrrell' means *on behalf of* Mr Tyrrell. The book was presumably more easily obtained from the printers in London, where Locke then was, than by Tyrrell in the country.
As for the alterations made to the text of *Patriarcha non Monarcha* in the press, both Laslett and Gough (J. W. Gough, 'James Tyrrell, Whig Historian and Friend of John Locke', *Historical Journal*, xix (1976), p. 585), have missed the essentially simple bibliographical character of the book. It is an octavo work, but half-way through signature K, at K4, p. 136, the regular run of signatures comes to an end and the pagination goes wrong, p. 136 being followed by p. 97. The pages are then numbered in sequence until p. 160, which is followed

Laslett's dating of the basic material in the *Two Treatises* to 1679–80. The significance of this for our purposes is that the Lockean section is devoted to a defence of Grotius from the attack launched on him by Filmer: the Lockean theory of property in its first public appearance was explicitly linked to the rehabilitation of Grotius.

The argument of *Patriarcha non Monarcha* at the relevant point turns, as Locke's argument in the *Two Treatises* was to be famous for doing, on consideration of

what kind of right God had bestowed upon Mankind at first, which was not an absolute positive, or unalterable communion of every man *pro indiviso*, every blade of grass in the world: (for such as a Fiction of our Laws suppose, among Tenants in common) for then the Products of the earth could have contributed nothing to the ends for which they were designed by God *viz*: the preservation and Propagation of the species of Mankind ... Therefore it follows that God bestowed no more upon any particular man than what would serve for the preservation of himself, and propagation of his species, and only in that manner as might prove subservient to that design ... for seeing things are not of any use or benefit unless applyed to mens particular necessities, and that this grant of those things necessary for life would prove altogether in vain, were it lawful for others to take from us, those things which we have already seized on, [therefore] ... if a man have already seized any of those common things for his own use, though he does not actually use them, those things cannot be taken from him without injury.[36]

Like Cumberland, and like (as I have argued) Grotius in *De Iure Belli*, Tyrrell was prepared to refer to this loosely as an agreement among men, but he emphasised that this would indeed be a loose way of talking:

if any man will call this first principle of natural Justice, a true agreement of Mankind, I shall not gainsay it, since such an agreement is but a rational assent of every particular mans understanding that the abstaining from the doing such a thing is every private mans interest, and likewise for the good of humane society. Thus among the *Indians*, few or none steal from each other (though they have no stone walls nor Locks to secure their things in) because they know Theft would bring in perpetual War, and confusion among them; and therefore it is all their interest to joyn against Theft, not only as a breaker of the laws of nature, but an infringer of this tacite agreement.[37]

[36] Tyrrell, *Patriarcha non Monarcha* (London, 1681), sig. L6v-L7v.
[37] *ibid*., sig. L7v.

by p. 209. However, if the regular run had been continued, it would have reached the beginning of P at p. 209. This is indeed the case, and the work then continues in a regular fashion to the end. Between K4 and P1 of the original work, a new section has been inserted, with signatures L-O, which is made to fit the old lay-out by some very cramped type at the end (O8v). This is all that has happened to the book, and is easy enough to understand in the light of the contents of the inserted section; it is largely a discussion of Filmer's 'Observations upon H. Grotius *De Jure Belli et Pacis*', in his *Observations Concerning the Originall of Government*, to which Locke's ideas would be particularly relevant.

On Locke's ideas on property in general, the major new book by James Tully will be absolutely vital reading – I owe a great deal to it, even if my interpretation of Locke differs somewhat from his.

His use of the term '*tacit* agreement' reminds us that Locke, in attacking the idea that property relations rest on contract, showed the absurdity of 'making an *explicit* [my italics] consent of every Commoner, necessary to any ones appropriating to himself any part of what is given in common'.[38] Like Tyrrell, his main target was doctrines which laid stress on explicit contracts, rather than the looser agreements of men like Cumberland.

The crucial question, and one which has rarely been put in this form by Locke scholars, is: how does the argument of *Patriarcha non Monarcha* and the similar argument of the *Two Treatises* differ from Cumberland's? (The comparison is particularly fair in that Tyrrell subsequently published a disquisition on the law of nature based explicitly on Cumberland.)[39] In both cases, after all, property is explained in terms of a right necessary to the fulfilment of a duty to preserve and benefit mankind as a whole, a duty which men are under naturally as well as civilly. It is true that Tyrrell and Locke give a much more concrete picture of what is involved, both with respect to the duty (which they anchor firmly in God's known will rather than in the vague 'nature of things' selected by Cumberland) and with respect to the acquisition of property through man's labour in the world (though too much should not be made of Locke's originality in stressing the role of labour – both the early Grotius and Hale, for example, took work to be the means of appropriation, as distinct from the 'mental act' proposed by some more traditional theorists). But this greater concreteness does not alter the fundamental outlines of the theory.

The answer to this question seems to be primarily that Locke and Tyrrell saw the consequences of this theory of property in a way that Hale and Cumberland, and even Grotius himself, did not. It was this clear-sightedness that made Locke's achievement (assuming it was largely his) so remarkable, and enabled him to publish the most satisfactory work presented by anyone in this natural rights tradition. Cumberland had argued rather weakly on the basis of his account of property that the existing distribution of *dominium* (by which he explicitly meant both property and political power, as did most people in the tradition) should be respected as the best available to maximise utility; Tyrrell and Locke perceived that a much more radical attitude to property should follow from a broadly Grotian position. As *Patriarcha non Monarcha* said,

this natural Propriety in things much less, that which is introduced by Law, or common consent, cannot exclude that natural right every man hath to his own preservation, and the means thereof; so that no man can be obliged in conscience, or commits a sin, if in a case of extream necessity, (even ready to perish) he makes use of some of the superfluous necessaries of life which another man may have laid by for the future uses of himself, and Family.[40]

[38] Locke, *Two Treatises*, p. 331.
[39] *A Brief Disquisition of the Law of Nature, According to the Principle and Method laid down in Dr Cumberland* (London, 1692).
[40] Tyrrell, *Patriarcha non Monarcha*, sig. L7v–L8.

Similarly Locke famously insisted in the *Two Treatises* on a 'spoliation condition':

the same Law of Nature that does by this means give us Property, does also *bound* that *Property* too. *God has given us all things richly*, 1 Tim. vi. 17. is the Voice of Reason confirmed by Inspiration. But how far has he given it us? *To enjoy.* As much as any one can make use of to any advantage of life before it spoils; so much he may by his labour fix a Property in. Whatever is beyond this, is more than his share, and belongs to others.[41]

It is the clear tenor of Locke's argument that the industrious poor are always *entitled* to the wherewithal with which to make their livelihood. It is of course true that men can possess more than they can immediately make use of, in the shape of money, but such holdings must always represent in a conventional form goods that they have made for use by other people. It is also true that societies can make explicit and positive agreements about the distribution of property, as about any other matters, and that the distribution can be altered thereby; but the general principles Locke proposes concerning consent apply to such agreements. In particular, men must *themselves* consent (they cannot be bound, as both Grotius and Cumberland implied they could, by the consent of their predecessors), and the agreements cannot override the general rules concerning the exploitation of the world by mankind which God laid down (thus an agreement to allow one person to engross all possessions would be invalid).

If Locke was clear-sighted in detecting that a Grotian theory of property would lead to a more radical conclusion than Cumberland had recognised, he was equally clear-sighted (and here he differed, as I have already remarked, from his friend) in seeing that it was not necessary for a radical to use the principle of interpretative charity either in this area or in the area of political relationships. It is a striking fact about the *Two Treatises* that their author never uses the traditional radical arguments against either the denial of aid to the needy or slavery and autocracy.

While Grotius had felt constrained to use interpretative charity to justify the right to seize commodities necessary for life, Locke realised that a theory of property of the kind Grotius advanced in *Mare Liberum* and which is still fundamentally present in *De Iure Belli* needed no such additional principle to generate a right of that kind. Similarly, he attempted to establish restraints on absolute government without employing the orthodox radical theory of inalienable rights – rights, that is, which it would be foolish though logically possible to renounce (a theory which as we have seen Tyrrell was prepared to use in the non-Lockean sections of *Patriarcha non Monarcha*).

Locke in fact used two kinds of argument at this point in his work, though they have rarely been distinguished, and he did not himself make the distinction particularly clear (it was the section on property,

[41] Locke, *Two Treatises*, p. 332.

significantly, that Locke himself esteemed, rather than any other).[42] The first and much the weaker of the two was to argue that it was logically impossible to consent to slavery or to the renunciation of the right of self-defence. He tried to show this by asserting that God's ban on suicide (which all could accept) entailed that one must always preserve oneself.[43] The difficulty with this, as his predecessors had usually perceived, is that it requires a much more complex argument to establish it, for *prima facie* there is a difference between disposing of one's own life and allowing another to dispose of it, just as there is a difference between murdering another person and letting him die.

The second and stronger argument involved bypassing this kind of issue entirely. He perceived that it is enough to rule out absolutism that the sovereign ought under no circumstances to act in an arbitrary or unjust way towards his subjects, given a general theory of sovereignty as created by agreement. For if there is such a restriction on possible actions by a sovereign, men cannot put themselves under a ruler who might break it: that would be to consent to another man's acting in an immoral way and would thus go against the fundamental principles of the law of nature.[44] All that was needed to establish the constraint on absolutism was thus a clear statement of what kind of rights men may possess over each other in a pre-civil society, that is, a clear statement of the right which both he and Grotius believed in, to execute offenders against the law of nature. Locke could never disentangle himself sufficiently from the conventional way of dealing with this problem to state his solution in this simple way, but it is the basic structure of his argument at various key points. And like his theory of property, it is a natural extension of Grotius's ideas (particularly as embodied in the *Mare Liberum*) into a region where Grotius himself by the end of his life was unwilling to go, the territory of a liberal and unabsolutist political theory. It is ironic, in view of Rousseau's strictures on Grotius, that the most faithfully Grotian political theory available from the presses of the late seventeenth century was that of Locke.

[42] *ibid.*, p. 15.
[43] *ibid.*, p. 325. See on this J. Dunn, *The Political Thought of John Locke* (Cambridge, 1969), pp. 88–9.
[44] See Locke, *Two Treatises*, pp. 402–3.

Conclusion

'The History of Morality'

At about the time that the heroic period of the new theory of natural rights was drawing to a close, its exponents began the attempt to locate it in an historical context and to assess the different part played by its various architects. Their activity led to the formation of a new *genre*, the History of Morality, which was to be eminently characteristic of the early Enlightenment. The first person to write such a history of the new school was Pufendorf himself, as early as 1678; he was followed by (among others) the author of probably the best example of the *genre*, Jean Barbeyrac, in 1706, by J. F. Buddeus in 1711, and by Christian Thomasius in 1719.[1] It was their view of their own intellectual ancestry that was to be the main influence in shaping the eighteenth century's interpretation of the whole movement. On the whole, all these authors had a clear and consistent picture of this history.

Barbeyrac's *Historical and Critical Account of the Science of Morality* is a good example: he argued that among the philosophers of the ancient world, only the Stoics had come anywhere near to giving an adequate account of man's moral life. Aristotle's ethical theories, for him, were vitiated by his incapacity to apprehend

just Ideas of the natural Equality of Mankind; and, by some of his Expressions, he gives Occasion to believe, that he thought some Men to be, by Nature, design'd for Slaves ... Thus this vast Genius of Nature, this Philosopher, for whom such Numbers have so great a Veneration, proves to be grosly ignorant of, and, without any Scruple, treads under Foot, one of the most evident Principles of the Law of Nature.

The Stoics, in addition to asserting the natural equality of men, had the concept of a *lex naturae*, and, despite their difficulties in elucidating it, came closer to a satisfactory theory. Consequently the most complete Stoic treatise of ethics, Cicero's *De Officiis*, was described by Barbeyrac as

[1] S. Pufendorf, *Specimen Controveriarum circa Jus Naturale ipsi nuper Motarum* (Uppsala, 1678); J. Barbeyrac, *An Historical and Critical Account of the Science of Morality*, prefaced to S. Pufendorf, *The Law of Nature and Nations*, trans. B. Kennet (London, 1749), and originally published as a preface to his French translation of Pufendorf (Amsterdam, 1706); J. F. Buddeus, *Historia Juris Naturalis*, published with P. R. Vitriarius, *Institutiones Juris Naturae et Gentium* (Leyden, 1711); *Paulo Plenior Historia Juris Naturalis ... in usum auditorii Thomasiani* (Halle, 1719).

'without Dispute, the best Treatise of Morality, that all Antiquity has produc'd'. But after the fall of Rome, Aristotle's influence had steadily increased:

From thence sprung the *Scholastic Philosophy*; which spread itself all over *Europe*, and, with its barbarous Cant, became even more prejudicial to Religion, and Morality, than to the speculative Sciences. The Ethics of the *Schoolmen*, is a Piece of Patchwork; a confus'd Collection, without any Order, or fix'd Principles ...[2]

The Science of Morality was not 'rais'd again from the Dead' until the early seventeenth century; and the early Enlightenment believed that the great heroes of the resurrection were Francis Bacon and Hugo Grotius. Grotius was the main hero – 'the first who broke the Ice' as Barbeyrac said; Bacon seems to have been accorded an important position first by Pufendorf, who interpreted Grotius's *De Iure Belli et Pacis* as an attempt to apply the principles of the *De Augmentis* to jurisprudence.[3] Pufendorf was presumably piously bracketing together two great contemporaries who seemed to have destroyed scholasticism. After Grotius, there were firstly the two English writers, Selden and Hobbes, to whom these historians accorded equal attention. Both were seen as unquestionably participating in the same exercise as Grotius, but there were radical flaws in both their works. Selden's *De Iure Naturali et Gentium*, despite having many good features, had an extremely obscure style and an idiosyncratic overall plan, while Hobbes's *De Cive* was an attempt to revive Epicureanism. Hobbes was extremely clever, but his work was essentially rather confused and his political conclusions, particularly about the power of the magistrate in religious matters, were unacceptable.

So it was the later writers, particularly Cumberland and Pufendorf, whom these Enlightenment historians believed to be the true heirs of Grotius; this was especially true of Pufendorf, despite the fact that his *De Iure Naturae* contained many criticisms of his predecessor. It was also true, Barbeyrac at any rate believed, of Locke: his notes on Pufendorf frequently appeal to Locke as an authority for the correct, *Grotian* position on such matters as property and the natural right to punish.[4]

The main feature of this interpretation is thus its overriding concern to establish Grotius's authority. It was the search for the authentic heir to Grotius that occupied these historians more than anything, and it was for fidelity or infidelity to Grotius that they praised or blamed subsequent theorists. It was essentially this history that Rousseau accepted when in the *Social Contract* he tried to repudiate the entire natural rights tradition by repudiating Grotius. Clearly, there was a lot in it – they were absolutely right to see Grotius as a figure towering over the entire school, and they

[2] Barbeyrac, *Science of Morality*, pp. 55, 63, 66.
[3] Pufendorf, *Specimen*, p. 9.
[4] See the Kennet translation (n. 1 above), pp. 366–7 for property and p. 762 for the right to punish.

also had the correct instincts about such things as the importance of Selden and the Grotian character of much of Locke's work. Where they went badly wrong, and where their mistakes have complicated all subsequent historiography, was over three questions: the medieval roots of the new theory, its potential radicalism, and the faithfulness to it of Pufendorf's main work.

The first mistake is understandable: they correctly divined the anti-Aristotelian character of the theory, and like many other people assumed that medieval scholasticism was genuinely Aristotelian. In fact, as we have seen, there was a great gulf between scholasticism and the more accurate reading of Aristotle presented at the Renaissance: when Grotius turned against Renaissance Aristotelianism, he was not (whether he was fully aware of it himself or not) turning against scholasticism. The recovery of the medieval roots of Grotius's theory was one of the major achievements of historians at the beginning of the twentieth century.

The second mistake (if we can indeed call it such) is more difficult to deal with. Just as Grotius had been politically equivocal, so (for example) was Barbeyrac: even Rousseau acknowledged that Barbeyrac and Locke, unlike Pufendorf, had doubts about the possibility of voluntary slavery and absolutism.[5] And yet it is also true that by presenting Pufendorf as the second hero of the movement, and by treating Locke's divergences from the authoritarian line as relatively minor and appropriate to footnotes on the *De Iure Naturae*, Barbeyrac implied that its dominant political attitude was a conservative one. The complete disappearance from this historiography of the English radicals also helped to make this point, for it removed the other major contribution in a liberal vein to the post-Grotian tradition. Clearly, this badly distorted the truth, and prevented the Enlightenment historians from fully recognising the Janus-faced character of Grotius. Nevertheless, one must not go too far in the opposite direction. The movement was fundamentally cohesive: Locke corresponded with Barbeyrac and praised Pufendorf, as did Tyrrell; Pufendorf admired both Selden and Hobbes; everyone admired Grotius. What they all had in common seems to have been more important than what divided them, even if it was by the end mainly hostility to a common enemy, the Renaissance and its ideological derivatives.

The third mistake is related to this last point. It is striking that the historians failed to see how far Pufendorf had in fact abandoned the entire tradition at one of its central points, and had laid the theoretical foundations for something completely alien, which was to culminate in Utilitarianism. Their failure is no doubt connected with the fact that Pufendorf himself was always concerned to emphasise his continuity with the Grotian tradition, both because of his own intellectual biography and

[5] *The Social Contract and Discourses*, ed. and trans. G. D. H. Cole, revised by J. H. Brumfitt and J. C. Hall (London, 1973), p. 95. (*A Discourse on the Origin of Inequality.*)

because he remained a convinced anti-Aristotelian at a time when that was still an embattled position. But we can see that this emphasis was misplaced, and as a consequence we can have many more doubts about the success of the whole Grotian enterprise than the Enlightenment historians had. It is remarkable how brief the two great *floruits* of rights theories were: the first *c.* 1350–1450, the second *c.* 1590–1670. Seen against a background of European thought as a whole, they are freakish and fitful, and their dismantling has been a matter of high priority for succeeding generations. But they have also cast a powerful spell as an alternative to our own settled and gentler theories: the curious fascination that Hobbes has exercised over all his subsequent readers may serve as a symbol of the whole movement's peculiar attractiveness.

Index